THE CHURCH 2001

The Church 2001

by

MICHAEL RICHARDS

Writings from *The Clergy Review* and other
sources, edited with additional material

by

PETER JENNINGS

 St Paul Publications

St Paul Publications
Middlegreen, Slough SL3 6BT

Copyright © 1982 St Paul Publications

First published March 1982
Printed in Great Britain by offset lithography by
Billing & Sons Ltd, Guildford, London and Worcester

ISBN 0 85439 202 5

*St Paul Publications is an activity of the priests and brothers of the Society
of St Paul who promote the christian message through the mass media.*

TO THE PARENTS OF ALL

CLERGY AND ESPECIALLY MY OWN

CONTENTS

IX. RENEWAL AND DEVELOPMENT

ENVOI

FOREWORD

ON the 20th December 1966, the day before my ordination as a bishop, I joined Cardinal Heenan for tea in Archbishop's House, Westminster. He then gave me the news, which he had himself, I think, received only that day (it became public property the same evening) that Father Charles Davis was leaving the Catholic Church.

Charles Davis was the Editor of *The Clergy Review* and a theologian much in the public eye. It was immediately urgent to replace him as editor, and the Cardinal's nominee was Father Michael Richards, a convert from Anglicanism who had taught at the school at Ampleforth and studied for the priesthood at the Institut Catholique in Paris. Since 1962 he had been teaching Church History at Allen Hall, the provincial seminary now stationed in Chelsea, but at that time forming part of St Edmund's College near Ware. Father Davis had also been selected as a member of the Preparatory Commission, due to meet in Italy in January 1967, to which the Anglican/Roman Catholic International Commission succeeded about two years later. Father Richards replaced Davis in this role also.

The Clergy Review is a monthly magazine, and the January 1967 number was ready for publication before Charles Davis left us. Father Richards's début as the new editor is represented in the present volume by the Editorial for February 1967. It is important to bear in mind that at that time the second Vatican Council's termination was still only fourteen months behind us, and *Humanae Vitae*, Pope Paul VI's Encyclical on birth control, lay a year and a half ahead in the future. The Editorial expresses a commitment to Vatican II which pervades the pages of this remarkable selection from Father Richards's articles and essays, so wisely chosen for this volume, and so helpfully edited by Mr Peter Jennings. Michael Richards is still a teacher of Church History (now at Heythrop College in the University of London). He would not be a good Church historian if he were not also an accomplished theologian. Nor would he be a useful editor of *The Clergy Review* if he did not recognise that academic theology is vital for the health of the Church, but futile if it does not keep its eye on the application of knowledge to the missionary and pastoral activity of the Church. This concern for practice emerges very clearly in his first Editorial: "The new shape and style of the Church's life will not come from the world, but from what we have learnt in the Council. As the Church grows, the world will be transformed. If our Church is too small, it is because we have been small minded. We have yielded to the pressures of the world. But the new pains are the pains of growth, we are yielding to the pressure of the Spirit".

Michael Richards is not only a distinguished editor of other people's writings. He is himself a teacher. And he knows by instinct, perhaps also by experience, that teachers can be bores. But in his own writing cheerfulness will keep breaking in; cheerfulness, humour, wit. And he knows the power of the unexpected, even at first incongruous, joke. He can be severe with Catholics who reject the spirit and perhaps the letter of Vatican II. But he can laugh at the absurdities of some "progressives": "Hairshirts are undergarments; worn, for greater comfort, as fancy waistcoats, they flatter the eye of those afflicted with a gullibility uncharacteristic of the Christian mind" (p. 19). Was he still thinking of so-called progressives when he wrote (p. 22): "The university background of some of our waspish laymen might lead us to expect them to launch out in this direction" (i.e. in promoting dialogue with unbelievers) "but they are happily pre-occupied with parish gossip and their noisy splashings in the holy water stoup"? The whole collection of articles ends with a hilarious piece entitled "Restaurants and Redemption: the Theology of Cuisine".

Paullo maiora canamus. What is the background to Michael Richards's theology? First, he was an Anglican and comes from an Evangelical milieu, an unusual and valuable equipment in these days when we are searching for unity with the Church of England. Secondly, his historical studies have brought him into contact with the significant English Catholic apologists of the Elizabethan period, particularly Stapleton. Thirdly, and presumably through his years at the Institut Catholique, he is unusual among English theologians for his familiarity with French theology, from the days of Bérulle and Olier to the present; this is important, in view of the influence that French theology exercised in Vatican II. Finally, he has studied the achievements of that Council itself, and penetrated through the letter of its documents to the spirit which moved within it. My impression is that he has paid less attention to Rahner and his school; and you will hardly find a reference to Lonergan in these pages.

This background is important. But can one attempt to sum up the unifying view-point which allows Richards to use these various sources without creating confusion? The simple and ultimate answer is, of course, that he has "faith", and assents to "the faith". Faith knows that it has an Object, even when it has not consciously identified this object. It also knows that this object has given a concrete expression of itself in history; and again it knows this even when it has not yet found that concretisation in its full subsistence in and as the Catholic Church. An intelligent adult convert like Michael Richards has the inestimable advantage of having found, or rather been found by, this subsistent Church which, in terms of some modern theology, is the "sacrament" of Christ, while Jesus Christ himself is, in a higher analogical sense, the sacrament of the Absolute Mystery *quod omnes vocant Deum*. I don't suppose that Richards discovered the Catholic Church as an absolute novelty; I think it more probable that he recognised it as something that he so to speak always foreboded. What it gave him was "the faith", the needed content of his supernatural believing (for to have faith, to believe, requires an object of faith and, since we are finite, a concrete expression of that object).

In the faith he found freedom. That, surely, is one of the deep messages latent in these pages. He has found that to be a Catholic is not to be confined by unnatural restrictions and constraints but to live in an atmosphere and an ambit which invites to a full and happy use of one's responsible freedom. (When I became a Catholic I was warned by a brilliant Oxford friend that I was committing intellectual suicide; and in some respects it felt to me like emotional suicide also. My friend himself became a Catholic about a year later; and my affective endowment has survived).

I think it worth emphasising that the freedom which Father Richards has found in the Church is a responsible one. It is not a slavish acquiescence or a "crucifixion of the intellect" in the sad sense often given to that phrase. His acceptance of the Church's infallible teaching and its infallible definitions of the faith is total and not reluctant. But he does not make the common mistake of imagining that her non-infallible teaching requires and deserves the same quality of assent. He can write quite sharply, though with respect, even about a Pope if he judges it necessary to do so. He is not like a prisoner in a communist country; he is more like an intelligent schoolboy asking awkward questions — partly, perhaps, for the fun of the thing, but more deeply because he cares about the truth and wants help to find the right answers.

How comes it that a highly intelligent and widely-read man of the twentieth century can be so total in his commitment — and so happy and vivacious in it? For the very obvious reason that the faith is meant for everybody and welcomes all truth and all responsible use of the intellect; and that the Church is called by God and animated by the Holy Spirit to be not a ghetto for a minority of mankind but the ever-developing home of the whole human race everywhere. The reader will note, in particular, that Michael Richards will not put up with the idea that Catholics should settle down for minority status in England and for a tolerance which we already enjoy but which goes, sometimes, hand in hand with an assumption that tolerance can never become assimilation.

Here we may find our author's special concern for what is called the "ecumenical movement". In any case, Vatican II explicitly recognised that behind this movement was the impulsion of the Holy Spirit, and officially committed the Church to join it. But for Michael Richards there is also, it seems to me, a personal reason, though one which many of us can share. He knows that since the days of Elizabeth I the cultural life of this country has been influenced by Protestant negations at the expense of our inheritance from the Ecclesia Anglicana of the Middle Ages. He also knows that this represents a deprivation for England and an impoverishment of its culture. He does not expect that the mass of non-Catholic Christians in this country would find their way into the Catholic Church as individuals without the help of the ecumenical movement. And holding, with Vatican II, that the universal Church is a communion of local churches, each of which is called to adjust itself to its locality (as the Church of the Fathers, sprung from Jewish roots, adjusted itself to the intellectual culture of Hellenism), he gladly looks forward to the discovery, by all that is best in the Church of England and in English Protestantism, that full communion in and with the Catholic Church would not be loss but fulfilment:

> All which I took from thee I did but take,
>   Not for thy harms,
> But just that thou might'st seek it in My arms.
>   All that thy child's mistake
> Fancies as lost, I have stored for thee at home;
>   Rise, clasp My hand, and come!

And on our side, too, recovered unity would mean enrichment. He is insistent that unity would entail not only that our non-Catholic brethren accept all that the Catholic Church has to offer them, but that it would mean that we also accepted all that they have to offer us. Neither side would lose anything except its negations. It should be added that, for all his education in French culture and thought and his abiding love for France, Michael Richards is profoundly English. If the Church in this country were really nothing more than an invading body from Italy (I was warned by a clerical head master not long before I became a Catholic that "he had a great regard for the Roman Catholic Church" but "it isn't English") he would still be a Catholic but less humanly at home than he is. He wants us to "indigenise" ourselves in the land and the history which, after all, are ours since we are Englishmen by birth or by adoption. And he has no doubt that England would be enriched by the recovery by the churches of full organic unity in this country. For such reasons, as well as for many others, the second Vatican Council was epoch-making for Michael Richards personally.

Michael Richards's concern for the recovery of visible Christian unity needs to be seen within the context of his vision of

Christianity as the whole created order renewed and elevated into the "supernatural" dimension. This vision happens to be reflected in a remarkable contribution to *The Clergy Review* (December 1981) by Donald Nicholl who has just succeeded to the post of Rector of the Tantur Ecumenical Institute in the Holy Land, an Institute which enjoyed the patronage of Paul VI. Nicholl's theme is that Christianity is precisely not a narrowing down of the totality of the experienced and the experiencible but a total acceptance (and, one would add, elevation) of this totality: "Behold, I make ALL THINGS new" Along with this vision goes, and necessarily, Richards's profound conviction and inspiring insight that the Roman Catholic Church is precisely not a sect, and yet is indubitably unique. This conviction is strikingly expressed in the article (pp. 80ff.) with the enigmatic title ". . . SUBSISTIT IN . . ." — a reference, as the cognoscenti will realise, to a key sentence in Vatican II's Dogmatic Constitution on the Church, in which — surprisingly to some — it is said not that the Church established by Jesus Christ *is* the Catholic Church but that it "subsists in" the Catholic Church with its bishops in communion with the successor of St Peter.

The article ". . . SUBSISTIT IN . . ." should be read in the context of a principle which is fundamental to Father Richards's total Christian vision: the principle that the goal set by God for our whole human endeavour, and indeed for the whole created order, is already present and operative within the historical order and more particularly in the historical and risen Jesus Christ and so in the Church which is his "body" (that is, his sacramental embodiment). Elsewhere our author, who makes very clear his total detachment from the "traditionalism" of Mgr Lefebvre, criticises Dr Küng for his failure to do justice to this "already here and now" presence and dynamic force of the "absolute future", the *eschaton* or ultimate thing. Biblical scholars will feel at home here, since in the earlier half of this century a war was raging between advocates respectively of "thorough-going eschatology", "fully realised eschatology", and "eschatology already given in pledge"; did Jesus preach a merely future kingdom, or did he proclaim an already achieved kingdom, or did he proclaim and incorporate a kingdom already operative in himself and his mission but awaiting a culmination which would crown its growth with the absolutely final act of divine grace?

In conclusion, I hope that this book will be read with avidity by very many Catholics, very many Christians whom we recognise as our separated but true and very dear brothers in Christ, and very many who would hesitate or even refuse to call or think of themselves as Christians but still hope that there may be some meaning and abiding value in existence. Christians could do worse, after a swift reading of the whole book, than take its contents, article by article, for daily reading, meditation and prayer (in the case of the concluding article, I would suggest that special prayer which we Christians call "grace after meals"). Mr Jenning's list of relevant dates will be of valuable assistance in such reading.

Bishop B.C. BUTLER
St Edmund's College, Ware,
Hertfordshire.

10 December 1981

PREFACE

THE title of this book may sound presumptuous. It was originally used for an editorial in *The Clergy Review* discussing a report on the implementation of Vatican II in England and Wales, and was kindly supplied by the ready wit of Fr John Mahoney, SJ, in the aftermath of seeing Stanley Kubrick's film. In its present application, it expresses, not an assertion, but a hope that the involvement of the *Review* in the labours of the present generation has contributed in some way to the future development of the Church and indeed, that having by then reached the biblical score of years, I shall see the outcome.

Peter Jennings's chronology will help readers to recapture the struggles, setbacks and achievements of the conciliar and post-conciliar years and to situate this or that piece of writing in its context; the book would certainly not have taken shape without his energetic involvement in its preparation.

The editorial board of *The Clergy Review* have always provided unfailing support; they will all concur in my singling out Bishop Christopher Butler for a particular expression of gratitude, not only for the Foreword, but for years of attentive interest and concern, without which the enterprise would certainly have flagged and have run into greater difficulties than it has in fact experienced.

I should like to acknowledge the permission given by the Editors of *The Times*, *The Tablet* and the *Catholic Herald* to reprint material which appeared originally in their columns; the fact is indicated at the appropriate places.

My thanks go also to Tom Burns, to the Tablet Publishing Company, and to all those who provide the life-support system for the *Review* at 48, Great Peter Street, without whose backing and professional labours the reading requirements of the clergy would have been far less efficiently met.

Mrs Marjorie Mathers, Mrs Audrey Andrews and Mrs Jo Skipp (for most of the fifteen years) all deserve a special mention in these acknowledgements for coping with my scrawl and putting it into readable shape.

Finally, I wish to express my deep appreciation of the encouragement given by Cardinal John Heenan and then by Cardinal Basil Hume, who, as Archbishops of Westminster, gave me my job and then allowed me, in spite of everything, to keep it. Their patient forbearance has often been tried; their over-riding confidence is all the more precious.

MICHAEL RICHARDS
Hugh's House, Buckden,
Cambridgeshire.

21 December 1981

THE ROLE OF THE CATHOLIC PRESS*

The real role of the Catholic Press is to provide a forum in which there can be the dissemination and exchange of ideas. I firmly believe the Catholic Press must have the same freedom as we accord to the secular Press.

I would beseech Catholic journalists, as indeed any journalists, to remember that when they criticize personalities in places of responsibility, they are dealing with vulnerable human beings who are fallible. The Catholic Press should be an example of honest criticism done in an understanding and sympathetic way.

CARDINAL BASIL HUME, OSB

* From an interview with Peter Jennings published in the *Catholic Herald*, 5 March 1976.

I

THE CLERGY REVIEW:
POLICY AND PROGRAMME

THE FIRST EDITORIAL:
PRIESTS ARE PILGRIMS

IT is easy to forget that the clergy are a charismatic lot. Lumped together, we file past, the long and the short and the tall: a motley crew, but unexciting. The onlooker does not usually remind himself that the Spirit of God had intervened in the personal history of every priest, calling him to live his life in the service of the Gospel. The seminary years tested his conviction. The Church, the Spirit-filled community, recognised and confirmed this certainty: he was chosen to build up the Body of Christ, the Temple of God. He joined a group of men who are not given unity in the same way as a social or cultural class is united; our corporate identity comes from the Spirit, who forms in us the character of Christ. The diversity of background to be discovered among the members of the priesthood is a sign of the free choice of God's Spirit; the variety of gifts used in the work of the Church is a sign of God's richness, not our own. If we are an odd crowd, not very regimental, it is because we represent humanity; if we are men of little brain, it is because we stand for the wisdom of God by which foolish men are saved.

A priest, like everyone else, often feels like settling down in some comfortable spot along his pilgrim's way. But the parish, the *paroikia*, is no more than a temporary place of sojourn in a foreign land. The immovable parish priest is a canonist's wry joke. The Vatican Council has moved him on. Certainly, the priest in every age bears witness to the eternal God and to his one way of salvation. The Gospel does not change. But man does. He can never stand still in this world. He can never cease to respond to the grace of God by which he is remade. Routine and habit are only useful if they free him for something else.

The response that we are called to make at this moment involves more in the way of a departure from habit and routine than we find comfortable. The sudden release of spiritual energy which we have experienced in the last few years has left us dizzy and a little lost. The fact of our calling is as clear as ever; but our minds have not yet fully grasped what we are meant to be doing next.

The new relationship with society which the clergy now have to find will involve them less in protecting a particular minority who respect them and more in speaking to a majority who do not know them. That does not mean that the household of faith will be neglected. There is nothing better in life than living among friends. But the Church is not a refuge. Those who praise the Catholic Church (from outside) as a bastion of truth pay us a double-edged compliment. The social links which reinforced the spiritual cohesion of the Church, the solidarity of the recusant or the immigrant or the exile, must now be exchanged for new ways of communication, in a society which has yet to be built. The life-pattern of the Church will still be recognisable, relating us through the history of the world with all who have been called into unity with Christ. The fruits of the Spirit will still be the same. But those who receive the Spirit will be different. They will find new ways of faithfulness to Christ, just as they will make new discoveries about God's world.

All this does not involve a leap in the dark, a sudden submission to some blind urge to go we know not where. Christian worship is rational worship. We cannot dispense ourselves from the labour of studying the conciliar documents. Most of us still have only a superficial acquaintance with what they have to say. Our task would be easier if we had taken theology more seriously in the past, and had more men in England in tune with the Council and ready to interpret its teaching. More is involved than reorganisation. 'Do not be conformed to this world, but be transformed by the renewal of your mind', wrote St Paul to the Romans. A deeper understanding of the Church is the key to most of our internal problems. It is also the key to the work we have to do in the world. The new shape and style of the Church's life will not come from the world, but from what we have learnt in the

3

Council. As the Church grows, the world will be transformed. If our Church is too small, it is because we have been small-minded. We have yielded to the pressure of the world. But the new pains are the pains of growth; we are yielding to the pressure of the Spirit.

February 1967

THE GREAT CONTROVERSY:
HUMANÆ VITÆ

NOW that the Holy Father has made his pronouncement on the principles governing the morality of married life, a word is perhaps called for first of all on the policy I have tried to follow on this and other matters since taking over *The Clergy Review*. I was quite aware then of the part the contraception debate had played in Charles Davis's own personal crisis and of the fact that this was the most difficult question I would be expected to handle. There has been no attempt at supervision and control from any outside quarter. Bishop Butler, as chairman of the Editorial Board, has, of course, given me unfailing advice and support, not to mention the invaluable help of an eagle eye in reading the proofs. But I have been left to do as I thought best by all those who might be concerned, and all I have to report is a skirmish with one author's superiors over quite another matter, which was settled amicably without change of text.

I have several times said that *The Clergy Review* is and must remain at the service of the whole Church. It depends for its existence and usefulness on the widespread support given to it by clergy and religious and by a substantial number of lay people. This is the best guarantee of its freedom and openness to all shades of opinion within the Church. If there is to be true dialogue, there must be places in the Church where the channels of communication are kept as widely open as possible, and this review attempts to be one of them.

I shall continue to welcome articles which speak from within the tradition of the Church as newly expressed by Pope Paul,

4

and those which propose for consideration any fresh moral principle which can claim a basis in the Christian scheme of things. For it is precisely a new fundamental principle which must be found if those who think there should be a change are to consolidate their position within the Church. Discussions about whether this or that statement is irreformable, or whether there can be a change, or whether this or that argument (the artificial/natural one, for example) holds water, do not really get us far enough. In fact, I hope I may be allowed to think that they sometimes fall into the rationalism, quibbling casuistry and legalism which moral theologians are now trying to avoid.

I must say that I myself, both in my marrying and non-marrying days, have never been able to see how anything other than the teaching given us by the Pope can be regarded as a full expression of Christian faith and life. But I would fight to the death (as Voltaire said) to defend the right of anyone else in the household of faith to think otherwise.

The root of our present difficulties lies not in this doctrine, which underlies Christian sexual morality and is in harmony with the picture of redeemed humanity given in the New Testament, as in the way Christian living is still too often taught, understood and practised. The Catholic way of life still appears to many in the Church, not to mention the countless numbers who have turned aside, to consist of a number of arbitrary rules of a not very obviously connected kind, to be obeyed uncomfortably under pain of mortal sin and ultimate damnation. Spiritual life thus degenerates into a Kantian, Stoic, or unreasoning attention to a variety of duties and commandments instead of being a loving relationship with God, a new life reborn in Christ.

The encyclical says that the Church

cannot renounce the teaching of the law which is, in reality, that law proper to a human life restored to its original truth and conducted by the Spirit of God.

That law is the law of the Gospel. Now what we must never do, and what we are only too liable to do, as current misunderstandings have once more revealed, is to make the Gospel even more of a burden on men's consciences than the Old Law ever was.

5

Within the New Covenant we have a sure way of salvation. The Pope and all the bishops of the Catholic Church are authentic and infallibly guided interpreters and teachers of the New Covenant. All Catholics must say that those who follow the teaching given in *Humanæ Vitæ* are in the right way. But no one can say that those who materially do not conform with the teaching given in *Humanæ Vitæ* or who disagree with it in detail are not in the right way as well. We must say this, if we are not to return to the Pharisaism which our Lord condemned.

Properly understood, the encyclical comes in several ways as a liberation. With all its firmness and clarity there goes a tone of voice which too many, accustomed, perhaps, to reading Roman documents through nineteenth-century spectacles, seem to have overlooked. The Pope speaks the language of persuasion and exhortation, not of command and censure. There is no labelling with 'grave sin' as there was in Pius XI's *Casti Connubi*. There is no attempt to argue from the idea that procreation is the primary object of marriage, as there was in the teaching of Pius XII. There is a welcome emphasis on characteristics of conjugal love other than its fruitfulness in new life.

Humanæ Vitæ must be read in the context of the documents of the Second Vatican Council, of Pope Paul's other statements, including his first encyclical on dialogue, and of his whole manner of exercising the Petrine office. His words call for a generous response: generosity of interpretation, generosity of application. It will not be a matter of wresting collegiality and lay participation from an unwilling Pope, but of receiving this encyclical in precisely the way he has always wanted the Church to receive such documents.

The Pope speaks to his fellow bishops of a work 'of education, of progress and of love' which lies ahead. And that is the only way in which Christian moral teaching can be put across. *Humanæ Vitæ* is an invitation and a guide; it is not a strait-jacket, to be imposed indiscriminately on all, irrespective of their degree of faith, their state of mind and their circumstances. It contains no threats and no condemnations. To the extent to which it persuades, it must be followed. And that is true of the entire Law of Christ. It will do immense good, not only on account of the doctrine which it contains and the manner in which it is expressed, but because of the fact that it will force us to think again about the proper way of educating men's consciences in Christian living.

The Pope and the bishops expound the way of salvation and do not deceive or mislead us. But they do not claim to say everything that can be said. No one whose conscience says otherwise has been excluded from the Church. There has been no talk of excommunication. Nor can there be. A man who denied that this is a truly human way of married life would not be a Catholic. But a Catholic who cannot personally accept this doctrine as the only possibility is still a Catholic. I do not believe that the authority of the Church, where moral teaching is concerned, can be exercised in any other way.

September 1968

FORTY YEARS ON

THE first number of *The Clergy Review* appeared in January 1931. The *Review* then cost one pound a year and was published by *The Universe,* which at that time was selling for twopence a week.

The first page announced that the magazine 'shall be devoted exclusively to the professional interests of the English-speaking clergy all over the world'. Canon Myers and Dr Flynn made this clear in their editorial: 'we are, in the first instance, seminary priests writing for seminary priests'. This fundamental character of the *Review* has not changed. We hear frequently nowadays about various forms of collaboration between priests and lay people, whether it is in parish councils, national commissions or in the diversity of movements and societies which further the work of the Church. It should not be thought, however, that the change since Vatican II has been as revolutionary as all that; lay people were writing for and reading *The Clergy Review* from the beginning. Another change has come about through the closer contact of our seminaries with the national universities and through the establishment of Heythrop College in London, all of which should eventually strengthen the higher education of the clergy and enable them to make their own distinctive contribution to the academic life of the country. With this thought in mind it is hoped that the

7

Review will contribute not just to the formation of the clergy, but to the general circulation of ideas within the Church and between the Church and the world.

The general mood of the English clergy is a sober and practical one. They are not given to chasing after new ideas and they are critical of new developments which savour too much of the ivory tower and the study. They do not believe that the Church is built up by startling innovations and in general one can point to the steady growth of the Church in this country to demonstrate that they are right.

New opportunities, however, call for a fresh orientation. Enterprise and flexibility of a kind which, let it be said, has already been showing itself in the years after Vatican II, will more and more be needed. We must be prepared to regard ourselves as called upon to exercise responsibility for Christian teaching and service on a national scale. Although this means putting a great strain on our resources, we must now realise that the integral Christianity which we represent demands a policy framed not by the needs of a sociological minority but by the needs of the total population in the midst of which we are placed.

The clergy of the future will be less inclined than they were forty years ago to think of themselves as a profession. Work for human welfare of every kind is everywhere becoming better organised and the techniques involved have become matters for research, study and systematic training. All this represents a movement of thought and practice in real accord with the Christian gospel. But the function of religion is going to be seen less and less as an institutional one of this kind, and it will be the concern of the clergy not to fit themselves into one particular compartment of public life, but to be present everywhere as a sign of what fundamental and complete humanity means, of the purpose which God has in mind for the human race, and of the means which he has provided for us to attain happiness and fulfilment. The clergy must be capable of providing inspiration, not just warnings and police measures. If this is to happen we shall have to be equipped to present Christianity as a genuine science of human living which stands up to all the rational tests which ingenuity can devise. A new affirmation of the full content of Christian teaching together with a practical human demonstration of the effect of belief and practice on personal balance and development — this means a great deal more than pietism and good works — must be made in the universities, and through them in the other places where minds and people meet to build our common way of life. The clergy must above all be concerned with the truth and reality of Christianity: not black-coated workers, but prophets.

January 1971

HOW I GAVE UP WORRYING ABOUT THE CIRCULATION

EDITING is not exactly a euphoric occupation, but it does have its moments. After a few years of *Sturm und Drang*, a certain calm, I devoutly hope not illusory or short-lived, has begun to set in. Circulation was an anxiety partly because the clergy's affairs have been in a pretty unsettled state anyway, and partly because publishing in general was going through a tricky time. Eventually, however, the worry lessened: figures didn't go down after all, and, with the watchful backing of an energetic publisher, one could say that the *Review* was never healthier.

But balance-sheets, I still thought, weren't everything. Even if the figures looked good by our own standards, what was being achieved? Was anything really circulating, not in terms of quantity, but in terms of public influence on the quality of life? Doubts still hung around.

T. S. Eliot's *Criterion* had a circulation of only 800. And didn't *Scrutiny* have even less? The influence of these periodicals is still very much with us and is everywhere acknowledged; reprints are made; theses are written; disciples pursue their cultural careers. *The Clergy Review* must be seen in the same light; with a much bigger subscription list, with a wider and deeper range of human interests, with a readership profoundly involved in the life of society at every level, how could one imagine that nothing significant was happening?

Only people who think of the clergy as mere technicians of the obvious can fail to appreciate what they are trying to

9

achieve. *The Clergy Review* is not a handbook wherein the members of a clerical closed shop may learn their private etiquette. It is committed to the construction of an entire way of life. Civilisation is our affair. 'Every venture is a new beginning'. In the general history of 'little reviews' and their readers, the career of this one will even now repay anyone's attention.

August 1972

FOR CLERGY, READ LAITY

PEOPLE often say that *The Clergy Review* should change its name. Surprised to find that its contents are not narrowly clerical, they suggest that many of those who would enjoy reading it do not make the effort because they feel excluded from a private ecclesiastical preserve.

One or two other periodicals have recently felt the need for change; *L'Ami du Clergé*, for example, is now *Esprit et Vie*. And new ones have sprung up, with attractively all-embracing titles: *Concilium, Communio*. Well-established publications, however, usually manage to adapt themselves successfully without altering their name. Before rushing into anything, it might be as well to enquire into the meaning of the one we have already.

In the New Testament scheme of things, the clergy are the whole Church: that part of humanity which has been chosen by God and visibly set apart as his People, the growing-point of unity throughout history for all mankind. The *cleros* and the *laos* are the same thing: one society, without distinction. *Cleros* can be used to mean a part of that society, but not the part we now mean; it denotes the people committed to the pastoral charge of those who have been given responsibility for the Word of God and made leaders of the community.

The fact that 'clergy' has come to mean a part of the church in contra-distinction from the laity, those who are officially in charge, instead of those who are committed to their care, is one example among many of our failures to grasp the extent of the change brought about by the Gospel; it is a return to a pre-Christian phase of human history. We have taken over and thoughtlessly passed on the social structure of the Roman Empire and the feudal system of the Middle Ages, not the Christian order of the New Testament world-view.

The clergy/laity distinction has set up many false problems for the Church, and will go on doing so as long as it is retained, since it represents a principle alien to the nature of the Church as a society. Talk of a 'distinctively clerical' or a 'distinctively lay' point of view is nonsense. A laity 'independent of the hierarchy' would not be a laity at all, just as a hierarchy without the laity would, in Cardinal Newman's words, 'look pretty silly'.

The true picture of things is the one set out by St Paul in 1 Corinthians: one Body and one Spirit, with a diversity of gifts. One of those gifts we have come to recognise as the gift of ministry, the sacrament of Order by which the whole Church is held together, in the first place through the preaching of the Word of God and in the second place through every form of community service.

Bishops, priests and deacons are as much part of the laity as everyone else; they work with them and for them, and never apart from them. They must not allow themselves to degenerate into a separate caste, with their own private, largely ritual, preoccupations. And they are as much in the world as anyone else. What can they possibly think they are doing in preaching the Gospel, if they are not occupied in actively changing the world into which they have been sent?

Rather than search for a new name, it will be better to go on working for an understanding of the kind of people that we are. We are not 'the Roman Catholics', a section of the community holding ourselves apart and living by our own peculiar tribal pattern, moral code and devotional style, outside the mainstream of English life. We already are the mainstream of English life, and always have been: 'hidden', in Ronald Knox's image, but the mainstream just the same. Already we contain an active cross-section of the English people; of no other distinct society, religious or otherwise, in this country can one say the same. But we shall not expand further, renewing the whole of English life, unless we abandon those distortions and deficiencies that are part of our present, inherited, way of life.

The Church must live under the continual correction of the Word of God; and there we learn that laycraft has as little justification for its existence as priestcraft. The only 'independence' anyone needs is an independence from the world as it organises itself in opposition to God; to win that independence we must all acknowledge one dependence, and one alone; obedience to Christ, in whose all-inclusive People diversity flourishes but distinctions are at an end.

February 1977

WHAT'S IN A NAME?

THE intercession for 'the clergy' in the second Eucharistic Prayer appears to many celebrants unduly abrupt and exclusive. So they add 'and people' or 'and faithful', to show that they at any rate have not forgotten the laity, and do not imagine, in these post-*Lumen Gentium* days, that clerics are the only people in the Church.

It is possible, however, to wonder if those who introduced this prayer, instead of committing a theological oversight, were not in reality being subtle, and expecting more of us than we have realised. Perhaps they were going back to the New Testament meaning of 'clergy'. For St Peter, the clergy are the lay people allotted to the care of one of the appointed pastors of the Church, who are warned not to lord it over their flock (1 Peter 5:3). So perhaps *clerus* in Eucharistic Prayer II was meant to signify the whole Church, the entire people who are now under the care of the Lord, whose portion they are. If that is the case, it should be translated by some such expression as 'your people', to avoid the contemporary misunderstanding arising out of the semantic reversal that the centuries have, as so often, brought upon us. 'Clergy and people', almost as much as 'clergy' alone, gives a wrong impression.

All this poses a problem for *The Clergy Review*. When it was founded, everyone knew who the clergy were: the ordained men with their white collars and their black suits who were the specially chosen share of God. And where the *Review* was concerned, 'clergy' meant the parish clergy, the seminary priests, the seculars, who needed their own private journal where the

12

concerns of their trade could be aired without much fear that the laity would be eavesdropping.

Now that Vatican II has given us a theology of the Church, and so re-established our boundaries and landmarks, we need to make sure we understand correctly the name by which the *Review* is known. So well known, in fact, that, despite pressure to the contrary, it was decided after due thought last year to keep it. People still say 'Why do you call yourselves *The Clergy Review*, when you publish articles that people would want to read?' The answer must now be: 'Perhaps your idea of the clergy needs a change'.

To help the change forward a little, it may be worth while pointing out once again that the 'clergy' are, in the meaning of the New Testament under which we live, first of all the whole Church of God, his chosen People, the instrument by which he intends to restore the unity of the human race. And so the *Review* is for everybody; it is meant to be of service to all.

In the second place, *cleros* designates the various ministerial responsibilities in the Church. This is the meaning the word has, for instance, in the *Apostolic Tradition* of Hippolytus. It still therefore refers to the people for whom the various ministers are in different ways responsible, and means nothing without them; it is a charge, a relationship linking an individual to those who are placed under his care.

And in the third place, the clergy can be said to be in particular those ministers who have received the sacrament of Holy Order and who are therefore the special servants of the Word and the Spirit, designated to bring about the existence and harmonious working of God's People. But this special meaning, once again, is nothing without the people; without the assignment made to the Apostles and their successors, the assignment by which (and by whom) they will be judged.

For *The Clergy Review*, perhaps, a revolution? No, rather a widening of horizons. If it is the whole Church that has been sent into the world, we must cease to call one class alone 'secular', or one class alone 'clergy'. All are for the Church: none more than those whose *cleros* it is to provide its daily bread.

July 1979

13

1981

THE approaching bi-centenary of Bishop Richard Challoner's death will enable *The Clergy Review* to celebrate its own fiftieth birthday next year especially by devoting attention to the man who was called upon to play a truly cardinal role in the history of the English Catholic Church. He withstood the tide that might have carried us away beyond survival; he renewed and handed on the tradition, and in his lifetime fresh growth and eventual health and strength became possible. He will be remembered especially, of course, in his resting-place, Westminster Cathedral. But the commemorations should be held throughout the country, with renewed prayers that an Englishman whose faith and character made him respected and venerated in his own lifetime, should be honoured in the worship of the Universal Church. The Venerable Richard Challoner is a worthy countryman and successor of the Venerable Bede. It is to be hoped that the publication this coming year of the results of fresh historical research and appraisal will help to earn him the place he deserves in our national tradition and culture.

1980 has been the fourteenth year since Bishop Christopher Butler began to preside over the labours of the *Review*, with its newly constituted advisory board and its newly appointed editor. He decided in the course of the year that it was time this particular responsibility came to an end, but the change has gone unmentioned until this month, when new developments can also be made known. I have constantly had cause to be grateful to him for the strength of his support, for his encouragement whenever needed, for his unerring eye for detail, for his counsel on innumerable occasions and for the freedom which the surety of his judgement has made possible. These have been strenuous and even dangerous years, and the fact that buoyancy has been maintained in stormy seas owes more than I can say (and, probably, than I know) to his wise and attentive presence, from which the *Review* and its board will continue to benefit.

The board now welcomes Bishop Cormac Murphy-O'Connor of the diocese of Arundel and Brighton among its members and anticipates an interesting and lively future as it pursues its work with the help of his experience and judgement.

There is one other change. I have now moved from the London parish where I have been based for the last eight years, St Mary's, Cadogan Street, and am living near Huntingdon, in the diocese of East Anglia. The work at Heythrop College, as head of the Department of Church History, continues. From this new home, I hope to become more closely acquainted with a variety of parishes and pastoral needs. The move to the country does not, in my own mind at any rate, indicate impending retirement.

December 1980

II
THE CHURCH IN ENGLAND AND WALES

A NEW GHETTO MENTALITY

UP to twelve or fifteen years ago, English Catholics stood shoulder to shoulder in determined opposition to the hostile world which surrounded them, and defended themselves valiantly against foes both real and imaginary. Letters to the editors of our national and local press were sent off by the sackful whenever the slightest sound of criticism was heard: all attacks were answered, all knots untied, all doubts dispelled. Discreditable episodes held against us from our wicked past were dismissed, if they could not be disproved, by recounting racy tales of Popes even more wicked and Inquisitors even more dreadful than our innocent interlocutors had ever imagined. Pamphlets poured forth reflecting and prolonging the dying echoes of wordy battles of long ago, deafening once but now forgotten. The convert who had wrestled long with the vital problems of God's existence, man's salvation, the reality of Christ and the presence of his Church, found that much of his new companions' energy was dissipated in coping with issues undreamt of by modern man.

It was said that we bore the mark of the ghetto: that we were going through the motions characteristic of a beleaguered garrison, unaware that the enemy had struck camp and moved elsewhere. Our unswerving loyalty to the cause, staunch and honourable as it was, made us blind to the new situation, to the opportunities for creative work, to the emptiness which we were called on to fill with Gospel life and truth.

Today, in the post-conciliar epoch, the ghetto mind lives on. But it lives in other men. The cramped utterances, the intemperate and peevish outbursts, the warfaring mentality which we associate with rootless and unhappy exiles, with men who feel themselves debarred from friendship and influence, with all who labour under a grievance, are now directed not

18

against the hard world outside, but against our fellow-Catholics. The ghetto that was self-defensive is now self-destructive. The world outside is as unimpressed as it was before. Annoyed once by our aggressive touchiness, it now smiles mockingly at this group of fools, at one another's throats over the colour of a bishop's socks.

The new ritualism forgets that anti-triumphalist display is as unpleasant as pompous worldliness and can be much more deceptive. The stage-entry of Tartuffe, *Laurent, serrez ma haire avec ma discipline,* should have warned us for ever against loud talk of the diaconate and of penance. Hair-shirts are under-garments; worn, for greater comfort, as fancy waistcoats, they flatter the eye only of those afflicted with a gullibility uncharac-teristic of the Christian mind. One does not qualify as a space-age bishop by the simple act of donning a pectoral cross in expanded polystyrene. Pope John, who walked the streets of Rome to visit the poor and the sick, as Pius IX had done before him, also brought back into use the cap of a Renaissance pope. Both he and Pope Paul have set before our bishops the example of St Charles Borromeo, a pastor shaped in the Tridentine mould, who was inspired and instructed by the English reformers and martyrs.

Those who today are trying to build in England a Christian people whose lives are penetrated by the renewing light of the Spirit, were trained, many of them, by the very men who formed the mind of Vatican II. They take the Council's decisions as their charter, but find their efforts continually hampered, blocked and obliterated by a barrage of cantankerous, sour, unquiet, ill-informed speeches and writings; uttered in the name of freedom, progress and the open mind, these effusions serve only to irritate, estrange and antagonise those whom (no doubt) they are meant to edify.

'He that goeth about to persuade a multitude, that they are not so well governed as they ought to be', wrote Richard Hooker, 'shall never want favourable and attentive hearers.' Our radicals have discovered this, and are delighted. Their writings may not sell on railway bookstalls, or in church porches, but they circulate none the less, in the national news-papers as well as in periodicals whose subscription lists con-stitute an inner ring of the enlightened. 'And because such as openly reprove supposed disorders of state are taken for principal friends to the common benefit of all, and for men that carry singular freedom of mind, under this fair and plausible colour whatsoever they utter passeth for good and current.' How bold, how brave, to belabour a bishop! 'They know the manifold defects whereunto every kind of regiment is subject, but the secret lets and difficulties, which in public proceedings are innumerable and inevitable, they have not ordinarily the judgement to consider.'

That they should succeed and go on writing is of course the fault of the rest of us. 'That which wanteth in the weight of their speech, is supplied by the aptness of men's minds to accept and believe it.' We read and listen, attracted, convinced, or perhaps afraid to be taken for men opposed to change. 'If we maintain things that are established, we have . . . to strive with a number of heavy prejudices deeply rooted in the hearts of men, who think that herein we serve the time, and speak in favour of the present state, because thereby we either seek or hold preferment.' Surely these men are letting in the light and demonstrating to all the glorious freedom of the adult Catholic man?

No, they are not. They are striking empty air, forcing open doors that were never locked, demolishing walls long since climbed and left behind, bare ruined memorials of an abandoned past. Those who refuse to imitate them are not time-servers, nor do they necessarily, as Richard Hooker did, defend things that are established. They are committed and honest men, who seek neither to blame others who seem to be standing still, nor, before the eyes of the world, to dissociate themselves from their brethren, nor to rail against the family which they have joined. Mere Catholics, they are content to let the weeds grow together with the wheat until the time of harvest. When they make innovations, they do not call attention to themselves by their noisy disparagement or destruction of everything left behind by others. When they sow seeds, they do not dig up what other men have planted. Their affirmations need no fanfare of negation to make them sound louder in men's ears. They know that they do no more than enter into other men's labours. They have no itch to enter into controversy, but there comes a moment when one grows weary of distracting polemic and of small men who complain and sneer, collecting easy pocket-money by peddling the backstairs gossip of their mother's household, like so many dismissed hirelings fallen on bad times.

There are many in England who are content to be Catholics; they find in Christ's Church the freedom of God's world and are concerned only to make that freedom available to others. The Vatican Council is God's way of lifting men out of their old routine, of enabling them to see further than the barriers erected for them by historical or political pressure. The vision of the Church which we have now been given helps us to forget the ways in which we have been confined; we can see ourselves now not as a social minority, set apart from the main stream of English life, but as men who work at the centre and heart of everything around us. We speak as a Church free of the State's constraining ties, free of the constrictions imposed by national perspectives or by parties tied to movements and controversies of the past, free continually to reform ourselves and to adapt our pastoral methods, as we have done, in so many ways, over the last four hundred years.

For separated Christians in England, we are the bridge-Church, having spiritual, liturgical and dogmatic affinities with all of them. The distinctive strands in Anglicanism, which have sought so long for reconciliation, will find in Catholicism a comprehensiveness greater than that which they already enjoy and value, matched by a unity which they are unable to establish for themselves. Scripture, Tradition and Reason, which so easily become warring principles within the Church of England, underlying the Evangelical, Anglo-Catholic and Modernist schools of thought, are active as well as united within the Catholic synthesis. Warmth of devotion, evangelistic fervour, attachment to the local church, sturdy non-conformity, depth of silent adoration, all these things Free Churchmen will find in the Catholic Church, which has a longer tradition of independence than any of them.

The educational ideals formulated in the nineteenth century, now rapidly fading, will be widened, deepened and renewed as we follow our calling in the teaching Church. Man in the image of God is more human than man alone. The humanism of Greece and Rome, or a humanism inspired by the natural sciences, are surpassed by the humanism of Christ, in which all the wisdom

21

of man is set within the knowledge and reality of God. One Church and one world, in which family and national loyalties are valued but never limit the boundaries of our vision, will now replace Empire and Establishment in the eyes of Englishmen.

The dialogue with unbelievers may be expected to develop in a new, more serious way in the years ahead. Many of them show an appreciation of Catholic thought and spirituality and a readiness to listen which matches the efforts we can for our part justly claim to have made already. The university background of some of our waspish laymen might lead us to expect them to launch out in this direction, but they are happily preoccupied with parish gossip and their noisy splashings in the holy water stoup. If they would turn their energies to serious writing and research instead of playing their silly game of startling the Catholic bourgeois, we might find ourselves being helped a bit further forward.

The seminary, for Cardinal Allen, was a place where the most liberal education of all was available to those who would come to ask questions, before learning to teach the Gospel to others. We wish for no higher ideal. We study to create for the glory of the Lord; no rude mechanics, but whole men in the service of God's people, the priests formed by Vatican II would thank the radicals to stop jogging their elbows and let them' get on with the work already in hand. The fortress fell down years ago; it is high time these ageing young men grew up and stopped throwing stones among the ruins.

The Tablet, 5 March 1966

A NEW BEGINNING

FOR long, weary years now the mind and life of English Catholicism have been plagued by the continual intrusion of a nagging mood of cynical criticism, which has destroyed men's confidence, sapped their will to work creatively and hopefully, and drained the energies of those who have tried to resist this acid, depressing and destructive movement of the human mind. Without a renewal of confidence in the Church, without a clear recognition of the fact that we are here faced with a violent temptation against the faith and against the

Spirit, there is no future for the Church in this country. It must be plainly understood that we have been allowing ourselves to become involved, far too deeply, in what was not a genuine, rational illumination, but a dark pessimism that fed itself only on purgatives and took delight only in acts of demolition.

In a Church which has been persistently trying to open up channels of communication, to consult widely before decisions are made, to give everyone their voice and their distinctive responsibility, there are still men who prefer to take the way of the pressure group and the conspiracy. This is a temptation into which those who like to be called progressives are as liable to fall as those who have been damned as conservatives. We are discovering, too, that there are some who will always raise their voices in contradiction, whatever they are asked to do; some of them have passed during their careers from one protesting camp to another.

Already, some are trying to write off Vatican II as out of date. Others, without going so far, set Vatican II against Vatican I and Trent, as if the Spirit of God were now speaking in violent contradiction with himself, wiping out the past and deflecting the Church onto a new route, in a state of partial amnesia.

The Church has been right to be patient with all the controversy, not to resort to repression or to the kind of name-calling from which many have had to suffer. But readiness to listen can be carried too far; it can be merely time-wasting; the moment comes when one simply has to stop listening and go off to get on with some work. If some people want to turn the Church into a talking-shop, that is their affair; they won't hold the crowds for long.

Pope John would not listen to prophets of doom. In this country, the dark clouds have been coming from more than one direction. The future lies with those who refuse to allow the sour thoughts of bitter men to enter their minds, who keep out of heat-producing ephemeral controversy, who leave contradiction to the publicists who live on it, and who recognise in the present disturbances the very attack we had to be ready for after a Council which set out to renew our faith in the Church.

To have faith in the Church means acting in terms of what we believe the Church to be, and not judging the Church and

23

other Catholics in purely human terms. It means a readiness to begin by learning from the Church, to approach the study of the faith in a truly scientific spirit, trying to discover the facts and not treating theology as a sort of game in which argument and taking sides are more important than arriving at a result. It means accepting the Church as it is and working with it, not writing off those who have as much right to be there as we have.

It means believing that the Catholic Church in this country really is the Catholic Church, and not some sort of sect that might become the Catholic Church if enough enlightened people got to work on it. It means being more interested in bringing the faith to others than in controversy within the Church; once the apostolic spirit has gone, then Church life of every kind becomes completely stale and sour. It means renewing the Church rather by bringing it into contact with new people and new ways of thought than by some purely internal process of cogitation. Pope John suggested opening the windows, not just rearranging the furniture in the same old overnight atmosphere.

A healthy conscience does not take long to examine. It is a sign of spiritual disease to be continually mulling over one's misdeeds and failings. Vatican II was meant to be a time of self-examination and renewal; we betray the Council and the lead of the Spirit that was given there if we remain for ever in a state of hesitation and distrust weighed down by our faults or the faults of others and unable to launch out with confidence. We shall do well to refuse to give the compulsive protesters and negative critics even the encouragement of our attention. If we can forget what we are and live in terms of what God is making us, then we shall find the new Church which is even now growing all round us.

October 1968

THE FORTY MARTYRS AND THE FUTURE

NOT very many years ago, Catholic and Protestant scholars engaged in violent combat about the interpretation of the middle ages. Deep confessional differences made it appear necessary to score apologetic points against one's religious adversary. It is difficult for historians today to imagine themselves falling back into such a frame of mind. The study of the middle ages has ceased to be a controversial issue and is pursued in a scientific spirit for its lessons about mankind and about the Church.

Students of the sixteenth and seventeenth centuries are moving rapidly in the same direction, though it cannot yet be said that the same feelings of partnership are being felt by all of them. Now that we are entering a new epoch in our understanding of the relationship between the Church and the world, between ecclesiastical administration and secular government, and are accordingly much more easily able to envisage the healing of Christian divisions, it is likely that within a few years the study of reformation and post-reformation history will be pursued in as objective a way as that of the middle ages, and therefore in a way much more nourishing and healing where human relationships are concerned.

The place of the Forty Martyrs within English life and the constructive role of their witness will certainly be very much better understood when the study of their lives is conducted in this way. The full significance of the celebration of their memory will, however, only become clear if the Church in this country is able to move into a new orientation of its activities, as boldly planned as that which the break with Rome brought about in the sixteenth century. The reconstruction of English Catholicism in the nineteenth century was for a very large part based upon mediæval and counter-reformation patterns. It is difficult to see how things could have been otherwise, and Catholics were by no means alone at that time in seeking inspiration for revival in the patterns of the past.

At the present moment we see more clearly that the mere resurrection of old styles is not enough, but we are still searching for a new identity and for the way ahead. If we are to re-build the Church it seems certain that we shall have to force ourselves as Catholics to think no longer in sectarian terms and to preoccupy ourselves not so much with the special care of a single group within the national religious life, as with developing a Christian style of living which is so attractive, reconciling and inspiring, that throughout our society people will be able

25

to recognise that they can find themselves within it and that national life itself can be renewed by it once the self-satisfied patriotism of the past has been forgotten.

Where the clergy are concerned, this means a re-orientation of studies and pastoral activities which it will take years yet to achieve. In particular, one must hope for a profound renewal of the secular clergy which will involve the final destruction of the idea that they are just plodding, obscure, responsible men of routine, whose job it is to keep the Church ticking over and who are not expected to be leaders or pioneers. If this is to come about it will be necessary to forge a new sense of the unity of religious and secular clergy in the priesthood, and it is much to be hoped that common studies pursued at places like Heythrop College, which opens its doors this autumn in London, will further this end.

It may well seem that too little thought and work is yet being put into this local renewal. Certainly very little ever appears about it in the national press and not all that much, in the sense of fresh thinking, in the Catholic press either. But I don't think I am mistaken or starry-eyed in saying that the new spirit and some of the new institutions are already there and that we have started to lay the foundations of a local Catholicism which is not content to live as a quiet minority, but which is becoming visible as a rich source of truly human life for the future.

October 1970

IT *IS* A RELIGIOUS ISSUE

THE nineteenth and twentieth century search for the economic motive in human affairs has brought a sane realism into the study of history, even including Church history. It has sometimes been necessary to resist or to correct attempts to argue that the history of religion is no more than the history of material supply and demand in an ideological disguise, but a religion which pays as much attention to the proper use of the riches of this world as Christianity does can hardly overlook the investigation of man's struggle for ownership, lust for power, and, where it exists, compassion for the weak and the poor.

Churchmen may often enough be right when they reject the cynic's explanation of their idealism as a barely concealed desire for personal gain. They can point to plenty of cases where the practice of genuine unselfishness has left a lasting mark on social behaviour. They should accordingly be wary of turning to economic explanations when wanting to excuse their own failures or deflect people's attention from their own direct contributions to the sum of human misery. It will not do for them to shrug off responsibility for conflict and violence by saying that the religious labels and battle-cries being used are really a cover for underlying material realities.

Religion is most certainly a powerful contributory factor in the appalling antagonisms unleashed in Northern Ireland; religious leaders cannot wash their hands by saying that what is at work here is false Christianity, or content themselves with uttering those pious platitudes which harmonise with the state of mind of ineffective intellectuals but which are quite inaudible to those human beings (the majority) who have passions capable of being roused.

English people either do not understand or are unwilling to face the fact that the unholy and explosive mixture of religion and nationalistic politics in Northern Ireland is largely of their own making: that what they see there is very much what was to be found in their own country before the Oxford Movement and ecumenism softened the climate, with the Orange Order and Ian Paisley playing the role of Exeter Hall and John Kensit, no doubt, but with a generalised feeling of religious prejudice, more gentlemanly but none the less devastatingly effective, acting to keep Catholics at bay.

Irish Catholics, meanwhile, sorely tried as they are, and rightly scornful as they have long been of the temporising feebleness of English Catholicism, need to watch that they do not fall into the same trap as those Englishmen who have identified the national cause with their religion and have slipped into Old Testament attitudes, into belief in holy colonisation, or even in the holy war.

Full Christian responsibility must be taken for what is happening in Northern Ireland, because it is in the name of Christ that injustice and violence have been committed. If churchmen, whether Catholic or Protestant, feel themselves so

27

involved in their nation's demands, so blinkered by their political sympathies, that they cannot speak or act for reconciliation, then let them keep quiet and meditate on conversion, which means the rejection of the past and continuing sins in which their Churches have been implicated. But if there are any churchmen left who believe that Christ and the Church he has given to the world are the means God has provided for making peace — churchmen whose membership of the People of God is more important to them than being an Englishman, Irishman or Ulsterman — then it is they who hold the key to the present situation.

Vatican Councils, Bishops' Synods, Priests' Conferences: so much escapist hot air, if Christians are unable to find a solution to the Northern Ireland conflict. It is easier to rearrange ceremonies than to help human beings. Vatican II changed the liturgy and wanted to change the world. The priesthood may be no more than a refuge in rubrics; can we make it instead an instrument for peace?

January 1972

ON NOT LIVING BY OUR WITS

EACH day that passes confirms the fact that the Church in England suffers above all from a lack of that simple, profound wisdom which comes from a truly rational and intelligent cultivation of the life of faith.

Practical wisdom we have in plenty: good business sense which knows how to read a balance sheet, handle bricks and mortar or cope with a committee. But when we are faced with questions arising out of difficulties over faith or out of the renewal of Church life itself, then we fall short every time.

The quick reply which satisfies an examiner, which turns the tables on an opponent in an academic disputation, which temporarily downs a heckler at a CEG meeting, which keeps TV interviewers at bay, which baffles but does not deceive the experts: this, the product of a certain type of Catholic upbringing, can win battles and live to fight again, but it will never win the real war.

The wisdom which listens to the Word of God and which listens to people, taking them seriously and not reducing faith to an all-purpose formula or regarding others as potential digits on a private scoreboard, this is what we should all be praying for.

We do not have it at present and on that account we are failing to deal adequately with the problems of interpreting the documents of revelation and of religious education, to take seriously the future of the ministry, to give the Church its proper place at the centre of English intellectual life and to grasp the opportunities arising out of the momentous changes in our ways of worship.

Contemplation will save us, not cleverness. The wisdom born from a true knowledge of the folly of the Cross can and must find ways of expressing itself in the service of God and of mankind; without it, we may stave off our opponents for a while, but we shall never win them over to our side.

January 1973

PRIORITIES

'THE first duty of a bishop is to preach the Gospel'. Trent said it, Vatican II said it; our theory is perfectly clear. Our practice is another matter. The first duty of a bishop, and therefore of a priest and of every member of the Church, is to preach the Gospel: to communicate to other people the truth by which they may be saved. Styles can change, our words can change; the Word does not change. Truth sets men free; the Church is the servant of all truth. But, in actual fact, that is not where our emphasis lies. Our money and our energies are spent on other things: not on truth.

The budget of the National Catholic Fund provides clear evidence of this failure to put first things first.

The Information Office receives the largest sum. One must add to this the £50,000 which is raised nationally for the Radio and Television Centre at Hatch End: half the total raised for the National Catholic Fund itself. We are spending all this money on communication and practically nothing at all on making sure we know what it is we have to communicate.

Education and Catechetics: £75; Seminaries: £448; Theology: £250. This is the measure of our national concern for truth. The nerveless mishandling of catechetics over a great many years; the niggardly, haphazard and improvident attitude to priestly training; the off-hand dismissal of the study of theology — or of anything else — as a hobby for effete intellectuals, who are to be humoured but not to be trusted or used: these glaring weaknesses in the behaviour and character of our Catholic community are clearly going to be left untouched and unremedied, however deeply they may undermine and render fruitless our other efforts.

If further evidence is needed, one can turn to *Co-responsibility and the Clergy*, the report of the joint working party of the Bishops' Conference and the National Conference of Priests. Co-responsibility for what? There is not one word in the entire report which suggests that bishops and priests share joint responsibility for getting the message of the Gospel across to the people to whom we are sent. There is no sense of mission, no awareness of the fact that the Church has a purpose beyond itself and its own interior management. The report deals only with the private life of the Church: teamwork, living conditions, in-service training, salaries and pensions; all of these are matters needing attention, but the fundamental issue is left out of account. The practical questions will not really be solved unless they are properly related to the work which bishops and priests are expected to do. The clergy need to renew their grasp of their overriding purpose; all the reassurance in the world about relationships, remuneration and retirement will be useless if bishops and priests do not concentrate on the work they are for and do not co-operate for the conversion of the people around them to the truth which they serve.

The writers of the report will plead that they left such matters to the other joint working party on pastoral strategy, and their report, *The Church 2000*. But here again, a serious attempt to express the mission and the message of the Church and to understand the society to which we should be speaking has not been made. It would have been enough if Vatican II had been thoroughly digested and put across in terms of our local responsibilities; but even this elementary piece of work has not been done. An interest in the study of the actual content of revelation, as distinct from some of its fringe-benefits, incidentals and accidental associations, has in this country been left almost entirely to the religious orders and, in a patchy and unconvinced sort of way, to the seminaries. We need the whole weight of the Church behind higher education, not just a benevolent but sceptical toleration. If theology is really so dangerous a topic, if theologians are simply people whose chief function in life is to demonstrate to the pious and obedient faithful the dangers of intellectual pride, then maybe the faith itself is not really as assured a plank of salvation as we like to think it is.

Whatever their degree of academic culture, the people who watch the Church with interest are not really such fools as some of us like to think they are. They will be convinced only by someone who knows and has a respect for what he believes as well as for his audience. When the Church as a whole, on a national scale, begins to take a serious interest in the intellectual validity and significance of what it has to say, then enquirers will have some confidence in turning to us instead of to one or other of our innumerable rivals. But bishops and priests together seem to have other priorities. Only one agency has a lower budget under the National Catholic Fund than catechetics: the secretariat for non-believers, with £58. The Church in England and Wales is at present more preoccupied with itself than with its message or its audience; but without a product, research, and an interest in the market, no firm ever flourished for long.

August 1973

THE CHURCH 2001

NEW TESTAMENT scholars often tell us that the early Christians were above all intensely convinced that their Lord was about to return and bring the world to an end; some, now out-dated, used to go on to say that the Church was an after-thought, a second best, set up as a substitute when hopes of the parousia had faded. It is refreshing now to hear[1] that the early Christians, whatever

[1] From David Stanley, s.j., for example: '*Koinonia* as Symbol and Reality in the Primitive Church', in D'Ercole, J. and Stickler, A. M., *Communione Interecclesiale — Collegialità — Primato — Ecumenismo*, Rome, 1972, 2 vols., I, pp. 83-99.

the degree of their eschatological tension, were even more aware of the continuing presence of the Risen Lord in the midst of his Church. To make plans for the future, to work out what the Church may be like less than thirty years from now, does not mean that we are settling down, becoming worldly minded, putting the thought of the Master's return out of our minds. It is really a normal response to the present moment, to the contemporary guidance of the Lord and his spirit. We do not know exactly what he will have made of the Church by the year 2001; but we do know that the relationships and the life of the Church will be recognisably those of the year 1 and of every other year. To make plans is not to decide for ourselves what we will make of the Church; it is simply part of our perennial attempt to think out what discipleship means, what Christianity itself really is, as distinct from what men have made of it, and what we in our time must do to express that discipleship. Plans for A.D. 2001 are in reality attempts to ask ourselves what Christ, the Word of God, requires of his Church in 1974.

This must mean, in particular, the Church in the British zone of influence which the *Review* mainly serves. This is our immediate context, the context of an English-speaking culture which has in so many ways defined itself over against Rome and the Catholic Church, which has thought of itself as necessarily opposed to the system of religious and political authority and government to which we as a Church are thought to be committed. 'As English is the natural tongue, so Protestantism is the intellectual and moral language of the body politic', wrote John Henry Newman in 1851; and we would be deceiving ourselves if we thought that the climate had really changed very much over the years since that time. We may have grown in all English-speaking countries and given a fuller and better account of ourselves since that time; but there are still mountains of accumulated misconceptions and antagonism to be cleared away. The 'Protestantism' in question is often, nowadays, rather an unbelieving, anti-religious, secularism than a body of thought with any Christian content; but it is still there just the same. Vatican II was all very well in theory, and has opened many hearts and minds so that conversation and collaboration have become possible; but we still have to translate all those words into actions and social reality.

We are thinking, then, of a religious and cultural area marked by Anglicanism and by the Free Church, Independent, traditions, which has produced its own political institutions, its own style of civilisation, deeply influenced by Christianity; we are thinking of the future development of this way of life, which has spread from sixteenth- and seventeenth-century England to North America, to Australia and New Zealand, to Africa and India, which attained a high level of self-confidence and influence in the nineteenth century and which is still as much alive and as fertile, if not as massive, as any other pattern of political and cultural life at present flourishing anywhere else.

It is a way of life which has defined itself, as we have seen, in opposition to Catholicism; what we are now working for is its continuation and progress within the Church.

That means, in the first place, that we shall have to reach out to understand the essential, positive Christian affirmations of Anglicanism and of the nonconformist churches who, like ourselves, have developed for one reason or another outside the nationally established church, in order that the Christians of these churches may find themselves at home within Catholic communion.

This reconciling function, which we are now called upon to exercise ecumenically within the divided churches, is also our responsibility in political and social fields. The theological differences which led to denominational division were also class and political differences. The present chronic state of separation and friction in English public life goes back to a church/chapel separation, with the chapels originally feeding both the Liberal and the Labour opposition to the possessing classes, who identified themselves with the national, established church. The lines of cleavage have become much more complex since that time. On both sides of the class barrier there is an anti-foreign, anti-Catholic state of mind that needs changing; in order that industrial peace and collaboration can be achieved in England, it will be necessary for the Church to overcome this prejudice and to act socially as a peace-making influence. Those who want to escape from the crude oppositions of English party politics today must somehow be shown that there is a Christian body of thought and political experience which in other countries has had a progressive and constructive effect on economic and political affairs. We have rightly kept clear of the formation of a Catholic party; but we have tended accordingly to avoid the task of finding some other way of being of service to the community in local or national government. Individual dedication is not enough; we need to show that Catholicism has something positive to offer by means of which we may overcome some of our least attractive political faults.

First Priority: Higher Education

It is the Church's activity in the field of higher education that is going to decide its success or failure in this reconciling and socially constructive role. The priority lies with the spread of true knowledge of the Word of God, with the study of the Christian faith as a body of teaching by which the human understanding is to be enlarged, enlightened and guided. The proper place of this teaching and way of life among other bodies of knowledge and forms of enquiry needs to be firmly established; and this can only be done by a much greater effort in universities and training colleges and in adult education of all kinds, to which the whole Church must become committed under the leadership of the bishops. It cannot be left to individuals or to subsidiary organisations in the Church, the bishops remaining on the touchlines simply to watch the state of play and to intervene if they think things are getting out of hand. This is a matter which affects the whole attitude to the faith of the entire Catholic community: are we dealing with a body of truth made known by God and essential to human happiness, and therefore more worthy of scientific investigation than any other field of enquiry, or is Christianity just a form of private piety, a body of social customs with a purely decorative or cultural role, which can claim its ration of time on television and must then give way to far more interesting and important investigations into interstellar space, the psychology of inter-personal action or the myths and legends of the North? Is Christianity something to be learned in infancy and then simply observed dutifully (or forgotten about) in adult life, or is it something to be grown into, essential to a mature and complete adult attitude to the world?

To many, an emphasis of this kind on the tertiary level of education will sound like pretentious intellectualism; Christianity, they will say, is for the simple and unlearned, and the small minority of university men and women can safely be neglected or humoured when need be, in favour of the plain, straightforward, ordinary good Catholics in ordinary parishes throughout the country. But this point of view is in fact unworthy of the Christian apostle and pastor. It is unworthy because it forgets that Christianity is truth, feeding and nourishing man's rational and spiritual nature, and it is unworthy because it forgets that all men, the unlearned as well as the academic, have minds which can grasp the profoundest truths and be guided by them once they are presented to them through the total complex of means which is used by the Word of God in his activity as teacher of mankind.

The only way of preventing the Church from degenerating into senseless routine, folk-religion or superstition is through teaching men, in season and out of season, that their roots are not to be set in national traditions, in religions or philosophies of human devising, or in themselves and their own personal whims and desires, but in the Word of God by whom all such partial truths or loyalties are judged. Theological research and teaching and the encouragement of every form of study of God's creation must be given first place in our activities today for the very same reasons as the Apostles had when they declared that their first preoccupation was the service of the Word of God. Without that service there can be no true Church; only a set of rules and observances, a conglomeration of human relationships kept together by inertia, by compulsive emotional pressures, by guilt-feelings, by fear and by self-interest. It is by knowing the truth and being changed by the truth that the Church comes into existence. If we do not succeed in translating this fact into real institutional form and into personal practice on a far wider scale than at present, then our prayers and devotions will rightly be regarded as no more than a flight from reality, not an urgent desire to know and love the truth.

The latest volume of Karl Rahner's collected writings[1] has a good deal to say about the passage in Vatican II's Constitution on the Church (*Lumen Gentium*, n. 76) which affirms that 'the Church of Christ is truly present in all lawfully constituted local communities of the faithful, who, united with their pastors, are, in the New Testament, themselves called "churches"'. He takes this passage as the text for what he has to say about the present shift in emphasis from thinking almost entirely in terms of the universal world-wide Church to a realisation that the Church is present and directly experienced in the local Christian community. This line of thought, together with what Fr Rahner has to say about the diaspora-situation of the contemporary church, has been behind much of what has been said and done recently about fostering *communautés de base*, small groups of Christians who know one another well and worship and act together. Fr Michael Winter made this a principal theme of his *Mission or Maintenance* (Darton, Longman & Todd, 1973). For many English Catholics, it may sound like a return to the catacombs from which they have only recently emerged. But it does deserve the attention of everyone involved in the apostolate in English-speaking countries, and should not be relegated too quickly to the status of purely academic continental theorising. Have we not thought in all our planning that the normal state of the Church is that of a vast, uniform, supranational organisation, recognisable (largely through adopted or preserved cultural forms) for what it is wherever it exists, so that only too often we have taken the shell or the skeleton for the living reality?

Now that we have dropped so many of the outward signs which once marked us off as Roman Catholics, we should be in a better position to make ourselves recognisable above all through the Christian openness and usefulness of our local communities. The local Catholic church should be known by the welcome which it gives and the breadth of its social concern, much more than by its use of particular liturgical or linguistic forms. The parish council exists primarily to foster the knowledge

---

[1] *Theological Investigations*, Volume 10: Writings of 1965-7, II, 409 pp. Darton, Longman & Todd, 1973.

and practice of the faith, and to make the Church useful to its neighbours, not to deal with the church fabric or new hymn-books; there can be sub-committees for that.

It is, after all, the members of these local communities, rather than the ministers who serve them for longer or shorter periods, who provide continuity of Christian witness in each place. It is they who translate what they hear and do on Sundays into effective Christian activity and by so doing build up the Church.

At the root of the Englishman's dislike of the Catholic Church there lies his conviction that it holds down human aspirations, national, communal and individual, that it debases and demoralises man, restricting human potential. It seems to him that every advance in human knowledge and happiness has been won in defiance of the Church, not with its support. The believing Catholic and even the simple unbelieving scholar tell him that this is untrue and unfair, but the beliefs and the prejudices remain. We have not yet done nearly enough to transform this antagonism into friendship and acceptance. If we can show that the faith brings with it freedom, responsibility and growth, and not the reverse, then we may arrive at A.D. 2001 with a single, greatly enlarged Christian community in the cultural area with which we are most directly concerned. That means teaching, trust, and then getting out of the way. Rather than setting out to plan the next generation's Church, we had better make sure that our own response to present needs is the right one.

March 1974

FIRST THINGS FIRST

DURING the last ten years, the Catholic community in England has altered its frame of mind; from being a rather self-conscious minority, defensive or aggressive, snobbish or just urbanely self-assured, according to temperament, breeding or background, it has become more relaxed, more extrovert, and more responsible, not just for its own affairs, but for the life of the nation as a whole, where it now occupies, no longer a marginal, but central position.

How can we make further progress? What must our priorities be, if we are to react appropriately to this new situation? Some

37

people lay emphasis on organisation, others on prayer, others on improving the quality of family life. Liturgy, the charismatic movement, service and re-education to remedy social evils: these, too, all rightly demand our attention, our effort and our time.

But the first priority is truth. None of these activities will have the results that we expect from them if the truth of the faith itself is neglected. The Church is above all concerned with being the means of communication for God's search for man. Television programmes in 1977 gave us plenty of evidence of the present interest in religion: of man's search for God. But the presentation of what God has done and is doing in Christ and in his Church was for the most part lamentably feeble. Theologians trot out hoary old critical objections to the credibility of the Gospels or re-interpret Christ's message down to vanishing point. Newspapers rarely treat Christianity with intelligent appreciation. Churchmen busy themselves with short-term campaigns in an effort to hang on to the flagging interest of their congregations.

The Church in England needs to strengthen its capacity to show that faith in Christ can only make sense, flourish and spread if it is the classic, perennial Catholic faith. We are not concerned simply to live our own lives more charitably and more spiritually; we are not concerned simply with defending our own position among the many religious options available today. We are in business to convince people that Christ is God: that Jesus is Lord and that only in his Name can salvation for the world be discovered.

Biblical scholarship and the theological understanding of the Person of Christ are the two areas where a special effort is needed in universities, colleges and seminaries. Besides that, European Catholic scholarship is too little known in this country; the strength of our case is unheard and we are left with the superficial, one-sided wranglings of the local, often lamentably provincial, theological faculties and publicists. Rigaux, Boismard, Feuillet, Mühlen, Ratzinger, Vergote, Klostermann, these are some of the names our publishers should be introducing to the English public.

The Catholic Church only continues to exist in the world because it is called together, kept going, and sent out by Jesus of Nazareth, who is the Christ of faith; by the Word of God, and by his Spirit. Catholicism is no optional choice among Christianities: it is the total faith itself. It can provide reconciliation for divided Christians and new life for our disorientated country; but only if Christ himself is preached and taught and communicated. The Church does not exist to serve the world in the first place. It exists to serve Christ. To give Christ to the world is our sole purpose, and only in that way can we hope to do the world any real and lasting service.

February 1978

ONE NATION

DISRAELI saw two nations; we are still divided. Division causes havoc in our economic and political life. Public figures call for national unity. Some hope that religion may revive and bring with it a renewal of the nation. Perhaps it will. But one thing is certain; it will not do it unless it is de-nationalised.

The use of religion to secure national unity kills both religion and the nation. The simple reason is this: man needs competition. Enjoyment of the sports pages in the papers should enable anyone with any sense to read the home news a little less tragically. The separation of the cause of Caesar from the cause of God introduced a principle of healthy conflict into human society which must at all costs be respected if the cause of justice is to be served.

After living through the horrors of the first half of the twentieth century, Europe has been trying to teach itself how to resolve differences without going to war about them, with some success. Each country is trying to do the same within its own borders. In Britain we are trying all the time to increase local and individual freedom, hoping that improved skills in management and negotiation will keep the nation afloat as well as guarantee fair treatment for all. It remains a ticklish business, but we have not yet gone under or given way to demands for greater authoritarian control, whether of the right or of the left.

But if the game is to go on being played in this way, the rules must be generally accepted. If the two or more sides in political and economic affairs are to talk to each other, and, for most of the time, work in co-operation, all must recognise that they have some common membership and purpose.

The appeal to the idea of the nation does not by itself provide sufficient basis for this social unity. Once nationalism becomes an all-embracing principle, then the worst crimes are possible. No one political party can safely be regarded as the expression of the national will. The nation needs a sparring partner; it also needs a referee.

The Church exists to provide the sense of common humanity which all must share if their conflicts are to be contained and resolved within the same agreed framework. It does not wish to be identified with this or any other nation, because that destroys its usefulness. It is essential for the nation that the Church should retain its own distinctive standpoint; it is as essential for the Church that the nation should provide a separate field of action within which its members can work out their own salvation. They have been called into the Church, certainly; but they have subsequently been sent out into the world.

An established Church is a Church that has blurred the dividing line between itself and the world, between itself and the nation which it should help to create. The Catholic Church has taken sixteen hundred years to learn that lesson; but learn it it has, as the texts of Vatican II explicitly declare.

Ever since the sixteenth century, at least half of the active Christians of England and Wales have been outside the Established Church, and, for much of that time, opopsed to it. English Protestantism, as much as English Catholicism, bears clear witness to the fact that the health of our country and the health of our faith do not in any way depend on the maintenance of the Established Church as a national institution. English political life has continually benefited from the fact that there was a Christian opposition to challenge the precise forms taken at various times by the alliance between Church and State.

The sense of belonging to one another that we all need if the nation is to work has of course been found by most of our fellow-countrymen in a shared anti-Catholicism as well as in sectarian and party Christianity, along with the national

40

Church itself. If the future of Christianity in this country lies with the growing-together and growing-up of a single local Church in communion with Rome — and it is difficult to see where else it can lie — that anti-Catholicism must be overcome.

Victory over this deeply-ingrained opposition can come quite quickly if we only pay attention to making known certain essential truths about ourselves. The first is our history: that continuing thread of local Catholic life which could become in a few years the shared pride of all who recognise and value a whole-hearted faithfulness to Christ. The second is our thoroughly mixed character as a community at the present time. Politically, socially, culturally, we are the most diverse single body of people in this country; and that goes for the public and private expression of our worshipping life as well.

The third truth is our rejection of any claim to aspire to national identification. The one Church of our country's future must remain distinct from all other institutions, both in order to give them the true freedom within which to function, and in order itself to have the freedom to pursue its own purpose: witness to Jesus Christ as the one source of justice, peace and fulfilment for all men.

Jesus gave the Church to the world in order that it might be saved; he also gave the world to the Church in order that it might for ever be prevented from seeking its own private salvation and thus losing its own soul.

If we are to be one nation, then we need one Church. If Christians are to become one Church, then they must all be committed to making one nation. And if both Church and Nation are to survive, it is certain that they must do so not as one body, but as two: as partners, as mutual critics, as friendly rivals. No patronising, no takeover, no merger: nationalisation is the kiss of death. One Nation calls for one Church; both call for separation.

February 1979

ENGLAND, THE CATHOLIC CHURCH AND EUROPE

NOW that the Cardinal of England (the sixteenth-century title should be revived) besides being President of the Bishops' Conference of England and Wales, has been elected President of the Council of European Bishops' Conferences, one can hope for the forging of much closer working links between Catholics in this country and those in the rest of Europe. Although Catholics in Britain have always had a European outlook, at the popular level as well as in the higher reaches of politics, literature and the arts, there is still a great deal to be done by way of making the reality of communion in the Catholic faith a practical reality of minds, hearts and common action.

Pilgrimages, shared training for the priesthood, 'supply' visits to parishes: these are the commonplace occasions of exchange between Catholics of this country and those of the continent. They need to be supplemented by more deliberate efforts to express our unity, to learn from one another and to co-operate in mission. Opportunities for experiencing the unity and diversity of our Catholic faith arise through the twinning of towns and larger communities. Catholic parishes and dioceses should be involved in the visits and meetings that take place as a result of the relationships that have now been established. These are by no means only commercial, social and sporting, but involve cultural and religious interests as well; schools, choirs, and international organisations such as the Society of St Vincent de Paul should be making their contribution.

The friendships that have been forged between Anglicans and continental Catholics in the interests of ecumenism should be enlarged so as to include ourselves. Indeed, unless the three-fold nature of the contacts that should be made is duly acknowledged, these relationships may well be counter-productive. Episcopal collegiality within the Catholic Church lays a duty of observing certain priorities on the bishops, say, of France, Belgium and England; in matters of mission and unity, as in other matters concerning the faith, they are bound to share a common policy of pastoral collaboration. One sometimes hears the claim that Catholics abroad are more liberal or more welcoming than those at home. Whatever the truth involved in this — and sometimes the affirmations made hardly do credit, if they are true, to the knowledge, good sense and loyalty of our fellow-Catholics — it is clear that 'tourist ecumenism' does not go very far towards healing the divisions in this country. When, as sometimes happens, odious comparisons are drawn, then the march towards local unity is in fact delayed.

Ever since Catholic Emancipation in 1829, the Catholic community in this country has been a growing one; growing in numbers, in quality, in achievement and influence. That has not meant that we have been without our obvious weaknesses, limitations and failures. They have been there too, and they always will be. Nor should we ever hope for general approval and acceptance. The essential thing is that in the midst of all our human deficiencies, freedom has meant growth and not decline. The National Pastoral Congress next year will provide evidence of that growth, as of the inadequacies that need remedying and of the new problems that must be tackled. It needs to be more than a National Congress; it needs to demonstrate and strengthen our bonds with Catholics throughout Europe, many of whom look to us for a distinctive contribution to the practical understanding of how our Church life should be carried on. Pastoral assemblies have not had a uniquely happy history in recent years; perhaps in England and Wales we can point the way to something better.

At any rate, when Catholics from the continent come to the Congress, it is to be hoped that they will find there plenty of evidence to wipe out the lingering idea that many of them have of us as a community that lives too much in the past and does not seize its present opportunities to act in a fully Catholic way in relation to the society in which it is placed. We need the friendship and support of Catholics everywhere, but particularly of those nearest to us, if the National Pastoral Congress is to help us to respond once again to the Word of God and to be seen more clearly by all our fellow-countrymen as the authentic Church of Christ.

The Bishops' recent statement on some of the principles that should guide the framing of a new Nationality Law, as intended by the present Government, deals with the rights that should be enjoyed by all British citizens, of whatever cultural and racial origin. It affirms that 'Britain has become irreversibly a multi-racial, multi-cultural society', and is concerned that we should not fall into a racialist conception of our national identity. But we shall not succeed in overcoming racialism unless we can provide ourselves with a more powerful alternative in the shape of some clearer ideas about our identity and our loyalties as a nation than we have at present. Simple toleration of other races and cultures will not be enough; the members of our society must also be convinced about working for a single British people with a shared sense of belonging and purpose.

It will fall particularly to the Catholic Church in Britain to provide that new sense of national identity, avoiding the nationalism that in the past harnessed the Christian faith in its service, with consequences for Christian unity that we are now painfully trying to remedy, and at the same time being unafraid to assert the need for Christian leadership towards the creation of a national community in which the many races and cultures can indeed claim their acknowledged rights, but are prepared first of all to recognise and accept their public duty.

September 1979

ENGLAND IS A CATHOLIC COUNTRY

THE Second Vatican Council, by making clear the originality of the Church of Christ among all the nations of the world and the universality of its mission, has by implication rejected nationalism, of whatever kind, as a political creed, and has set in its right proportions and perspective the duty of patriotism, without which none of us can live in justice and peace. The Church, wherever it is, works for the common good, both in its local reality and in its general expression, without which none of us can live in the safety of our homes. And to the extent that any country of the world can, in that view of things, be called Catholic, England in 1980 is a Catholic country.

The security, justice and peace of the English people will come to depend on the strength, dedication and service of the Catholic community and cannot be sought with any hopes of success in any other place. What is true elsewhere in the Christian world, and ultimately everywhere else, is true also here.

It is true, in the first place, because of the quality of our Catholic community. We can see this perfectly clearly by a simple test against our own private standards. If we take the most obvious and easily recognisable sample, and compare like with like, a village in East Anglia, for instance, with a village in Tuscany — where, indeed, the local church might be thought to have a head start on us — there can be no doubt about where the faith is better understood and worship more worthily offered. In East Anglia the congregation does not gossip throughout the entire Mass, sermon, consecration, communion, the lot, even when two priests are doing their best in the sanctuary. In East Anglia, men of all ages take a full part and go to communion; they do not while away their time in church squatting on their haunches in the side-aisles or standing about, half-in and half-out of the church, while the women chatter in their seats.

In England, especially if we are converts, we tend to jump to the defence of casual continental Catholic ways, saying that there the people feel at home in church. But there is no need for such absurd attempts to defend the indefensible, to 'explain' Catholicism, right-or-wrong. If some foreign Catholics behave at home as they do in church, it is hardly surprising that they prefer life in the cafés.

The Catholic Church in England is a strong worshipping community, well on its way now to gathering in the fruits of our local traditions, and to creating new forms of expression, musical and literary, for the future of England's celebration of the gifts and glory of God. On that first count, England is and will be Catholic.

In the second place, England is Catholic because the Christian understanding of human life is expressed in the laws of our country and in the practice of our constitution. Whatever is solid and worth handing on in our national tradition depends upon the experience and thought of men and women who have lived within the Christian world of thought and have drawn their theory and practice from Christian sources. Whatever damage was done by the dividing of the churches in this country,

45

the fact remains that a positive appreciation was retained of the place of Christianity in public life, and from here was transmitted throughout the world. There are many glaring faults in the way we exploited Christianity in the service of our national ends, as did other nations. But the Christian message itself has been too strong for those who misused it, as Christ assured us it would be; and it is still vigorously present in this country and throughout the world to correct our faults and to inspire and reform our way of life.

Today, the Catholic Church in England has before it the work of appraising our national political and legal tradition and of continuing the construction of that tradition according to the law of God, establishing it in his justice and nourishing its deep-rooted life through the practice of his law of love. On that second count, England is and will be Catholic.

In the third place, England is Catholic in sheer force of numbers and energy. What other Christian community can fill a cathedral, mediaeval or modern, as we can? Which other Christian intellectual tradition flourishes as ours does among the graduates and undergraduates of our universities? Where do the clergy of other denominations receive as warm a welcome as they do among the Catholic people? Which other English church has built up its own life and contributed to the service of the community at large, all out of current income, with no inheritance or endowments to draw on, no Church Commissioners, as we have? Which other reading and talking public can support as many newspapers and reviews, both learned and popular, as we can? We do, of course, not stand alone in any of these fields; but the signs are that before long no one will stand in them at all unless they are Catholic.

England is not a post-Christian society, but it most certainly is a post-Protestant, post-C. of E., post-Victorian-public-school, post-Imperial one. Its Christian present and future will be worked out in terms, not of Empire and Nation, but community and Commonwealth. To that end, it may not matter whether we are in Europe or out of it, but it will matter very much whether we are in the Church or out of it. England's Catholics have before them the exciting and inspiring prospect of bearing the supreme responsibility for the life of our society and for its strong, determined perseverance in Christian hope.

46

In Cardinal Hume's words,

the Church in England needs to have confidence that it has something to say and to give and there are many who wish to hear and to receive.

But, characteristically, the Cardinal is too gentle and too modest. The Church can and must have that confidence. Both the permanent mission of the Church and the demands of the present day make it imperative that we abandon our hag-ridden preoccupations with minority rights and set out to teach and to undertake the duties of full citizenship in the England of tomorrow.

January 1980

'. . . A GREAT MULTITUDE, WHICH NO MAN COULD NUMBER . . .'

A CLERGYMAN once remarked that people should stop describing the Catholic Church as only fit for children because that made it sound suspiciously like the Kingdom of Heaven; by the same token, the recent survey of Catholic opinion carried out by the University of Surrey[1] may perhaps be read as a confirmation of the lasting truth of the parables of the Sower and of the Wheat and the Tares. Demographic studies of past periods in our history have shown very similar patterns; neither the Church nor human nature change very much. One trouble is that hardly have we started to cope with our own generation than another one comes along: a comforting, not a discouraging thought, except for those tidy and meddlesome people that always seem to want to anticipate the Day of Judgement.

Convinced as I am of the pastoral usefulness of these enquiries and their subsequent analysis, I must confess to a sneaking hope that the pollsters and the clipboard-carriers, however charming, will leave us alone for a while now and

[1] *Roman Catholic Opinion.* A study of Roman Catholics in England and Wales in the 1970s.

go off after some other significant group, like football fans or weight-watchers or Wee Frees or students of sociology. Anything that reinforces our self-consciousness is to be discouraged. I am all in favour of our getting a great deal more dispersed in the lump of British society, in the firm belief that the faith will not thereby be weakened, but will rather be given a proper chance to spread about and take root elsewhere.

The mind of a Catholic should be directed first of all to the Word of God in order to gain the knowledge that will produce true discipleship, and secondly to the realities in the world around us that need to be changed by the power of the Spirit. Catholicism is not meant for private enjoyment amongst ourselves, but for communication. It is not enough simply to affirm, proclaim, or stand by the truths that we see in the Gospel; we must also live with, and for, the consequences.

There is plenty of evidence about that Catholics do in fact take this responsibility seriously, devoting themselves to the care of other people and working in defence of human rights and in many forms of public service, as well as defending their own right to teach and practise their faith. But perhaps what we need now is not more publicity for this, more acknowledgement of our distinctive contribution, but less. We need to fade into the background; in other words to 'fall into the ground and die'.

We need to involve ourselves in the service of the community, not to prove anything or even to 'make a Catholic contribution', but simply because of the needs that are there. The need to be a united and hardworking people if the nation is to survive at all; the need to bring all Christians into one Church, so that our worship may be more worthily offered, and not belied by our divisions; the need to remove the present unhappiness from a family life that is losing its cohesion; the need to bring English and Irish Catholics together in the search for peace and justice in Northern Ireland; these needs and many more should be our concern, and not simply the need to look after our own.

It must also be said that social surveys and journalists' comments on them do not grasp the real heart and mind of faith. They may well distort our self-awareness by their insistence on the Church as an institution and their itemisation of Catholic

48

life, which in their questionnaires, graphs and tables becomes a series of statements to be believed, laws to be obeyed and duties to be performed.

Catholicism is not really about regularity or commitment or being on parade or countable things at all. It is about quality, not quantity; about sin and salvation, weakness and strength, suffering and ecstasy, death and life. It has to do with our most urgent every-day, all-day, human desires: usefulness, happiness and love. What so many commentators, administrators, ecumenists, media operators and other observers do not see or appear to understand is the integrated simplicity of Catholic existence. The Church of God is not a sub-culture or a particular life-style: it is life itself, it is Jesus Christ spread abroad and communicated.

A complete survey of Catholicism in England would have to be based on a cross-section, not of 'Catholics', however defined, but of the whole population, to discover how in their attitudes they relate, consciously or unconsciously, to Christ. 'Everyone who does what is right is acceptable to God', said the first Pope; and the Church starts well beyond even those limits.

Catholicism is the passion to be human. Catholic priests and religious are, most oddly, absent from those questioned in this latest survey. Perhaps their invisibility is a parable of the fact that the Church must always slip through the census-taker's net. 'I am so much a man that I am no more than human', said St Francis de Sales. Ultimately, you cannot define, describe or otherwise pin down the Church; you can only catch it alive in the instincts, judgements and choices of your own heart.

April 1980

'. . . THAT NOTHING BE LOST'

THE National Pastoral Congress was not by any means the first Congress on this scale to be held by the Catholic Church in England and Wales. We have had plenty of great gatherings to stir our enthusiasm in the past. But it was much more than yet another milestone in the series of significant events that have strengthened our sense of purpose and marked our history. It was a new beginning.

It was a new beginning because in Liverpool the entire church of England and Wales met for the first time simply to do that which makes it the Church: to listen to the Word of God and to be renewed by the Spirit. This is what gives the Church its original and distinctive character: it is not an organisation on ordinary human lines, built up in layers or split into parties, but a single Body of Christ, with multifarious forms of life and service, and a single Spirit. The bishops were there to listen with everyone else as members of the Church; our common purpose was to hear more clearly the message that the Lord of the Church is giving to us. Those who try to interpret what happened at Liverpool in political terms — government and opposition, bishops versus the rest, clergy over against laity, tradition in conflict with innovation — can only stop short of understanding the real character of the event. The Church was not divided within itself and against itself any more than an individual is divided when he stops to take stock of his life before God and to make resolutions and plans for the future.

The Word of God speaks within the Church: the pattern at Liverpool was the simple pattern of our faith. We do not look back to a past that we now have to reconstruct; we are not left to argue interminably over the interpretation of written texts that do not explicitly resolve our problems; because we recognise ourselves as part of the one People of God, we are confident that the Spirit will continue to guide our listening and our obedience to the Word.

This was the Church as Vatican II has given us to understand it. We have been reflecting on those conciliar documents for fifteen years, so there was plenty of long-term preparation, as well as the short-term campaigns of study and search for structures of life that led us to Liverpool. Once there, everything came together: the Church, not just as a profession of faith, but as a reality, in its true balance and harmony.

It was a new beginning for ourselves, but it was also a new beginning for all Christians in England and Wales. The four centuries that lie behind us saw many initiatives in Christian living that have borne fruit in new ways of devotion, new areas of evangelisation, new efforts to serve Christ in our fellow men. These now need to be brought together into unity, and that unity is being ever more urgently worked for in this country.

Within the Church that met at Liverpool, one can see a living synthesis of all those separate efforts to grasp the Gospel way of church government, to be more attentive to the Spirit, to represent Christ more faithfully to the world. No one who is aware of our Christian history in England and Wales can fail to see the immense significance of this Congress in our national history, as a manifestation of the Church in its completeness and in its spiritual diversity. Divisions have arisen in the past through over-emphasis on one or other part of the Church, often inadequately understood: on hierarchy or on priesthood, on individual conscience or on popular rights, on Bible only or on free-ranging, disembodied Spirit. Here instead we had an effective sign of the way in which all elements of the faith and of the community that the faith calls together, exist and work together for the glory of God. The fragmentation of English religion will in the years ahead find in this living unity its means of reconciliation and its source of renewed life.

And the Congress was a new beginning because it expressed within and for the Church Universal the distinctive contribution of our own two nations. The blend of the Christian faith and of the character of the peoples of England and Wales has once again produced its recognisable fruits in a certain style: of moderation and at the same time of firm independence of mind, of deep yet controlled feelings and of practical common sense. The bishops who now have to decide what leadership to give us can have confidence not only in the Word and in the Spirit but in the people whom Word and Spirit have brought together. The Church did not meet to tell them what to do; the Church met to pledge itself to follow Christ and to be the place where together we might see where he is leading us. As successors of the Apostles, the bishops have received the first of the charisms by which the Body of Christ is being built up among men: they are both Servants of the Word that they declare to us, and Shepherds of the People that they must gather together and guide. At Liverpool, it was the second of those functions that came to the fore, and now we await the continuation of the corporate exercise in discernment to which we were all committed.

In deciding how best the Church in England and Wales can now move forward in shared responsibility for fostering

51

Christian unity, for strengthening marriage and family life, for feeding and stimulating the life of faith, for social concern and for the major political problems of our society, such as Northern Ireland, the bishops can place great trust in the sturdy and energetic community that has grown up around them, in the talents, the gifts and the awareness of what is involved in following Christ, that are to be found amongst us. The most important of their decisions will concern the continuing formation of that community, so that together we may really possess 'the mind that is in Christ Jesus'; their principal service is the communication of the Word of God, for the guidance, under the Spirit of God, of the People that the Word calls together.

At the First National Catholic Congress, held at Leeds in 1910, prominent among the societies represented was the Ladies' Needlework Guild. People may be tempted to think that in our passion for modernity Liverpool forgot such graces of the past. Certainly not. The banners were splendid. In their colour and in their pride, they summed it all up. Every parish must have one.

July 1980

LIBERATION THEOLOGY:
THE ENGLISH CONTEXT

LIBERATION THEOLOGY is usually thought of as an exotic growth, flourishing in foreign parts where the special circumstances of Church and State call for particular remedies: the affirmation of forgotten or neglected aspects of the Christian Gospel, so that the revealed law of God may be more faithfully obeyed. But if it is an authentic way of understanding and practising the message of Christ, freshly thought out and presented in terms of twentieth-century needs and mentalities, then it will have its application at home as well as abroad. We cannot be content with a patronising concern that other people should find solutions for their problems. Our first obligation is to our own local field of operation; but our thinking so far has not involved itself anything like enough with these immediate surroundings, with the realities of our English culture and society that should provide today's materials for a native expression of the Christian way of life.

The liberation that is needed in England is in the first place a liberation from the identification of Englishness with a particular Christianity of a somewhat selective kind, so that we may recover in this country the integrated life of the total Gospel of which a free and united Church should be the effective sign. Faith in the living God should set us free from the inherited burden of past mistakes.

In the England of 1980, Catholic faith does not imply the simple prolongation of one strain in our national life of the past four hundred years, but rather the possibility of escape from the fragmented situation in which we find ourselves into a new, changed state of affairs in which Christians will live together in common obedience to the ever-contemporary Word of God. The sovereign freedom and independence of the English Catholic Church give it the opportunity and the responsibility of being the growing point of the future unity of English Christianity. Liberation theology will involve the close study of the distinctive theological emphases and special concerns of the separated traditions in order that they may be given new life within a restored synthesis. It will show the way towards an end of division, and above all towards the end of a political situation that has been the root cause of that division.

Opinion in the Church of England at the highest level is moving towards accepting the final stages in a process that has for many years been severing the links that once gave the State a special relationship with the Church. This particular liberation would make available to Anglicans the freedom enjoyed by ourselves and by the other churches: freedom to make decisions about reunion and about their own internal affairs, and, most importantly, to speak to the English people in terms of the Word of God and of the Church of God alone, bringing to bear on English life the judgement and the salvation in the service of which the Church must be for ever independent of other interests.

In the second place, and more profoundly, liberation theology involves an exploration of the innumerable ways in which the Gospel and the grace of Christ set us free from everything that holds us back from reaching our full development as

53

children of God called to the fullness of growth in Christ. It involves a deeper investigation of the meaning of salvation than the reforming movements of the sixteenth century were able to achieve, with their narrow concentration either on throwing off what were thought to be restraints imposed by man on Christian truth, or else on defending and fostering these same beliefs and practices, understood rather as healing gifts of God. It involves the enrichment of a spiritual tradition that has concentrated on individual guilt and anxieties and on the temptations of the flesh, provoking thereby an introspection which can be a barrier to Christian growth and which needs the corrective provided by social morality and a concern for public justice.

Liberation theology does not turn the Church aside from its true purpose of bringing God to men, limiting its horizon to this world and to the provision of secular comfort. Liberation theology discovers both the extent of human need and the extent of God's provision for our predicament. It sets the Church free from the restraints and limitations which national or cultural identification have imposed upon it, enabling the People of God to be themselves and thus to be the liberators of the Family of Mankind. In England, it will help us to rise above that complacent pride which has led us to set national sovereignty above the will of God for his Church and which continues to blind us to the historical facts of our own contribution to the Irish *impasse,* as to other continuing political problems. It will save us from enslavement to the myriad cults that at present exploit the naïve religiosity of the English mind. It will provide the permanent critical opposition that the whole of our political life must have if it is to remain sound. And in doing these things, it will save us from death, the death that many of our contemporaries offer us under the guise of reform: death of the young, death of the old, and the death of our will to give life.

Liberation theology is nothing less than the attempt to grasp in all its length and breadth and height and depth the way in which the dire threat of death to the soul itself has been destroyed by the supreme cause of all freedom; the Resurrection of the Body of Christ.

October 1980

THE ENGLISH CHURCH AND PEOPLE

EVER since Bede's *Church History*, the words of the title have, with varying emphases, indicated the existence of a partnership that can in the future be as fruitful for the benefit of our country as it ever was in the past. I say 'partnership', presuming a distinction, because we must hope that the idea that Church and people are but two aspects of one and the same reality will soon fade completely from the English mind. Catholics in England, like other non-conformists, have never accepted that way of thinking. Throughout the Catholic world, one effect of the Second Vatican Council has been to make the Church everywhere more conscious of its own personality and independence, and therefore more capable of fulfilling a creative role of service in the communities to which it has been sent.

But if that partnership is to flourish in the future, with a united Church gathering together all Christians in this country, we shall have to make somewhat more of an effort to live up to our present calling, becoming the Church for the entire local community, whose needs by way of united purpose, shared social awareness and public morale are as urgently felt now as at any previous time.

That means that a deeper sense of national responsibility must permeate the Catholic body at every level. It is not enough always to be expecting that the bishops will do the talking and will provide the leadership. If work needs to be done, then the persons who see that need must simply get on and do it. This, too, would be a practical expression of the mind of the Second Vatican Council.

And in all that we say and do we need to start from the fact that we are fairly and squarely at home in this country. This is a security given to us by Catholic faith; a stability which we must have if we are to provide for our national life the solid foundation that it so much needs.

In our thinking about the problems of the nation, we shall have to become more aware of the damage that can be done by an *a priori* doctrinaire approach of the kind that is steadily being dropped now in missionary theory and practice. There is a great danger that as in our contacts with other religions in the past, so in our present relationships with other churches, with political parties and with intellectual and social movements of every kind, we rush straight into judging them by our own first principles. And we make a further mistake if we assume from the start that others do not share to one degree or another those same principles. What is needed now among the English people is a positive discernment of all those human and Christian values that must be the starting point of future development As in all good missionary dialogue, we should be as anxious to discover what we can receive as we are to convey to others what we have to give.

Since this country has for so many centuries been sustained by Christian tradition, we can surely expect to have at least as much to learn in England as we can hope to learn from other traditions elsewhere in the world. Yet there is in the Catholic body extraordinarily little awareness of our immediate neighbours and extraordinarily little by way of attempts to think and act in response to local needs. We are aware of the work of foreign Protestant theologians or of what is being written and done in Latin America, but we are not yet developing an ecumenical theology or indeed any kind of theology in the service of our own people. It is Irish-English relations, it is a political life fed by something more constructive than class conflicts, it is an education for local and national citizenship, it is the defence of human rights at home as well as abroad, that require the attention of our thinkers and pastors.

The episcopal appointments made by John Paul II — the choice of Jean-Marie Lustiger as Archbishop of Paris is the latest example — show that he is looking for men with leadership, intellect and pastoral skill and concern, even if this takes him away from the well-worn stereotypes of the past. It is very much to be hoped that he is now turning his thoughts towards England and his coming visit, and that he will realise how people who can put the English Catholic Church at the heart of the public service of the whole nation can also profoundly affect the development of the Church wherever the English way of life has in the past been a powerful influence. However unlikely it may seem to those who want to keep their Catholic life enclosed within a comfortable but marginal pattern of existence, the future now lies with those who will help to build the nation along with the Church by treating them both as partners in dialogue and in friendly competition.

April 1981

THE TRADITION OF FAITH

THE Catholic Church understands tradition in a special way of its own: particular and distinctive, but at the same time open and universal. In this we differ from many rivals. And amongst ourselves, too, we suffer from misunderstandings that give rise to public contestation and to distress for those who have the pastoral care of the Church, as well as for individual believers.

Tradition, for us, is not a secret source of hidden information, to be made available only to sworn members of a privileged group and kept carefully from the ears of profane outsiders. Not only Freemasons, but gnostics of many kinds, old and new, and devotees of esoteric forms of philosophy and religion, hope for successive revelations of occult and arcane mysteries. But this is most emphatically not our way; faith confers no separate superiority.

Catholic tradition must not be confused, either, with keeping to customs or beliefs simply because they have been accepted and observed from beyond living memory. It is not the same as conservatism, preferring always more of the same to the new and the different. It does not stand simply for the preservation of things past. It must not be identified with the cast of mind that in politics or in cultural life appreciates only some chosen epoch when all was very much better than it is now. It must certainly not be allied with any theory that uses religion to put beyond criticism and to render unchanging some preferred social structure.

When St Paul handed on to those whom he was teaching that which had been handed on to him (1 Cor 15:3), he was relating himself to a moment of creation in the recent past, and he was asking that his message should be given to the whole world. The mystery he had come to understand had been made known in his own time. From being the fierce defender of the religion of his fathers, he had become the bold and patient messenger of a fresh and contemporary message. Age and changelessness were in themselves no virtues. The new had acquired the sovereign right to be heard everywhere.

The message that we are concerned to receive in its entirety and to pass on to others is in fact both old and new, both special to individuals and applicable to all. And it must further be said that these attributes, recommendations as they are, are still not enough to persuade us into acceptance. The Gospel commends itself not by its incidental attractions or benefits alone, but by the compelling indications it gives of its inherent truth, recognisable by everyone who is open to grasping the reality of our situation as human beings. We do not believe it because it has always guided the society and culture of which we are a part, nor because it has come to us through immemorial custom, nor yet because it takes us out of a rut and promises a relief from routine. We welcome and proclaim Christ because he alone can give us what we really need: salvation from our sins, words that we can trust, and lasting fulfilment. Christianity is, quite simply, the best there is; and it is no good trying to defend it on any other grounds.

We are, for instance, making an inadequate case if we argue for keeping up the teaching of Christianity in our schools on the ground that we are a Christian country and should pass on to our children our traditional way of life. Such an argument would tell against the Church in other countries where other traditions prevail. The only basis on which Christianity can be defended as the inspiration and guide of education is the fact that it is true and that no other set of beliefs offers as much to mankind.

It would also be a mistake if we allowed ourselves to think of Catholicism as one particular pattern, one traditional spirituality, to be set alongside other spiritualities in the general Christian spectrum or in the religious context as a whole. The Catholic faith is not just for particular temperaments; nor does it require the adoption of any particular aesthetic, linguistic or national style. While our English Catholicism, for instance, has inherited its own particular ethos, we are by no means bound to confine ourselves to it, preserve it unaltered for ever more, or require it of anyone else. Converts are not to be asked to adopt recusant attitudes. The simple single-mindedness of the Gospel is already, and can become more fully, the unifying factor of a rich diversity of human patterns of response. Catholicism in this country should not look upon itself as just one distinctive strand in a wider national tradition; it is the fundamental God-given means by which all strands in that tradition, past, present and future, may be made to flourish together. And Catholicism in all countries must learn to serve national communities as much by its own independence as by its readiness to identify with each people's needs. Discernment here, for the pastor, is one of his gravest responsibilities and most difficult tasks.

As John Paul II has said, we cannot solve this year's problems with last year's answers. Tradition, in the Christian sense, looks forward. The eternal Present of the Gospel is the means by which we build the future. Whatever our natural cast of mind, it corrects our prejudices and limitations and opens up potentialities we had not discovered. It leaves us free, wherever freedom opens a way to fresh creation.

This note needs to be sounded very much more clearly whenever guidance is given to the Church over matters of general policy. In the liturgy, for example, the overall purpose of expressing the English way of life through the worship of God must be brought home to us if we are to overcome traditionalist objections to what has been done so far. There have been mistakes; but no one should lose sight of our valid aim or in desperation try to substitute for it the preservation of an idealised past.

The tradition of faith calls us to forget as well as to remember. Not for us the hesitation of the backward look. Heaven-haven lies ahead.

September 1981

THE SOVEREIGNTY OF GOD

THE chief concern for us in Britain at present should be the business of renewing our awareness of the authority of Christ in the national life and of adjusting our relationships accordingly. Christianity is not a private faith, but a public one: a faith that makes a people.

This renewal must obviously in the first place be the concern of the churches: of those who explicitly and visibly acknowledge the sovereignty of God. But in pursuing that renewal we will have to become more aware of the sectarian way in which so often we press our claim for a share in it. It is not a matter of re-asserting authority and of trying to regain lost ground, but of rediscovering authority. We must learn to understand that we cannot confine the Word of God within a political constitution. The Queen and Parliament cannot be assimilated, as they were for centuries, with ecumenical councils of the Church. To keep its soul and its very competence to serve, the Church must be capable of ordering its own life in the light of God's Word and that alone. There must be a great drawing together of Christian witness in obedience to the living God, who seeks always to lead us away from everything that clogs and diminishes our free response.

In this renewal, it is the role of the clergy not to allow themselves simply to be enrolled as official chaplains to national institutions and interests, and certainly not to seek a share in government, but above all to teach the Word of God in its fullness and to demonstrate its power wherever human beings are at their weakest. It is their responsibility not to live off the fat of the ninety and nine but to use their resources to go in search of the one that is lost. And in many sectors of our society those proportions are reversed. A Catholic priest, a servant of the Word of God, a pastor of the People of God, is necessarily a pioneer, an explorer outside frontiers, an urgent communicator of all that he has found.

And this is true of every priest, diocesan or religious, home-based or traveller, simply because of his sacramental consecration. He is chosen to be a sign; by making the Word of God present within his parish or wherever it is he works, he must open that territory to world horizons, leading everyone from their narrow local habitation to their place within the universal scope of God's love.

While it concerns the churches first of all, this renewal must however not be a private affair; its purpose involves the whole of the society in which we take our place. It entails the clear demonstration in every department of our national life that the teachings of Christ provide the inspiration and the guidelines we need. This could of course mean reducing the Gospels to no more than useful handbooks for worldly success, and this is precisely what many false prophets still do. The teaching of Christ includes the authority of Christ: that is the key point to which we must not be afraid to refer, again and again. God is good for us, yes; but only if we recognise who he is and remember the account that will be demanded for all that he has given us. So much Christian piety, spirituality and devotion is sheer self-indulgence and is sold as such. But society needs to know that God has laws which are not broken without disastrous results. He provides not just good advice, but the hard-and-fast rules of the game.

There is not much sign of penitence in our national life at present, nor yet of demands from Christian pastors that penitence is needed. But the kingdom of God demands constant conversion. The key men of our society are not the police, keeping law and order externally so that we can all pursue our own interests in comfort. The key men of our society are the Christians, whatever their social role, who seek to know the will of God in public life: that must be our programme. This is not clericalism. This is no rule of the mullahs. This is the rule of the living God, through those living men and women who become, as he did, servants: servants of the people, because first of all servants of God.

October 1981

III
COUNCIL AND CHURCH

HANS KÜNG ON THE CHURCH

THE *Church*[1] is the first volume in the ecclesiological section of a new series devoted to ecumenical research, edited by Hans Küng and Joseph Ratzinger. The publishers and translators realised the great *tour de force* of bringing out the English edition in the same year as it was published in Germany. Reading it for review has taken a little longer, elsewhere as well as here; long discussions are now appearing in theological journals, mixed and tempered in their comment, after the enthusiasm of the religious press.

The disappointment which has been widely expressed has arisen out of the fact that the book is not, after all, a masterpiece. After being given so much that was so rich, of such high scientific value, so effective in opening up relations with other Christians, so purifying for our thought and action in the Church, we were hoping for a mighty synthesis, a setting-out in strength and power of the Council's themes, a book which would make us say without doubt, 'A new Möhler, a new Scheeben, a new Karl Adam, is here'.

Dr Küng's purpose has in fact been more limited. One must not judge him for not doing something he did not set out to do. This is not a complete study of the whole mystery of the Church as it was set before us by Vatican II. As the subject index shows, he does not deal with chapters VI, VII and VIII, on religious, on the relationship between the pilgrim Church on earth and the end of pilgrimage in heaven, and on the Blessed Virgin Mary in the mystery of Christ and his Church. In view of the importance for the balance of our faith of this last-mentioned conciliar link-up between mariology and ecclesiology, the omission is perhaps surprising, but it is a fact which shows the necessary incompleteness of this work.

[1] Burns & Oates (1967)

Nor does he discuss at any length the views of other theologians, Protestant or Catholic. Close reference to other writers is patchy; it is to be found in the first eighty pages, and then again from time to time throughout, but for most of the time other men's names are confined to the extensive bibliographies. Although the book is dedicated to Dr Ramsey, his writings are not discussed; nor do other Anglican theologians fare any better. When one looks further for an examination of Orthodox or Lutheran or Reformed ecclesiology, one draws another blank. This is not a work of direct ecumenical dialogue, like Congar's *Divided Christendom*, or Van der Pol's study of the Anglican Communion, or Tavard's *The Quest for Catholicity*, or Leeming's *The Churches and the Church*, or Lambert's *Ecumenism*. It certainly is not a manual which the seminary professor can use as a skeleton plan and source of information for his lectures; nor is it a systematic treatise developing a logically coherent doctrine of every nook and cranny as well as of the supporting structure of the Church, to be looked at and admired like some cathedral of the Middle Ages.

Although Dr Küng says that he is considering 'the *real* Church as it exists in our world, and in human history' (p. 5), the historical aspect of the work is in fact one of the weakest; the work of men like Hubert Jedin and Joseph Lortz on the human reality of the Church in history hardly seems to have impinged at all. Jedin on Trent, for example, is not mentioned; nor is Lortz's *Geschichte der Kirche,* a magnificent study by one of the modern masters. And the sociological school associated with the name of Gabriel Le Bras, responsible for a splendid series of monographs and general studies of the people of God as they have actually lived their Church life, does not even get a bibliographical mention. The sweeping historical judgements, the breathless gallops through vast tracts of time, give us no more than a superficial contact with our ancestors in Christian communion.

The book must be read as a call to sincere and genuine response, an end of purely verbal professions of faith, a volcanic eruption in the midst of the placid round of ecclesiastical and academic life. Dr Küng cannot possibly expect us to accept with docility everything that he says; he is not that sort of theological master. He is principally concerned with administering a salutary shock to the institutional Church, with showing us that the beliefs we hold about ourselves are a challenge to authentic and fruitful action as well as a given reality.

The Church, Sinful and Holy

It is precisely at this point that the fundamental principles of his theology need close examination. In bringing us face to face with what we really are, does Dr Küng do justice to the full given-ness of salvation, to the extent of God's commitment to his world? What he has to say in his chapter on the holiness of the Church will provide a suitable test sample. Throughout this chapter, following his customary dialectical method, he contrasts the sinfulness of the Church, which comes from men, with its holiness, which comes from God. He is at pains to bring out the extent of that sinfulness throughout Church history; all this is a welcome change from those treatises which seem to refer only to an ideal Church, where men as we know them hardly appear. He is right to make absolutely clear that all sanctification comes from God alone, and that complete holiness will only be ours in the Church at the end of time. But he does not sufficiently bring out the fact that we are at the same time both 'sanctified' and 'called to be saints' (1 Cor 1:2). There is a fundamental personal sanctity, which we have been given through baptism (Eph 5:26) and which is the basis and constant stimulus of our continual response as we grow towards our full stature. Ephesians 5:27, does not simply suggest that it is the duty of the Church to be 'holy and without blemish' (p. 325); the text is here referring to a present reality. *Lumen Gentium* speaks of the followers of Christ as 'sons of God and partakers of the divine nature, and thereby saints in very truth'. They have the obligation 'to retain the holiness *they have received as God's gift* (my italics) in the life they lead, to bring it to perfection' (n. 40; cf. n. 48: 'The Church is marked on earth with a genuine, if imperfect, holiness'.) Dr Küng quotes this passage (p. 326), but I do not think his understanding of this real communication of sanctifying grace to the believer is adequate. Texts like 2 Corinthians 5:17 — 'if anyone is in Christ, he is a new creation; the old has passed away, behold the new has come' — or Galatians 2:20 — 'I have been crucified

66

with Christ; it is no longer I who live, but Christ who lives in me' — affirm an objective change in the believer. This change comes from Christ, involves a continuing relationship with Christ, is never our own achievement, is still tending towards perfection — and it exists here and now. At present it is hidden and it will finally be manifested (Col 3:3); but its hiddenness does not make it any less real at the present moment, and its ultimate manifestation does not mean that it will only then be given. In the Christian, sinfulness and holiness are not at opposite poles of a dialectic; holiness is at the centre, in possession, and sinfulness is being driven out.

This doctrine does not give rise to complacency or pride, but to constant humility; to conquer triumphalism, it is not necessary to insist overwhelmingly on the eschatological nature of our sanctification. We are put in our place just as well if we remember our constant, here-and-now dependence on the creative and redeeming grace of God.

We find the same restricted recognition of the contemporary victory of God's grace in the Church, when we look at the chapter on the Body of Christ. Dr Küng says that Paul's remarks about the community as the Body of Christ appear rather in the context of moral exhortation (pp. 227-8) than in the context of an 'explicitly theoretical ecclesiology' (pp. 227-8). This is true; Dr Küng is right to stress it; and he does not forget that the members of the Church 'ought to be "one body" because they already are "one body" in Christ' (p. 229). But the fact remains that he is far more interested in the moral imperative than in the indicative, the state of affairs on which all action must be based. He says that

> the connexion between Christ and the Church as his body is not a physical substantial one, as in gnosticism, nor a symbolic metaphorical relationship such as the Stoics would have understood, but an actual historical relationship in the Old Testament sense (p. 230).

The first two affirmations are perfectly correct; our union with Christ is not substantial, nor is it metaphorical; but to say that our present relationship is simply an historical one in the Old Testament sense is quite insufficient, and constitutes a radical flaw in Dr Küng's understanding of the Church.

When he says that the relationship between Christ and his Church does not exist ontologically and statically, but historically and dynamically (pp. 237-8), he is separating and opposing two ways of understanding the union between Christ and the members of Christ which are both needed, together, if the relationship is to be understood. The union between Christ and the Christian, between Christ and the Church, is not a substantial, ontologically necessary, organic union in identity; nor, on the other hand, is it simply a union of obedience, expressing moral dependence. In Christ we truly become the adopted sons of God; this is a union by intentionality, transforming the point from which we start as well as the process by which we move towards our goal; it is a relationship in which we receive Christ and are transformed by him, while our individual identity remains. It is characteristic of personal relationships that in them we communicate and share ourselves; we do not simply exchange gifts distinct from ourselves. The relationship between Christ and the Christian is established in the first place by Christ's gift of himself to us, making us capable of growth in his grace.

This union by intentionality is, then, an ontological union; but this does not mean fusion in some sort of pantheistic mysticism. It is a union by participation, by relationship, and by real exchange, contact and imprint. This is the only way of beginning to do justice to the union which we have *in Christ*, as the New Testament has established it, a union which is both 'static' and 'dynamic', which possesses us and which guides and drives us ever forward in our progress towards our fullness in Christ. I think it will be found that Dr Küng's disjunctive doctrine of grace (which 'surrounds' and 'embraces', but does not change or transform), and his failure to reach beyond the dialectic of his method to an understanding of the new, permanent, on-going personal covenant between God and man, between God and his Church, now established in Christ by the power of his Holy Spirit, weakens the whole structure of his work. It accounts, for example, for his failure to treat of the Church as sign, 'the universal sacrament of salvation' (LG n. 48). It also accounts for the absence of any positive treatment of the relationship between Spirit and Institution in the Church.

As a challenge to Catholics to live up to their vocation, as a quarry of information, as a source of intellectual stimulus, as a warning against complacency, this massive book is doing great service. But it is too pessimistic, too much on the dark side of the dialectic; there is too little straightforward contemplation of the mystery of the Church, too little dialogue with other theologians, Protestant or Catholic. It is not written as a handbook, and it would be disastrous if anyone took it as his guide to driving and maintenance in the service of the Church. It is, rather, a mighty roar from the touchlines, one which should send us all back to Scripture and to Vatican II to see exactly who it is has been misunderstanding the game.

May 1969

THE PAIN OF LIVING AND THE DRUG OF DREAMS

WE shall soon be reaching the tenth anniversary of the opening of the Second Vatican Council, and are no doubt in for a spate of self-analysis, balance-sheets, recrimination and Micawberism. After the honeymoon period when the neighbours suddenly seemed to like us, there has come the harsh time of readjustment: their friendly presence has receded and we have come to find one another's company irksome and frustrating. All of us have wanted reform, and all of us have found that the others are standing in the way.

The whole experience has been a lesson in the truth of Our Lord's saying about not imagining that we can add to our stature by making resolutions. As well as learning a few home-truths about ourselves at Vatican II, we dreamed all sorts of wonderful dreams and came to all sorts of decisions about making the world conform to them, only to collapse from exhaustion shortly afterwards through trying to keep up with the programme.

Patience is called for. People who think that we should have done more since the end of the Council six and a half years ago are out of touch with the basic realities of human nature. Individuals and institutions do not and cannot change as rapidly as all that.

69

But apart from this particular mistake, one which is often made by academics who, not content with their prophetic role, want to seize the reins of power and change the world by administrative decision as well, there is a more serious blindness which prevents us from seeing what Vatican II really accomplished and what is happening to the Church at this particular moment.

We had been working with a mental picture of the Church as a tidy machine-like institution in which theology, canon law, rubrics, appointments, marriages, ordinations — everything — worked in a smooth and hidden way so as to give us a sense of order and security in an untidy and frightening world. It did not matter if people got caught in the machine from time to time; according to the utilitarian principles which governed our affairs, individuals had to be sacrificed so that peace might be preserved. The best churchman was the one who could best adapt himself to the workings of the machine, either to use it or to be used by it.

When this dead but not yet prostrate view of the Church is coupled with a particular political and social theory about the pattern of society, we have a form of Catholicism but not Catholic faith, an integrism which confuses many things that should have been distinguished, a nationalism which brings the people of God into disrepute, a conservatism which suppresses the disturbing paradoxes of the New Testament or a progressivism which refuses the reconciliation that the Gospel rubs our noses in.

At last we have realised, in an agonising but ultimately salutary awakening, that the Church is not a machine that we can use as we will. We have discovered that it consists of people and that people cannot be shelved as easily as an office file.

The churchman whose home was the Church on earth is now homeless. The churchman whose home is the Kingdom of Heaven, and who lives in the world where that Kingdom is available, is as much at home as ever. Human nature is the same as it always was; the Church is the same as it always was; only those who still love the great Catholic dream can be shaken by what Vatican II and a little experience have done to put our feet on the ground.

July 1972

70

THE ONE TRUE CHURCH:
ULTIMATE IDEAL OR PRESENT REALITY?

IN our efforts to build the Church over the last hundred and fifty years, to go no further back in history, we have been persistently hindered by a theoretical and practical confusion, conscious or unconscious, which has masked the true nature of the Church and stirred up opposition where it need never have been aroused. In attempting to bring in the Kingdom of God, we have imagined that it is to be identified with a particular way of ordering human society as a whole. In France, for instance, from the French Revolution right down to the present day, it has been the soul of the nation as such that was to be saved through the application of Christian principles. The way of life issuing from the French Revolution and the way of life promoted by the Church confronted one another as two rivals for the control of the whole of French society. The same way of thinking has been found over and over again elsewhere and has even been accepted in this country, where the Church has not in recent centuries occupied the same position in the public history of the country as it has elsewhere.

Along with this confusion of the Church and the political and social order has gone a view of the Church which saw it as an ideal perfect world where everything was correctly regulated and where one's mind and heart could accordingly escape for respite and consolation from the troubles of the life in which we are involved. This ideal world could most easily be controlled in the sphere of the liturgy. It was easy enough to have a tidy ceremonial, with rubrics for every eventuality that could be foreseen. An attempt was also made to devise an ordered system of dogmatic orthodoxy in the same way, where everything was pre-ordained and any new insight had only to be fitted into the appropriate pigeon-hole, or else rejected if there was no place where it would fit. The same thing happened in the field of moral behaviour; there was an accepted practice which left little room for the unconventional, whether his standards were higher or lower than the prevailing norm.

Victims of this double mistake are to be found in the 'integrist' groups that are resisting the implementation of Vatican II: they are still thinking in terms of a society which

71

would be totally ordered on lines laid down by the Church, and in terms of a Church which, for them, is already completely defined in its constitution and in its doctrine. But it is not only the extremists who make this mistake. We are all liable to be victims of it in one way or another. Do not we all often imagine that the best way to cure social ills is to build up a Christian society by the application of Catholic principles? We may think that we are seeking in the first place the Kingdom of God, but we do, nevertheless, tend in spite of ourselves to be Catholics primarily because it is a way to solve some social or personal problem. We are not members of the Church on the Church's own terms. We are not building up the real Church; we are using an ideal Church for our own purposes, for some particular aim which we think is important but which may not in fact be the true aim of the Church.

Extra Ecclesiam Nulla Salus?

The one true Church of God is a unique social reality within which a Christian works out his mode of existence, develops as a person, and discovers not only other human beings but God himself. Now this reality is in one sense unnecessary; one can be a human being without having any explicit relationship with the Church or knowledge of it. One must be born of human parents to be human oneself, but one has no need of baptism. One can get married and die without any assistance from the Church. One can apparently have all the essential social relationships needed for normal growth without knowing any members of the Church.

We have to ask ourselves, therefore, what 'the necessity of the Church for salvation' can mean. Does salvation take place only in a somewhat problematic dimension outside this life which the Church helps us into? Or does it refer to our present achievement as persons? If we can have a satisfactory life in this world without the Church, is there some different fulfilment in another world which is the Church's special affair? Or does the Church guarantee or at least make possible some special kind of fulfilment in this world? If it does, in what way does this alter our fundamental human situation?

72

The pattern of social relationships into which we enter as church members adds something to our ordinary life which we can in fact manage without; we can eat, have friends, work, earn money, make love, be fathers and mothers, speak, think, perfectly well without it. It adds an entirely new set of relationships to those which we have already, simply as human beings: membership of a community including people whom we never see or communicate with directly and including people whom we do not need for our ordinary everyday life — persons we meet at church, persons we hear about doing this or that elsewhere and whose activities would have no interest for us were we not members of the Church. So it adds an extra area of interest, just as an archery club or an interest in gardening can add an extra area of activity and social contact to our lives.

But it effectively changes the rest of our relationships as well, and this change, quite literally, makes all the difference. Being a member of a tennis club may have nothing to do with my work, providing purely and simply a means of changing my preoccupations from professional activity to play. Being a member of the Church is not, however, simply an additional occupation of this kind; it involves all our other activities, changing our attitude towards them and the way in which we carry them out.

Needless to say, this is a description of the state of affairs as it ought to be. It is perfectly possible — and it frequently happens — that the Church is apprehended not as this lucid transformer of all other human societies, this bestower of meaning on activity which might otherwise appear pointless, but as an intruder into a world which apart from the Church may appear entirely satisfactory and complete. We may find that the Church interferes with some freedom we should like to claim or upsets some way of running society that we should like to adopt. But if the Church's own standards and appreciation of itself are adopted, this is how it will relate itself to the rest of reality: not as a part of it, not as something separate and superimposed, but as an influence permeating reality as a whole and altering its whole quality and orientation. It is because it has this general relevance to the whole of human society that it so often comes into conflict with other groups. Restricted interests, groups which find it necessary to exclude other persons

73

and to compete with them if they are to gain their ends, cannot accept the interfering presence of a group which challenges them to widen their concern and, in fact, to put the concerns of others before their own.

If the Church aspires to influence the whole of human society, how is it that it is not a totalitarian organisation, one to be rejected as a curtailer of human activity? What is the difference between the Church and other organisations which seek to dominate and control the whole of society? On what grounds do members of the Church commend it to other people as a beneficent influence?

The difference between the Church as a world organisation and others seeking power and control is that it contains within itself its own means of self-correction, recognising as it does that it is not an ultimate but must always refer itself to an external source of authority and value. Members of the Church do not regard any other member as exercising complete control over them; they are held together not by acceptance of a human means of organisation to which power of control has been given but by a common acceptance of the same God, made recognisable in Christ. The authority of Pope, bishops, parents, or religious superiors in the Church is not absolute and dictatorial but is only a part of the general dispositions arranged by Christ for ordering human life. All authorities in the Church accept the same authority over themselves as do their subjects. And by the true standards of the Church, it is always possible that any individual member of it may be a more authentic representative of Christ than those who are in public office.

This may sound like a façile prelude to an apologia for the misdeeds of the Church in the past or at the present time. But it is in fact the only realistic basis on which membership of the Church as a life-enhancing society can be defended. Mere membership does not guarantee our ultimate acceptance; we cannot join so as to be dispensed from all human effort for ever more afterwards. Being a member of the Church involves the incessant struggle to live up to the standards of Christ in our relationships with other human beings. And in this search for perfection, resistance is bound to arise, either from ourselves or from other people. If we have particular insights into truth, or imagine we have, we shall have to fight to communicate them and get them accepted. We shall have to take the risk of being in the wrong, because of our own stupidity or blindness. The mere fact that our motives are good (or we think they are) is not sufficient. Motives and resolutions have to be tested in practice.

To accept the Church as the community within which to live out the full scope of our life means that we are prepared to face the facts of our own limitations as members of the human race and to develop not as ego-centred individuals but as persons who find themselves in relation to other people. The fact that no restriction is made as to who these other people are is a sign of the unrestricted unselfishness which is the key to our own completeness.

The Church: True Humanity

'No salvation outside the Church' must therefore be taken to mean 'no salvation outside humanity'. There is no salvation outside the community that embraces the whole human race. The Church's role is to direct men's minds towards that wholeness; there is no salvation outside acceptance of that Gospel message. The Church rightly makes claims to be the exclusive source of salvation because in clearly verifiable fact no other organisation offers so universal a programme for mankind; all other bodies, even Christian ones, are more restricted in their aims or potentialities.

A look at all Christian groupings other than the Catholic Church will reveal that in some way or another they are limited by their national or cultural attachments, by their dependence on the theology of a particular founder or dominant teacher, or by their appeal to a particular group or spiritual family. Only the Catholic Church constitutes, in reality as well as potentially, a truly world-wide society, which, in spite of national or class ties in particular local situations, nevertheless rises above those ties, and can without danger to its own inner coherence cut itself loose from them.

This does not mean that the Catholic Church does not recognise that it is, sociologically speaking, one group among innumerable other ones, one Church among many others. It would be absurd not to acknowledge that fact. But what it does say is that its own doctrine and inner momentum fit it for the position of being the Church for all the world, and that that potentiality is to some extent at least realised in the Church's contemporary expression, and has indeed always been realised. This is as true of the aspirations and policy of the tiny church of the Acts of the Apostles as it is of the Church of Vatican II.

The present sociological variety of the Catholic Church also brings out its actual and potential universality. No other religious society has roots to the same extent in every social class (in spite of considerable fluctuations and gaps in many places) or appeals to such a wide variety of psychological types, from the gregariously minded to the individualist, from the intellectual to the manual worker, from the fervently emotional evangelist to the quiet contemplative.

This is because it is held together not by an efficient organisation or by a common language and a common way of doing things, though these human aids to understanding and collaboration can all help in its work. It is held together by a shared listening to the same message, which calls into being everywhere an open pattern of social relationships within which a fully Christian way of life can flourish. It is a message which everyone hears conversationally in his own way and to which everyone responds in his own way. And the fact that one is hearing it correctly and not distorting it can be decided by the extent to which we are or are not brought into harmony of thought and action with the whole Church — and not only with the constituted, organised Church, but with all work for the good of men everywhere.

It is this attention to the one message that makes the Church an organisation with its own means of correction, not a self-sufficient body, judge in its own cause. It is for every individual to get hold of the message and make of it what he can; this effort demands attention to and respect for the viewpoints and insights of others, but it may also be directed towards changing the viewpoints of others. The process of change will necessarily encounter opposition, both from other ordinary members of the Church and from those to whom responsibility for discerning true expressions of the faith from false ones has been given. These authorities may give an adverse judgement on what is put forward to them; it will be up to the individual to decide whether he must persist or whether he should think over the possibility of a revision.

But what of the infallibility which is attributed to the judgement of the Church? Is it not claimed that the Church can act as final judge, and, therefore, it would seem as judge in its own cause? Can it really be said to be a genuinely open society?

In the first place, it can very easily be pointed out that no completely open society exists in human affairs. There is always an umpire, an editor, a Lord Chief Justice, a Privy Council or a Supreme Court, whose decision is final. The gift of infallibility means that, as in all societies, there is a place from which the buck can no longer be passed on. The important question that has to be decided is the distinctively Christian significance of this particular gift in the Church.

Infallibility gives security; but not the security of a closed mind. Those judgements which are held by the Church to be unchangeable expressions of the Church's faith, whether they come from Councils or from Popes, are held to be protected from error. That means that they demand our serious consideration as reliable guides to the faith; it does not mean that they are exhaustive, or even adequate, statements of it. It means that you will not go wrong if you take them to be true and think and act accordingly. But you are never guaranteed against your own misinterpretation or that of others; the whole labour of working out what documents mean is still with us. The only help that infallibility gives is the assurance that in trying to interpret them, we are not wasting our time.

What infallibility makes us certain about is the ultimate coherence of the Church and of its powers of expression; this is an invitation to enquiry, not an end to it. It is more than indefectibility, since it applies to the message itself. We do not say simply that the Church will not fall away from the Word; we say that the Church hears the Word, can express it and must proclaim it. The unique reality which is the Church is held together by the unique Person of Christ, the Word of God. The conversation which he has begun with the human race is worth while because the Word is sure and because he is not final. He is for ever; there will be no end to our talking.

April 1974

77

THE ORIGINALITY OF
CHRISTIAN TRADITION

CHRISTIAN apologists of the 1930s and 1940s — the Hilaire Belloc, C. S. Lewis and Dorothy Sayers generation — often warned their contemporaries that England's Christian tradition was in a state of decline and that unless we were able to revive it, society could not last. Christopher Dawson's historical studies backed up their theme: without the continuing influence of religion, which he regarded as the dynamic element in culture, and in particular, without the Christian religion, civilised life would come to an end.

Often enough, it was held that this decline dated from some specific point in the past, when there had occurred a damaging break in the flow of European civilisation. Some placed it at the Reformation: others at the end of the seventeenth century, with Paul Hazard's 'Crisis of the European Conscience'; others again said that it had happened in 1789, or in the course of the Industrial Revolution. David Jones wrote of this break in the preface to *The Anathemata*, saying that 'in the nineteenth century, Western Man moved across a rubicon which, if as unseen as the 38th Parallel, seems to have been as definitive as the Styx'.

The decline of culture, a break in culture, tradition running out, tradition severed; religion for bridge-building, religion for reconstruction, religion for revival; the diagnosis and the prescription were put forward in the twentieth century as they had been in every previous one. Historians nowadays question the diagnosis, and give good reasons for their disbelief. For the sake of the prescription, Christians welcomed the gloomy verdict. But they should, for their own reasons, be sceptics, too; among their articles of faith, it is an intruder.

There have always been men who mourned the passing of their fathers' gods and sought stability in a return to the ways of old. That was how Jews and Gentiles argued against Christianity; since it was new, it was false. Very soon, Christians used the same argument. Since theirs was the religion that had established the State on a firm footing and had given good morals and prosperity to their forefathers, it should be maintained; Christianity became traditional.

In England, Richard Hooker argued on these lines, seeking in his *Ecclesiastical Polity* to preserve much of the Church's corpus of venerable customs and constitutional laws, and urging upon the Puritans (since he could not appeal to Scripture) respect for the long generations of the past. His blend of political conservatism with Christianity, fusing State and Church into a single society, became the *leitmotiv* of a whole line of English thinkers. It was given a new impetus by Coleridge in revolutionary times and fresh life in the twentieth century by T. S. Eliot; in Europe, it was favoured and adapted by men such as Joseph de Maistre, Auguste Comte and Charles Maurras. For the traditionalist, the backward look is decisive. Morals, politics and religion, inseparably one, made us great in the past, and can continue to do so for ever.

But this is a perennial and a damaging confusion; Christian tradition and conservative traditionalism are not the same thing, any more than belief in the Church and loyalty to a particular nation can ever be the same.

The past of which the Church must remain aware is its own past as People of God. Not Byzantium, not Holy Russia, not England's green and pleasant land, not France, Spain or Italy, not Ireland, not the Holy Land itself: these are not the source of the Church's contemporary faith. The Church is quite distinct from all the civilised societies to which it has given inspiration and support.

It is, moreover, an essential principle of the life of the Church that we are not saved, any more than we are damned, by what our ancestors have done. We can learn from their achievements, but the one essential benefit that we cannot inherit from them is our own act of faith. We cannot acquire true religion as we learn our native tongue; we do not believe in it rightly if we think it will make us sons of any earthly, conquering fatherland.

The Church's tradition is the Church's perseverance in unity with Christ. It is our response to the command he has given us, to hand on, in actions as well as in words, the message and the life which we have received.

It is the Church's continuing existence, held together by its common speech, the Word of God, and by its common Spirit. At the heart of the diverse political and cultural forms that have flourished and still flourish on the earth, it represents the essence of true civilisation. It has not broken, and will only break when the end has really come. Three Romes have fallen; the West may fall; but neither the world nor the Church, with the purpose it passes on, are yet at an end.

The Times, 19 April 1975

'. . . SUBSISTIT IN . . .'

NO WORDS of men should be more carefully weighed than those used by an Ecumenical Council. Many are the battles of interpretation and assimilation that still remain to be fought out in the Church. The significance and importance of the recent Council's explicit preference for *presbyter* rather than *sacerdos* or *clericus*, for example, has not yet been understood or acknowledged by all members of the Synod of Bishops; and if the Congregation for the Clergy has grasped the meaning of the conciliar terminology (which it can hardly have failed to do), it has so far conspicuously turned a blind eye.

Another instance often recurs in conversation: people have been struck by the fact that the Second Vatican Council did not say that the unique Church of Christ *'est'* Ecclesia catholica, *a successore Petri et Episcopis in eius communione gubernata*, but *'subsistit in'* Ecclesia catholica . . . (LG n. 8). Did this mean some alteration, some mitigation of those exclusive claims?

There were many, even in enlightened ecumenical circles, who thought that the Catholic Church's claim that it *is* the Church of Christ meant that all other churches were *not*, in any sense at all. If the change of wording can help them to realise that when anyone says that something is so, he is not making a corresponding denial of everything else, so much the better.

But beyond that, what does *subsistit in* mean? To begin with, it certainly does not mean *non est*. The obvious sometimes needs stating. Nor does it mean that the unique Church of Christ is eking out some sort of diminished life at a very low level in the Catholic Church: subsisting, so to speak, on bread and water. That is not what the Council meant, though to hear some people you would think that it did.

Both in Latin and in English, *subsistere* means to stand firm, to exist in a vigorous, affirmative, particular and very solid form;

it is a strong word, not a weak one. It gives *est* flesh and blood; it certainly does not render it thinly abstract and metaphysical. It expresses continuation in existence in a definite circumstance, condition and place. Where *est* might be found too static, too complacent, *subsistit in* conveys life, growth, presence and action.

Any idea that this constituent part of Catholic faith implies a denial of values existing elsewhere should have been sufficiently dispelled by the rest of the very sentence in which the phrase *subsistit in* occurs; it is made clear that holiness and truth are to be found outside the structure of the Church and play their part in building up Catholic unity.

The message that the Catholic Church has been created to pass on to the world involves us in a more wide-ranging and positive appreciation of human values than does any other religion or philosophy. Without the unique claims of the Catholic Church, mankind could rest content with narrow horizons, leaving others out of account, loyal only to party, class, colour or nation, and turning their eyes from the demands of world-wide solidarity. If all religions are equally true or untrue, then we can be content with our own little set of beliefs, incurious about others; if the Catholic religion is true, then all others have permanent importance, since every scrap of wisdom they contain must be sought out and brought into a living and growing synthesis.

It is a simple fact of life, easily verifiable, that only the point of view of Catholic faith makes us give full value to the truths by which other Christians live. We deny no positive belief of any of the Christian churches; they on the other hand only keep their distance from us by rejecting some part of our belief. To be a Catholic is the only way of making sense of the Christian phenomenon without suppressing any part of the evidence. To accept the Catholic Church is to be obliged to seek out and to treasure everything else. One is a Catholic precisely because one is required by Catholicism to reject nothing except negation itself. Any other position is sectarian, partial and incomplete.

Catholic unity is both static and dynamic, given and lived in anticipation: never one without the other. A Catholic can never be brought to say that unity is no more than an ideal held out before us by Christ, a pious hope, something that may be realised one day; he knows that it is a gift to be accepted here and now, one that can come eventually to perfection because it already exists and has started to move in that direction. This is true of every aspect of Catholic faith and life; everything, our very existence, our salvation and sanctification, our union with Christ, our vocation in life, our marriage, our children, every enterprise we undertake, every death, every entry into new life, is in the first place the gift of God.

There is nothing pretentious about saying that the Church of Christ subsists in the Catholic Church, simply because such a statement begins from what God has done, not ourselves, and forces us to give full value to the contribution of everyone else. The message the Apostles were told to take to the world included the fact that they themselves were not indispensable. The Catholic Church carries within itself its own self-correcting mechanism; it exists by the principle of God's initiative, and it knows and proclaims that God's initiative precedes it everywhere.

Many English Christians think that unity can only be brought about by the abandonment of Catholic claims. Rome has only to set aside its authority and its pretensions and all will be well, all will fall neatly into place. The reverse is the truth. Only by a full understanding and acceptance of those claims, by Catholics themselves in the first place, can unity be brought about. If Christian unity does not already exist somewhere, then it cannot ever exist anywhere. Because it does already exist in the Catholic Church, then it can and will be found everywhere, both now and in the centuries to come. *Subsistit in* means that the unity of the Church is a growing point, not a resting place; it gives us more, not less, to feed on; it is the only solution that asks all the real questions.

August 1976

ON PICKING OUT THE PROPHETS

'I DON'T propose to come to your lectures, Father. You only give us the party line.' The emancipated sister who spoke, had, of course, no thought of paying a compliment. But since the Church has only managed to keep itself in business so far by sticking to what the Apostles saw, received, and passed on, her remark could be taken that way. Every theologian wants to be understood as an interpreter of the Word of God, no more, no less. He cannot do that without fidelity to the Church which the Word of God continually calls into being and sends out to represent him.

Some writers nowadays set out to appeal to the great mass of readers over the heads of the experts and scholars. They claim to tell us what 'the authorities' of every kind know but do not wish or dare to tell: von Danniken or the Bermuda Triangle authors, for instance, have had great popular success with curious but uncritical minds. The same has been true in the theological world: ephemeral fame has over and over again been achieved by the catchpenny device of appearing to be the only expert who is prepared to tell the tale.

Today as always, the test to be applied to the authors, lecturers and publishers who compete for our attention is to see whether they accept the living rule of faith, the Catholic Church that speaks to the world the integral Word of God. In the New Testament scheme of things, this rule of faith applies to all of us — to prelates and professors as to everyone else. And, since one ought to be specific, it appears that it is being set aside today as much by Hans Küng as it is by Archbishop Lefebvre. As a Presbyterian friend remarked the other day, 'That Archbishop Lefebvre has been to see the Pope, and he has come back as jaunty as ever'. 'Jaunty' is what Hans Küng is as well. Whom does he imagine he is taking in, when he interprets Catholic doctrine down to vanishing point, and then says 'I am a Catholic'? Hans Küng has written one good book: *The Council and Reunion*. Since then his work, vigorous and talented as it is, has been cock-eyed and one-sided, using one half of Catholic truth to lambaste the other. He acknowledges no superior — that goes without saying — and he acknowledges none of his peers either, since he is as out of tune with his fellow scholars as he is with Rome.

It is part of a theologian's responsibility to 'withstand Peter' when necessary out of loyalty to the Word of God; this review has always been ready to act in that direction, whatever it might be that called for comment. All such criticism must be conducted within the context for dialogue that is provided by the communion of the Church, with a view to improving the Church's presentation of its message and thus of commending its gospel authority to the world. Serious scholars and teachers do not want to waste their time tidying up after Hans Küng, particularly when he pays so little attention to anything his colleagues may say. We have had enough internal controversy over the last ten years; it is time we put it behind us and got on with addressing ourselves to the world outside, as fellow-members of the Church and fellow servants of Christ's message, not as lonely mavericks who will fit in with no one.

A Catholic theologian or a Catholic review that systematically leaves Rome out of the dialogue must expect to raise doubts in people's minds. We need pastors and teachers who will commend the Church as it really is, as part of the Gospel; we can do without those whose purpose in life appears to be making the Church look silly. Westminster has more, much more, to offer than Tübingen, and if the Church in this country were to start to teach, it would earn the gratitude not only of Catholics who are tired of obsessive fanaticism but above all of the world that waits for a word that comes from communion as well as conviction.

But the fact of the matter is that Küng himself seems to expect an immunity from criticism that none of us has a right to ask. One could take him more seriously if he were able, like Cardinal Newman, to identify himself with the Church, whatever the discomfort. The results of Newman's fidelity can be seen today; his light will continue to grow. If Küng allowed himself to be more obviously one of us, there would be more chance of his being accepted as indeed a true servant of the Word of God.

January 1977

THE NEW TESTAMENT

IGNORANCE of the real nature of the New Testament is one of the most obvious mental gaps preventing many contemporary spokesmen for Christianity from uttering anything other than fumbling, earnest, jocular protestations of their half-belief. If Malcolm Muggeridge understood what the New Testament is, he would never have called his latest book *A Third Testament*. If Don Cupitt understood it, he would not have attempted to find a 'Jesus' who stands apart from his Church. If Antony Burgess understood it, when he made Our Lord speak in the Zeffirelli film of 'What I must call my Church', he would never have added that note of reluctance.

The work of Jesus is misunderstood from the start if it is not realised that he deliberately brought a new people into being, a people held together by himself, the Word, in dialogue with them and among them, a people filled with his Spirit; and that he thereby established the new and final ordering of the relationship between God and man. The fundamental source of our knowledge of Jesus, from the very beginning of his mission, and still at the present day, is his living Church. He did not write a book; his words and his actions wrote in the hearts and minds of men, and, with him, a community of friends told the world who he was. He never meant us to be reduced to reconstructing his life out of the documents and monuments of the past. He is present for all time in his Church; and the way of access to him, for all men, is through belief in its testimony, through faith in its life, through hope in its future, and through love of its aim and goal.

The New Testament is not a collection of books; it is an unbreakable personal and corporate union with God through the blood of Christ. Those who wrote the books of the New Testament, under the inspiration of God, lived within that union; and they looked always to the Church, to the people who were the New Testament, as the source of what they said, as the evidence for what they believed, as the authority for what they taught, as the place of their access to Christ. The books of the New Testament, read in the context of the Church, the Temple of Christ's Body, are the privileged and authorised guide to our knowledge of him, and will never cease to convey new depths of significance to those who study them in the light of an active life in the Church. But the guidebook is not the reality itself. The new relationship which Christ established with men: that is the unbroken reality into which we must enter if we are to see Truth.

Some Catholic scholars have forgotten this essential characteristic of their faith and talk as if it were possible to extract a lesson from Scripture, positive or negative, which could then be viewed separately from what the Church believes and teaches. The Church therefore becomes in their eyes no more than a supplementary authority which supplies information that they may either, on non-biblical grounds, be prepared to accept, or, on the other hand, may from their own standpoint wish to reject. A position of this kind is a hang-over from pre-conciliar days; it certainly does not represent the far more balanced and profound view of revelation presented by Vatican II.

Jesus Christ in his Church, under the guidance of the Spirit: that is the primary datum for Christian scholars, whatever their special discipline or area of study. It is the principle of all Catholic research and teaching in universities, of all pastoral training, and of our entire mission; in the present century, those who accept it have produced remarkable results in all fields of theological enquiry. It is lack of acquaintance with this achievement that makes university theological teaching in this country so dry, so uninspiring, so provincial. For twenty-five years and more, no Catholic faculty in the world has allowed itself to live in the kind of ignorance of Protestant scholarship that still today is taken as normal, where Catholic scholarship is concerned, in the universities of England, Scotland and Wales. The acceptance of the true New Testament principle as the key to the knowledge of Christ demands, and has been seen to demand, an openness to the entire content of the Gospel and to the full ecumenical range of its purpose.

The Jesus of history and the Christ of faith are one and the same person. And it is also true that there is no Jesus Christ without Christians, no Messiah without his messianic community, no Son of God without the sons of God, no Shepherd without his flock, no Master without his disciples, no High Priest without his priestly people, no Mediator outside the Temple in which true worship is offered, no King without his Kingdom. Jesus Christ willed to be known to the world in and through the Church which he sent into the world. Because men do not open their eyes to the Church of today, they do not discover the Jesus who told us to look for him only among the living.

June 1977

86

THE CHURCH IS THE GOSPEL

THE attempt, so often made, to search out a primitive, pure Christian Gospel, is a mistake. Many of those who make the attempt occupy positions of eminence, but it is a mistake none the less. It is a technical mistake because it misjudges the materials involved. And it is a religious mistake because the New Testament outdated it from the start.

Christ abolished book-religion. He left no written rule, no meditations, essays, manuals, nor correspondence. His predecessors and his followers expressed themselves in writing. He could have done the same, but he did not. The Word he gave was himself; and so that we might understand, he sent his Spirit: the spoken word and the moving spirit, to make men one in mind and heart. Records, writings, documents, monuments: all of these demonstrate and explain this new social bond, but they do not take its place. The teaching, the teachers and the taught: the living Church, and not the written word, is Christ's chosen means of communication. What Newer Testament can there be? To press forward would be an illusion; to move back a betrayal.

Christ did not expect to be understood immediately. It is clear from the records that he meant both time and experience to be used in the effective transmission of what he had to say. The writings of the New Testament represent years of further thought on the part of those who heard him. That was his intention; for he had made his disciples part of his plan.

Scholars now think that they should pick out from beneath the layers of words the ones that were spoken at the start and rely on those alone. They relegate to secondary importance or less the contribution that the writers themselves made to the setting-out of their theme. Christ had more confidence. Precisely because he came to bring mankind together, he arranged to be heard through his hearers. If we do not accept their handling of his words, then we treat him as one of the scribes or as a lonely prophet. But it belongs to his words that they were effective: his hearers responded. We cannot listen to him without listening also to those who heard him before we did. We cannot answer him without joining in the answer that they gave.

In the Acts of the Apostles, often enough, 'the Word' is 'the Church': The Word grew, 'and the number of disciples was greatly increased in Jerusalem' (Acts 6:7). The Word includes those who heard it. The Word, the seed of the Gospel, has the power of growth; and what grew was the Church. The Word was visible; the Church was audible. The Word had left the written page and had become the common language, the shared way of life, of a new society.

In the face of fresh demands, that society knew how to speak with authority; no longer, like scribes and Pharisees, did they interpret a law they could not change, but they followed the new law of the Spirit, and sought new understanding, new phrases, wider freedom and greater conquests.

Just as natural growth — the seed, the vine — provides the characteristic images of our developing apprehension of God, so the organisation of material life provides the key to understanding our developing activity in the service of God. The Church is a hunting and a pastoral society; it is the fishermen and the shepherds, the farmers and the gardeners, who foster its life, not, once again, the scribes.

As well as abolishing the specialised priesthood, Christ set aside the professional interpreters of the Law and gave the Law and the Spirit to everyone. But he did not do away with specialisation, for he also gives many particular gifts. One of them is the service of the Word: responsibility for the spoken summons that calls the Church together. The Apostles put that service first. The service of the Word is also, indivisibly, the service of the Church: this is the ministry of the New Testament, by which Word and Church are still passed on today.

If Christ is reduced to being an object of archaeological research, it becomes impossible to make sense of him. The first principle to be followed — and it requires the subsequent application of every scholarly technique — is the one he himself laid down: that he would be found among the living. Any other arrangement would have been neither new nor lasting. A religion meant for all humanity uses scholars as it uses others; like everyone else, they must learn from a Christ who knew what he was doing when he wrote his will and testament, not on paper, but in the flesh and the spirit of man.

November 1977

CRUCIFIXION is death in agony; it is death in public; and it is death as an outcast. The God of the Christians died the death given to slaves, criminals and enemies. That is the fact from which we cannot free ourselves. We did not start as a community; we began with one whom a community rejected. We did not start as a culture: we began with one of whose form of punishment the cultured did not speak. We did not start as a nation; we began with one whom those who led the nations excluded from their city.

Service can be honourable; not so slavery. The Church was once a solitary slave who died the death ever fearfully present to the minds of all slaves, keeping them slaves by the horror it inspired. He did not save them from that death, but asked them to accept it: to take it up and embrace it with joy, because he had turned its inescapable terror into an endless beginning of bliss.

The Church is built of slaves: of those who know and accept rejection. That is why it is the only society for which there are no outsiders. Many governments of today's world are opposed to it because they must live by creating enemies. In their prison cells, their torture chambers, their punishment and extermination camps, they offer human sacrifice to their gods. And the attacker of governments, the terrorist, also solves his problems by finding people to hate. His god destroys, just as the god of dictatorship and privilege must needs destroy.

But the God of the Christians knows no limits. We trust him because he went beyond the barriers to bring back all those whom men turn into foreigners. He became an alien, showing men what they had done to their God and what they were doing to themselves.

The Church brings everyone in. It cannot compromise with any who would restrict its horizon to one nation, one culture, one class or one teacher. However large, however homely, however welcoming, it must remain a stranger to those who still want frontiers.

On Good Friday, the thought of physical suffering can fill our imaginations but leave us in our sins, like many another tale of violence. To be purged by that pain, we must accompany it to the end. We must go beyond the limits of human loneliness. We must be separated from our very selves. Only then can we live again.

There is no resurrection without that death. There will be no resurrection of the Church without that drive beyond the frontiers, without that search for those who are outside. The handicapped, the sick, the oppressed, the persecuted: these are the ones whom God has chosen for himself, the ones of whom he makes his people.

In their favour, he has used, not power, but weakness. Their weakness became his strength. He does not change the world by the world's methods: by making slaves, by setting limits, by enmity and exile. An end will come, judgement will come. But we cannot anticipate that day; we cannot take over the power of the Creator.

The Church is not an Empire. Universality is not imperialism. It means possessing nothing, but serving and fostering everything. Division means a narrowing of horizons; insistence on the presence of unity is a remembrance of the fact that barriers have been destroyed.

In his Son, God has shown us where our long search ends. It goes further than we thought: to the ends of the earth. Not a circumnavigation through pleasant places, not an escape to an oasis, but a journey through a desert place to visit those whom the holiday-maker does not see. And it goes less far than we would wish: no further than our own street. To make those who are not yet God's people into his people; to bring near those who are far off: that was the work of the Cross. We have made God an outsider; but he has overcome our worst, and calls us all inside.

March 1978

CERTAINTY

FAITH is not a 'fundamental option'. It is the foundation itself. Misunderstandings in ecumenical discussion and malaise in the Catholic body frequently arise from a faulty appreciation of the gift on which everything is built.

When I first began to read the Anglican review *Theology*, it was edited by Alec Vidler, who at that time was a devotee of Paul Tillich. He wrote an editorial about Tillich's book *The Shaking of the Foundations*, making its message his own: faith means disturbance, the dark night, the earthquake, the storm. A little while later I was in digs in Bradford, in the home of the sister of an Anglican clergyman, whom she looked after, and who was bedridden and dying. She went out one day to hear Dr Vidler at the parish church, and I shall always remember her comment when she came back: 'He seems to think one cannot have real faith unless one always lives in a state of doubt'. She knew better than Paul Tillich and Dr Vidler; the faith that carried her through the trials of her life was a secure certainty: a foundation that was not shaken.

Faith is not a wager or a leap in the dark. Images and comparisons of this kind may serve in the run-up to faith, but they must not be taken as an accurate expression of faith itself. Where God is concerned, there are no odds to be calculated. We move from obscurity to light, not the other way round. Faith is a rational act, resolving uncertainty; it is the bedrock judgement.

If we regard being broken as the essential religious experience and doubt as the equivalent of faith, then we are simply dramatising our hesitations. Faith means being cured, not being shattered; *terra firma*, not a landslide; not being lost, but being found.

The judgement of faith is an unconditional assent to the meaning of the signs conveyed by the Church, witness to Christ in the contemporary world. It brings us into a context of rational understanding and discourse, in which we come to know and understand the Word of God, spoken in our own words.

It is a misrepresentation of the loyal Catholic mind to say that in this context it must offer unquestioning obedience, under discipline, to all official edicts. The obedience of faith is intelligent and questioning: it seeks to understand, in order that it may offer real assent to what is required and taught. From the beginning of his pontificate, Paul VI had made it clear that this is the kind of attention he expects to be paid to his own teaching and to all teaching within the Church. It is one of the tragedies of the time since the Council that his guidance has not been followed by many of those who should have been his most ready interpreters.

An alternative view, just as misleading, has been proposed. It sees the Catholic mind as set, not in unquestioning obedience, but in perpetual judgement over the utterances of authority, in order to measure them against its own understanding of the mind of Christ and to reject them if they are found wanting. Such an attitude has no place within the Church; it is self-destructive, hindering every possibility of advance. Its voice is still heard too loudly and frequently among us, and it has produced the intellectual confusion and frustration that afflict us today.

Faith does not close our minds in suspicion of authority, any more than it blinds us to the inadequacy of what authority may say. It is the primary understanding that makes communication possible. Worship, which is the heart of faith, respects the other person who addresses us, and listens, not in order to scrutinise and resist, but in order to hear, to discuss, and to reach a common mind. When God teaches in his Church, we are given the standpoint from which every other judgement must be made. There is no higher ground from which to survey and criticise. Within the teaching and learning activity of the Church, we are asked not for unthinking acceptance, but for comprehension and responsible collaboration.

When teaching and disciplinary documents, from Rome or from the bishops of any part of the world are received by Catholic journals in this country, as they have been in recent years, with flat contradiction, or are impatiently waved aside, then faith itself has been forgotten. Faith builds a community; these reactions tear it down. People have not heard what has been said, and have prevented others from hearing it, simply because they did not know how to exercise the founding virtue of faith.

Once the gift of faith has been received and the commitment of faith has been made, there can never be any valid reason for setting it aside or for abandoning that commitment. Faith is the gift of God, who never breaks his promises or withdraws what he has given. Certainty of that kind is precisely what we need to cope with the terrors that can so easily overwhelm us. The recovery of certainty is an urgent necessity in today's Church. The listening ear of faith is the first qualification for all who would speak; those who speak without it do not deserve listeners.

May 1978

HERMENEUTICS, HISTORY AND
ORAL TRADITION

IF I had been St Basil the Great, by 'oral tradition' in this context I would have meant 'unwritten' apostolic traditions, which he describes in his Treatise on the Holy Spirit as 'that unpublished and secret tradition which our Fathers preserved in a silence out of the reach of curious meddling and inquisitive investigation'. 'For', he says, 'if we were to attempt to reject the "unwritten" ordinances of custom, on the ground that they have no great force, we would be, without knowing it, injuring the Gospel in its most vital points themselves, or rather we would be reducing the "kerygma" to a mere name.' 'For "dogma" is one thing; "kerygma" is another thing. The former is kept secret; the "kerygmata" are made public.'[1]

And this might be seen as an appropriate topic for a church historian. Not for him the refinements of philosophical analysis, of logic, epistemology and metaphysics; nor the close study of the written records of two generations or so, in the New Testament documents: nor even the investigation of the writings that transmit the altogether longer experience of the Old Israel; to him belongs the necessarily cruder task of coping with the vast mass of documentation left behind by the *tempora christiana*. Cruder, let us say, because of quantity, and because it is a labour that concerns itself with texts that have not been officially canonised as inspired and are not therefore supremely authoritative; and the 'oral tradition' bit of the material is, of course, the least important of all, if one is a Protestant or a modern historian, since everything spoken and not written down is for the Protestant, 'merely human' and for the historian, 'notoriously unreliable'.

These salutary reflections on the humble insignificance of the historian would however at that point have been interrupted by St Basil himself, if he had been able to hear them. 'Have you already forgotten', he would say, 'that I said that "oral tradition" was very important, since without it "kerygma" is but a name? These Protestants you speak of sound to me like

---

[1] From the treatise *On the Holy Spirit*, ch. XXVII, tr. Amand de Mendieta, *The 'Unwritten' and 'Secret' Apostolic Traditions in the Theological Thought of St Basil of Caesarea*, 1965, pp. 2-6.

the Pneumatomachian disciples of Eustathius of Sebastia against whom I was writing.'

Twentieth-century Protestants, or some of them, would then chime in: 'Yes', they would say, 'we have read the writings of Fr Maurice Bévenot, SJ, and the Documents of Vatican II, and we agree that we should no longer think like Calvin or like Bishop Jewel in this matter; without oral tradition before the New Testament was written down, and, indeed, even after, we would lapse into Fundamentalism or fade away into the Higher Academic Thought'.

And then secular historians would rally to the support of their ecclesiastical colleague. 'Modesty', they would say, 'is all very well and possibly becoming, but don't forget that the anthropologists are making us bring back Oral History in a big way. The study of Oral Traditions has its own methodology. In many societies, they are our most easily available source for reconstructing the past; they are known to be the basis of many written sources; and, in pre-literate societies, they are frequently preserved and transmitted with the utmost care. Read your Jan Vansina and take heart.'

Urged on therefore by these reminders that Tradition, and even Oral Tradition, is no longer seen as a supplementary benefit, to be drawn on occasionally, perhaps, by theologian or historian, if real need arises, but without too much reliance on its lasting usefulness, and has instead moved to the centre of our scientific preoccupations, I would suggest that the question 'What material does the theologian study and interpret?' must be given the answer 'Tradition, and Oral Tradition at that'.

We have to remember that the Word that there was at the beginning was a spoken word, and that the Founder of the Church and of our civilisation was not a writer but taught by word of mouth: 'he began to speak'; 'he opened his mouth and spoke'.

If that is the case, then the Church historian is studying exactly the same object as every other operator in the theological field. His sub-division is chronological, not methodological; he is studying the same Word as the Old Testament or the New Testament specialist, the only difference being that he is listening to a speaking of the Word that took place at a different point in time. Church History has in the past been described as the

Cinderella of theological disciplines, but everyone knows what eventually happened to Cinderella, and I leave it to others to supply names for the two ugly sisters.

Interpreting the Spoken Word: Walter J. Ong

Given, therefore, the fact that he is dealing with material the predominant characteristic of which is that it was, or is, spoken and heard rather than written and read, what are the principles that the interpreter has to bear in mind?

Walter J. Ong is one recent author who has taken up this theme. He has studied it from the point of view of a specialist in Renaissance literature, particularly in the art of rhetoric, as he has tried to restore to contemporary scholarship a sense of what it means to deal with an oral/aural culture rather than a visual/typographic one. He has pointed out, for instance, that

> The centrality of the spoken word as a point of reference for the various senses of the word of God is due not only to the fact that the spoken word is always primary (writing and print always refer directly or remotely to the word as sound) but also to the fact that the Bible, from Genesis through the entire New Testament, including its epistolary parts, registers the oral culture still so dominant when the Bible came into being . . . The oral state of mind and psychological structures so evident in the Bible are strange to us, as we now know, not because we are 'Western' but because we are typographic folk, more intensely alphabetised than were the ancient Hebrews (*The Presence of the Word*, pp. 188-9).

Because they did not take this point seriously enough, it seems to me that neither Theodore Boman nor James Barr, in their discussion of the auditory/visual, Hebrew/Greek, Semitic/Western distinction, really go deeply enough into the question to be able to produce a satisfactory solution. Whatever the linguistic or cultural modes of transmission and expression, we do not interpret Biblical literature correctly unless we understand that it represents speech, and a particular understanding of the relationship between speech, creation itself, and man's situation within the created order.

Walter Ong's discussion of the Reformation period in the light of the history of changing attitudes to the word also throws light on our present-day attempts to get interpretation right. As he says, historians of the Reformation 'have assessed the effect of printing in a quite external fashion: printing "spreads ideas" . . . put the Bible "into the hands of the people" ', and so on.

But the interior change in psychological structures tied in with the shift of the word from a written to a printed culture is at least as important as the physical spread of inscribed texts (p. 264).

He examines this 'shift of the word' in four areas of Reformation controversy: (i) Scripture and tradition, (ii) the sacraments, (iii) the preaching of the word and (iv) authority.

(i) *Scripture and tradition.* Ong points out that the Protestant stress on the primacy of the written word — *sola scriptura* — 'reflects quite patently the growing confidence in the word-in-space' (p. 272). While this was of course complemented in Protestantism by an insistence on oral communication, on preaching, this has in fact led to the sharp separation at the present time between the literalist interpretations of fundamentalist groups with their highly oral, tribally transmitted standards of orthodoxy, and academic biblical scholarship, interpreting the written page but lacking a spoken tradition, except in highly restricted circles, within which to communicate it.

The Council of Trent managed quite a strong emphasis on the oral character of the message, which *Dominus Noster Jesus Christus Dei Filius proprio ore primum promulgavit,* and then 'omni creaturae praedicari' iussit; but the phrase in *libris scriptis et sine scripto traditionibus,* even without the *partim . . . partim* formula, did leave the way open for that restricted view of the Bible as written as printed and Tradition as not which we are now laboriously trying to discard (see Denz. 783).

Vatican II, with its clear affirmation about the primacy of oral tradition, (see *Dei Verbum,* nn. 7-10) has of course made a massive advance on this text, the full significance and value of which still has to be discovered and appreciated.

(ii) *The Sacraments*. In oral cultures, Ong points out, the spoken word is 'necessarily an event, an action, an indication of the present use of power (since it is something going on, and is thus of a piece with other physical actuality'. The efficacy of the sacraments in Catholic teaching (they are efficacious words in the doctrine of Aquinas and of Trent) 'is therefore more readily comprehensible to oral-aural man — or to modern man who understands oral-aural cultures and the actuality behind them in depth — than it would be to cultures tyrannised over by the alphabet and more particularly by print' (pp. 279-80). 'The extreme Protestant attitude to the sacraments, however, is thoroughly in accord with the typographic state of mind, which takes the word to be quite different from things' (p. 280).

(iii) *The Primacy of the Word*. Ong here recognises that Protestants did indeed lay great stress on the efficacy of the word in preaching, so that it would seem that the old oral-aural sense of the power of the word here reasserts itself. He could however have gone on to point out — unfortunately he does not — that for all their stress on preaching they did in fact by their theology of grace severely limit the efficacy of the word, which no longer really produced the effect it signified. Readers of Karl Barth, who has rubbed off on Hans Küng, will know what I mean. The theology of the word that was preached by Bossuet, for example, in the seventeenth century, provides plenty of evidence of a more powerful sense among Catholics of the efficacy of God's spoken Word in relationship to the community of the Church and to the lives of individuals.

(iv) *Authority*. Ong's comment on the rise of Protestantism is a further indication of his main theme:

> The movement from an authoritarian to an objectivist state of mind . . . is in great part correlated with the shift from habits of predominantly auditory synthesis to habits of predominantly visual synthesis (p. 283).

He goes on to say that 'An oral culture' (and here, of course, he has the Catholic Church in mind) 'tends to be communal, non-individualist and authoritarian'. His view of the Church corresponds with this somewhat depressing picture; but I am after all commending the virtues of an oral culture, so must take him up on this one. Underlying his somewhat depressing judgement is the notion that a Catholic hears the voice of authority as 'God's voice speaking *through* (my italics) the Church' (p. 284), and that he 'has resort to the word *of* (my italics) an objectively existing Church' (ibid.). Vatican II did however say that the *Magisterium non supra verbum Dei est, sed ei ministrat* (*Dei Verbum*, n. 10), and so the Catholic hears *in*, and not *through* the Church, a Word that is not the property of the Church, but rather possesses the Church as its own creation. The oral culture of the New Testament carries within it numerous corrections to that 'communal, non-individualistic and authoritarian' character attributed to oral cultures by Walter Ong.

The Power of the Spoken Word: Marcel Jousse

Having used his book to raise some of the issues connected with the discussion of our reference as interpreters to a tradition that is fundamentally and essentially an oral one, I should now like to turn to the teacher whose work will surely come to dominate the study of this theme and its many ramifications in the years ahead. Walter Ong owes a certain debt to him; so does Birger Gerhardsson in his *Memory and Manuscript*. The name of Marcel Jousse is only just beginning to be generally known in France, and he has hardly yet been heard of over here. He died in 1957, and had taught for twenty-five years at the Sorbonne, at the Ecole des Hautes Etudes and at the Ecole d'Anthropologie. Two books recently published gather together his largely oral teaching. His work is based on a study of the origin of language, using above all his observation of those predominantly oral cultures that remain, and, along with this, an investigation of the semitic oral culture as we find it recorded in the biblical documents. I will not attempt to present his theories in anything like a complete way, but will make one or two remarks about the nature of oral culture and oral tradition arising out of a first reading of his work.

The first is this: oral tradition does not limit itself to the spoken word. Talking is not the only thing we do with our mouths. We also eat. Oral tradition is partly transmission by eating and drinking. For the anthropologist this presents no difficulty. When you think of the importance of eating in the Bible, from

> You may eat indeed of all the trees in the garden. Nevertheless of the tree of the knowledge of good and evil you are not to eat, for on the day you eat of it you shall most surely die (Gen 2:16-17),

to

> On either side of the river were the trees of life, which bear twelve crops of fruit in a year, one in each month, and the leaves of which are a cure for the pagans (Ezek 47:12; Apoc 22:2)

and

> Then let all who are thirsty come: all who want it may have the water of life, and have it free (Apoc 22:17),

passing on the way by Wisdom's invitation

> Come and eat my bread, drink the wine I have prepared! (Prov 9:5),

then one begins to think that theologians concerned with interpretation have perhaps neglected the principal carrier of tradition, the sacred meal by which the People of God is not only sustained, but also defined. A people is made a people of a particular kind by what it eats or does not eat. One of the New Testament themes came alive in Peter's mind when he had his vision of every kind of animal on the rooftop and heard the voice telling him to kill and eat: 'What God has made clean, you have no right to call profane' (Acts 10:16). The early Christian community, we are told, 'went as a body to the Temple every day but met in their houses for the breaking of bread; they shared their food gladly and generously . . .' (Acts 2:46). 'Sharing their food' follows directly on 'the breaking of bread'. The Jerusalem Bible picks out for comment the adjective 'gladly': 'Joy is the sequel of faith'. Fair enough; but it would have been more appropriate to emphasise the fact that sharing food (of all kinds: nothing is unclean) is the sequel to the eucharist.

This means that for a theological interpreter the food by which the Church is kept alive is a central and indispensable object of study. The sacraments cannot be an option; to treat them as a ceremonial extra or a denominational concern is to blind oneself to the data from the start. No anthropologist would ever make that mistake. We cannot possibly interpret the Christian thing unless we understand what it is that Christians eat and drink, and the significance of their eating and drinking when seen in the context of everything else that we can discover about what food and drink have meant for man. Edmund Leach has applied structural analysis to the book of Leviticus and indicates the interest of continuing this investigation into the history of Christian ritual: 'The theological literature on this subject is vast but anthropologically naïve' (*Culture and Communication*, p. 93). The argument of his book is, he says, 'compatible with the general position of Mary Douglas and with the vastly more detailed analyses of Victor Turner' (p. 96), an indication perhaps of the value of this approach when it comes to curing theologians of their overdose of abstract verbalism. Louis Bouyer made a start along this line of investigation some years ago with his *Rite and Man*, and one or two people have followed him since then, but we still have a long way to go.

Marcel Jousse made this remark in a lecture in 1944:

Vous n'avez pas le droit, anthropologiquement, de nier la Présence Réelle et le Transsubstantiation. Et cette solution je vous l'inflige comme anthropologiste . . . (p. 263 n.).

And here he is supported by Jacques van der Loew:

Le mot 'symbole', qui, dans la mentalité moderne, a pris le sens édulcoré d'allégorie, reprend ici son sens primitif, son sens réel . . . Une preuve du complet changement de sens qu'a subi ce mot se présente, par exemple, dans les discussions théologiques où l'on prétend que le 'Sacrement' (c'est à dire, l'Eucharistie) doit être pris dans un sens purement allégorique, symbolique et non pas comme existant en lui-meme. Cependant, pour la mentalité primitive, 'symbole' est juste ce que ce mot exprime; une rencontre et identité de deux réalités. Cela signifie, primitivement parlant, que c'est la même chose, que 'cela est'.

Une théologie libérale enseigne que le pain et le vin ne sont que le symbole du corps et du sang du Christ, mais la théologie primitive enseigne que le pain et le vin *sont* le corps et le sang du Christ (*L'Homme Primitif et la Religion*, p. 45).

Talking of eating leads one of course to table manners, and I would like to quote Jousse on this theme as well. He is talking of justness, exactitude, if gesture is to be real, clear and efficacious:

Cette justesse surveillée et cette efficacité prévenue vont se transposer dans ce qu'on appelle les Liturgies. Là, toutes les actions sont, pour ainsi dire, préformées par la grande 'politesse' transcendentale qui vient de la Tradition, de ce conformisme résultant d'un usage éprouvé et approuvé. Il faut que tous nos gestes soient porteurs d'un sens et que ce sens soit exact . . . Nous avons trop ignoré que la Liturgie est fondamentalement une pédagogie . . . Toute la pédagogie religieuse devrait être une pédagogie anthropologique . . . La religion, je l'inscrirai en facteur commun de tout (18-12-1944; *L'Anthropologie du Geste*, p. 19).

And at this point we can bring in a contribution from our side of the Channel. In *The Anathemata*, David Jones has a striking echo of Marcel Jousse:

This man, so late in time, so curiously surviving, shows courtesy to the objects when he moves among, handles or puts aside the name-bearing instruments, when he shows every day in his hand the salted cake given for this *gens* to savour all the *gentes* (p. 50).

All this does not mean that we are running away from words. On the contrary, one is concerned here with giving words their full force and function in human life. And to do that, says

Jousse, we need an anthropology, and above all an anthropology of gesture:

> Le Péché Originel, et Capital, de notre civilisation de style écrit, est de se croire la Civilisation par excellence, 'LA civilisation unique' (*AG,* 33).
>
> L'Homme est la mesure de toutes choses. Le Cosmos, dans son expression globale ou orale et sa mise par écrit, ne peut s'exprimer et se grouper qu'en fonction de l'Anthropos. C'est pour cela que nous pouvons dire et redire: l'expression normale du réel, c'est l'Homme bilateralement mimeur (*AG,* 205).
>
> C'est face au Cosmos, inséré dans le Cosmos, que l'homme, ce 'MIMEUR' innombrable, va élaborer sa Tradition (*AG,* 37).

A word is an oral gesture: a gesture using our breath, our throats and our minds. A word is a physical action, with a physical effect. This fact underlies the transmission of oral culture, and in particular the transmission of biblical culture. And so from eating we move on to expression and memorisation. Eating and speaking, 'taking in' and learning, are inextricably joined together.

> Come eat my bread,
>> drink the wine I have prepared!
> Leave your folly and you will live;
> Walk in the ways of understanding.
>
> (Prov 9:5-6)

The parallelism of scripture, reproducing the bilateralism of man, the law of balance and equilibrium, is the means by which the teaching of the Old and New Testaments entered into its hearers and teachers, becoming part of them. Learning by heart meant what it said.

In the milieu of Palestine, the learning process of the rabbinical schools made use of two rhythms. From a position of repose, the pupil could move either forwards and backwards, the rhythm of the Burden, or from side to side, the rhythm of the Yoke. This mnemonic pattern underlies many passages of Scripture and is vividly employed in one of Our Lord's sayings:

                    Come to me all of you
For you are burdened   and heavy laden
                and I shall refresh you.
Take my yoke upon you   and learn from me
for I am gentle   and lowly in heart
            and you will find rest for your souls.
For my yoke is easy   and my burden is light.

(Mt 11:28-30)

The lasting force of the text of Scripture, as well as the meaning itself, depends on the use of patterns and rhythms of this kind. The studies of Marcel Jousse will renew our approach both to biblical interpretation and to every aspect of the way in which its message is passed on, assimilated and given living expression.

The interpreter is not a solver of puzzles; he is a translator. He helps those who wish to communicate but do not understand one another, by translating the language of one into the language of the other. Such translation must at the very least not be a betrayal, and can be an enhancement. The Septuagint translated the Hebrew Old Testament; the New Testament continued the work of translation, and that translation continues in the Church. The interpreter must not forget what it is he is interpreting: Oral Tradition. And as he interprets, he is making himself in a part of that same Oral Tradition, passing it on, translating it, to the next generation. We hand on what we have received; a true interpretation does not forget or destroy anything of what it has to communicate, but can and indeed should draw out its riches more fully.

The work of the interpreter was summed up in the words of St Paul:

You yourselves are our letter of recommendation, written on your hearts, to be known and read by all men; and you show that you are a letter from Christ delivered by us, written not with ink but with the Spirit of the living God, not on tablets of stone but on tablets of human hearts (2 Cor 3:2-3).

The Gospel written in men's hearts: in Père Congar's two-volume *Tradition and Traditions,* this theme is the subject of an appendix. It must, I think, become the central theme in any future study of the Word that builds Christ's Church. It is the source of our oral tradition; it is expressed in our theology; and it is the effect produced by every interpreter who uses the hermeneutic technique and the expressive art of the New Testament.

July 1978

References, Further Reading: Auerbach, E., *Mimesis. The Representation of Reality in Western Literature,* (Berne, 1946); Barr, J., *The Semantics of Biblical Language,* (London, 1961); Boman, T., *Hebrew Thought compared with Greek,* (London, 1960); Bouyer, L., *Le Rite et l'Homme,* (Paris, 1962); Cazelles, H., *Ecriture, Parole et Espirit.* Trois Aspects de l'Herméneutique Biblique, (Paris, 1970); Childs, B. S., *Memory and Tradition in Israel,* (London, 1962); Edwards, Adrian, 'V. W. Turner: A Pathbreaker in the Forest of Symbols'. *The Clergy Review,* LVII (1972) 410-8; Gerhardsson, Birger, *Memory and Manuscript.* Oral Tradition and Written Transmission in Rabbinic Judaism and Early Christianity, (Uppsala, 1961); Jones, David, *The Anathemata,* (London, 1952); Jousse, Marcel, *L'Anthropologie du Geste,* (Paris, 1974); Id., *La Manducation de la Parole,* (Paris, 1975); Leach, Edmund, *Culture and Communication,* (Cambridge, 1976); Ong, W. J., SJ, *The Presence of the Word,* (Yale U.P., 1967); Scheffczyk, L., *Von der Heilsmacht des Wortes,* (Munich, 1966); Van der Loew, J., *L'Homme primitif et la religion,* (Paris, 1940); Vansina, Jan, *Oral Tradition,* 1961, (Penguin Books, 1973).

DON'T LET THE DEVIL HAVE ALL
THE BEST WORDS

AT last year's Conclaves, the express wish of some of the more qualified observers and commentators was simply for a confident Pope who smiled and gave us hope. Their wish was granted. The smile of John Paul I brought happiness. The smile of John Paul II brings the same happiness; his courage has lifted the spirits of us all.

A warning must on that account be sounded against ominous signs that the prophets of doom to whom John XXIII refused to listen are with us again. Rallying cries are being raised; reiteration is replacing dialogue; labels are being applied so as to discredit and to spread hostility. Words that every Catholic should respect for their true meaning are being rejected and left to the enemy.

One of these words is 'liberal'. 'Liberal Catholic', is once again becoming a term of abuse; and it has been suggested that by his utterances the Pope has excluded everyone who considers himself a liberal Catholic from membership of the Church. But to relegate 'liberal' to outer darkness represents not simply an impoverishment of our vocabulary, but a failure to understand the faith itself.

If the God of the Christians is not generous, open-handed, unsparingly liberal in his gifts, then since the New Testament we have been getting our wires singularly crossed. Every rejection of Christ's teaching there has ever been in history has come from a refusal to accept the breadth of his vision, the extent to which he expects us to stretch our sympathies and our love. And these have not only come from outsiders; many apparent attacks on Christianity have in reality been rebellions of the human spirit, prompted by the Divine, against the attempts of churchmen to constrain or to use for selfish ends the message of Christ.

The liberal Catholicism of the nineteenth century, preceded by that of the Enlightenment, was not a watering down of the faith, but an attempt to make sure that it was communicated and received in the way most appropriate to its meaning and to its purpose. Those liberals who think it necessary to cut loose from religion, have never in fact found a firmer basis for the freedom they rightly desire than the one which is provided by the Christian faith and safeguarded by the Church of Christ.

Those who attack Vatican II today are men who refuse this liberality, who want to use the Church as an instrument of repression, and who have their own Procrustean standards of orthodoxy, by which they presume to judge all others. They forget that God judges men not by what they think, still less by what they know, but by what they do. They forget that the Church is a place where we are to be left to grow together until the harvest. Their efforts can truly be seen as dia-bolic, divisive, and destructive of communion, instead of sym-bolic, striving to connect, to join, to give and to receive.

Without the knowledge and spirit of Christ, man's efforts on his own to be a liberal always seem to end not in toleration but in a harsh authoritarianism that tries to bend others to its own idea of the good life. Liberality needs the full Catholic faith if it is to be sustained. Many efforts are being made to narrow down that faith, both in the name of 'progress' and in the name of 'tradition'. These, too, are good Catholic words that need rescuing from their false friends. For the moment, let it be reaffirmed that a religion without liberality cannot be Catholic, and that liberal values, now as always, are best preserved and promoted by those who accept the truth of Christ and live in the freedom of his Spirit.

December 1979

IV
WORSHIP

RITUALS OF HEAVEN OR RITES
OF THE JUNGLE?

THE liturgical changes of the last few years went reasonably smoothly in the small country church I look after on Sundays: some good-tempered grumbling, that is all. But the introduction of the new order of the Mass has tried patience beyond its limits, and it is now only too clear that all is not well. Some like the changes; some would like them to go on; but many are profoundly unhappy.

I was at a wedding a month or two back. The bride and bridegroom, both practising Catholics in their twenties, intelligent and very modern-minded people, wanted a Latin Mass. They brought some of their friends to play Mozart. Many of the congregation were Anglicans. All the old atmosphere came back: reverence, silence, prayer. People were taken out of themselves. This, they said, was the real thing.

Those who are upset are holding on somehow; but the 'other world' has faded. And I am speaking of committed, active people, not droppers-in to a Mass at Christmas time.

Unless we can rapidly discover and communicate to one another the point of the new patterns of worship which the churches are bringing in, we shall lose a whole generation or more of Christians; and that means finally losing England for Christianity itself. Myth and magic will take over. When the rational worship of Christianity fades, man will not be left in a clean, aseptic, secularised world; a primitive sub-human, savage, 'sacred' way of life is already returning and there is no visible sign at present that the process will stop.

Explanation of details, historical information about when this or that ceremony or prayer came in and why it should now go out, even theological commentary, are all pretty well powerless to help. People do not want bits of information; they want to see the unity of it all; they want to find God.

Years ago, Aldous Huxley was pointing out that if man is to find God, his emotions must be captured; to seize the spirit, worship has to lay hold of the senses. Once the appeal of the baroque or the Byzantine had faded, the Church would, he thought, have little left to offer. Man's universal search for mystical experience would take other paths. He has been proved right, up to the hilt. What is the use of a basic English Mass when what people really want is the fascination of music, mysticism and poetry: sitars and sutras, Allen Ginsberg and the discothèque? Man cannot live without incantation; left to himself, he chooses the ceremonies of Haiti or of Canaan as his way to ecstasy. Nothing short of the ritual of the courts of heaven will ever succeed in taking over from the rites of the jungle.

If Christian worship is to live today, we shall have to break through to the heart of it all: we shall have to find the mindstorming, light-giving, love-catching Person who is there, filling us with his all-absorbing love for the Father, sending us his spirit, lifting us up into the total transforming experience of God, an experience which fills and stimulates and fills again the appetites of all the seven ages.

The Mass is the language of God; it is shot through by the word, by Christ himself who speaks to us there through the other persons we meet, through his own words, through his own self-offering. It is the place where we can hear, take in and grasp the word of God, where the word can speak in us.

The reverence we pay to the Blessed Sacrament must expand and fill the church so that all are penetrated by the desire simply to listen and to know what God is doing and saying. New forms of words must not degenerate into programmes for us to perform; they must be new expressions of the love of Christ: the love of the bridegroom for the bride. Today, the Church has become a nagging wife; we must find again the blissful joy of lovers who are content to be together.

Within the words and the actions, we must discover the Real Presence of the Holy Spirit, the one Person in many persons who unites us to Christ and to one another. He takes us up into an action which makes us holy and hands us over to God.

109

At last we are human, at last we are wholly ourselves, at last we are united with the source of all happiness.

In all our worship, the Holy Spirit, so often forgotten, must be heard and honoured now. Only he can ensure that the many vernaculars will not become a Babel, that the voice of men will not replace the voice of God, and that the silence of Heaven will calm and captivate our noisy, troubled hearts.

The Times, 16 May 1970

FLASH BULBS IN NOTRE DAME

PRIESTS rarely go to Mass. They forget what it is like to be in the congregation. Palm Sunday in Paris this year brought an opportunity of being at the receiving end for once, of watching others do the work. Memories of being in the choir of Notre Dame for Vespers, of walking in the procession while the crowds looked on, of seeing visitors standing on chairs for a better view, and of being distracted by guides showing parties of British school-children round during High Mass, made me wonder how things were going to be this year. I was pleasantly surprised. A sprig of box to be collected from a bench near the door, the duplicated text of Lauds available on a stand at the entrance to the nave, a seat well forward near the altar; crowds, informality, but a sense of occasion. Singing, reading, ceremonies: simple, plain, spirited, with a great many communions. A Cathedral liturgy which was not just a social occasion or a performance. There were some small annoyances, like the mother and daughter just in front who talked throughout, breaking off momentarily to sing odd snatches of the Latin Creed and Sanctus; apart from that, all might have been well, even uplifting.

But. Yes, there was one. A big one. So important that it was enough to ruin everything. The flash bulbs. They never stopped. And they were enough to undermine all the good work that had been done on the liturgy. People didn't jostle or stand on chairs so that they could see. They popped and flashed instead, even at the elevation, when there was no bell, only silence, enough silence for the popping to take over. Communication and participation were thrust out; this was the world of spectator sport after all.

The cameras with their flash bulbs reveal the fact that even in Notre Dame de Paris, even in the best-known and most visited cathedral in Europe, representative of a part of the Church which prides itself on its forward thinking, its pastoral and apostolic pioneering, its scholarship and its sense of catholicity, the liturgy is not understood for what it really is.

At any other gathering, political, social or cultural, is it thinkable that spectators would be allowed to let off flash bulbs from beginning to end of the proceedings? At a concert, a play, a lecture, a debate, at any meeting for serious business, they would be regarded as an intolerable intrusion. Why does the Church permit the most personal and authentic of its activities to be reduced to the level of a carnival parade?

The Mass is not a free entertainment offered to the world; but by giving photographers *carte blanche* to fabricate and carry off their souvenirs, the Church is behaving as if it were. The Mass is an invitation, yes, an invitation to all men; but it is an invitation to hear the Word of God and to take part in a corporate act of worship, not to intrude and to turn a family occasion into a public display, to treat Catholics as so much zoological material, so much folk-lore, for sticking in an album back home.

The fundamental fault is that we are not understanding the Mass as a real occasion: only a ritual one. At Notre Dame, one could see that by the fact that the bishop who should have been the president, the head of the community, the leader of the proceedings, was reduced to the level of a puppet, brought out now and again to perform some ceremonial action and then put back again on his throne. His sermon was feeble, apologetic; he talked like a timid salesman who has lost confidence in his wares to an audience of whose attitude he was unsure, not like a father aware of the respect and love of his family and clear in his mind about their corporate purpose.

The practical ignorance of the meaning of the Mass which is so clearly revealed by this acceptance of flash bulbs and by the blurred, insecure outline of the principal celebrant, is with us, of course, in England as well. Sunday after Sunday, one sits through the readings at Mass watching the church slowly fill up. A third or a half of those eventually present drift in after the Mass has begun, paying no attention themselves to the words of Scripture and effectively preventing anyone else from

111

paying attention. We do not yet think of the Mass as a corporate celebration, as a social action in which each of us must play our part. If we arrive late for a concert or a theatre we are, quite rightly, excluded. If we are invited to dinner, we arrive on time. We attach importance to these occasions and we remember our manners. When God invites us, when we go to meet him in his Church, manners are forgotten. We regard going to Mass as attendance at a ceremony giving individual assurance, and we count on others to tolerate the casualness with which the pressure on our consciences can be relieved.

It would be no bad thing if when we found ourselves arriving late we turned round and went home again to avoid disturbing others. It would at least show that we knew the meaning of what happens inside.

The Mass is a real meeting, opening the way and setting the style for all other meetings. But we take it less seriously than the rest of our business or pleasure. The cameras in Notre Dame make those who pray feel odd men out in their own home; the puppet who does not really preside turns a programme for action and words for communication into a mechanical performance. A street market is not a community; a tourist does not really belong. Every family has to shut its doors some time. If we were to shut our doors and remember about not interrupting other people's conversation, we would be better placed to discover the presence in the Mass of the One whose words and actions are, for us, meaning and reality.

June 1973

THE MYSTERY OF THE CHURCH

LITURGICAL change can only really be justified by considerations of faith and doctrine; on matters of taste, one can reasonably expect to argue for ever. Are the present alterations a better expression of the reality in which worshippers are to be involved? Do they get rid of false mystification so as to confront people with the real mystery? Have they succeeded in straining off any comforting but obscure phrases which may act as sedatives or shields from the true power and glory of God? Are they faithful to that new arrangement of human affairs that Christ referred to when he said that we would now be able to worship in spirit and in truth?

There are mysteries from which the prophets of the Covenant, Old and New, have always told us to turn away: sacred groves, high places, hidden rites, secret initiations that lead on treacherous and deceiving paths. There are mysteries which darken and conceal; and there are mystics whose search for a refuge from the world and from themselves requires the hatred of both: the perennial gnostic and the everlasting manichee. There are liturgies that we have made mysterious by turning them protectively into linguistic monuments. Before we put our worship into words and music, ritual and vestment, we must be sure that we know and begin to understand the true nature of the mystery we celebrate. It is easy for us to repeat high-sounding words which may indeed provoke a catch in the throat in the college chapel, but which leave the heart unchanged.

Christianity took the term 'mystery' and developed its meaning, making it stand now not for secrecy, obscurity or concealment, but for declaration and making plain. The plan of God for the world was at one time hidden from man and inaccessible; but now he has committed himself to a course of action within human society which he has announced and explained. We know now, said the Apostles, what he intends to do and how he intends to do it; we have seen, as clearly as it is possible for human beings to see it, what he is like; we have been told to give this knowledge to the world.

The Church did not take over the old mystery religions; it rejected them as vehemently as the Old Israel had rejected the agrarian fertility rites of Canaan. The Church did not line itself up with the old mythologies; its thinkers learnt from and joined in the contemporary philosophical critique of the ancient gods. The mind of the Church was focused on personal, human, historic reality; and in that reality the mystery of God had been made known, by meeting the thoughts and confirming the guesses of human myths and mysteries.

The message of the Church was given all at once in simple, public proclamations of the faith within which men could discover themselves. The cross taken up by Christ had in turn to be taken up by others; and what they learnt in taking it was the shape of their own lives.

The 'mystery' of Christ's presence in the Eucharist, in his Word, in the Church, is not an enigma, a puzzle, designed to keep our brains busily occupied and unaware of the tedium or the horror of everyday life. It is not a problematic presence, but a real one; the Body and the Blood of Christ which are the chosen sign of that loving obedience which, he said, was food and drink to him, and the sign of our obedience, too, if we do, as he did, the will of the Father who sent him.

The Statement on the Eucharist drawn up by the Anglican/ Roman Catholic International Commission (but not, alas 'Series III'), has succeeded in expounding this reality in terms which avoid the literalism into which some Catholics and some Protestants have fallen. We do not dramatically re-enact the Passion of Christ; we do not didactically use bread and wine to put ourselves in mind of past events and future glory. Christ himself uses the bread and wine we see as his contemporary means of accessibility to us: the Body by which he is present (that, after all, is what bodies are for), to nourish us, and the Blood by which his life keeps us alive. It is not anything we have made; it is his own act of presence which is, effectively, the sign of what he has done in the past, is doing now, and will do in the future.

For us, the mystery still to be made known and understood lies not in this real, meaningful presence, but beyond it in our acceptance, when, in faith, we allow it to guide the personal pattern and direction of our lives.

This is how Christianity has always marked itself off from Gnosticism or from the mystery religions, from Valentinus or Hare Krishna, mescalin or scientology. The real presence of Christ sends us back into the real presence of our own lives. Rescued from the depths, the body of our mortal flesh takes on clarity and significance. Christianity, in John Toland's words, is not mysterious; but that becomes true only if we consciously and willingly permit its public facts to take the place of our own private fictions.

The Times, 28 December 1974

114

THE FUTURE OF WORSHIP:
REMAKING THE ENGLISH TRADITION

IT would be a great mistake to regard the present changes in our English Catholic style of worship as no more than the dutiful implementation of Vatican II, a transition from a Latin-based culture to an English one, or a shift from individualism to an emphasis on community. Very much more is involved. We now have the opportunity and responsibility of building a pattern of worship adapted to our local mentality and style that can form future generations of English people in the Christian way of life.

We are re-making a tradition; and tradition properly understood, is not simply the preservation of the past. It is an activity of the present day, which, while it inherits from the past, is directed towards the future. It is our own personal share in the whole historic process of handing on the faith. We receive the faith from others; we live out our lives in terms of that faith; we pass it on to others. And as we do this, the faith, the Gospel, the Word of God, grows. This is an essential New Testament conviction. It is of the very nature of tradition, in the Christian understanding, that it does not consist of pure conservation. Everyone who stands in the tradition must add to its working-out and its expression. Just as, under the Old Testament, men eventually learned that they were not damned by what their forefathers had done, so the New Testament has made it clear that we are not saved by what they have done either. It is up to us to make our own bit of the running.

Tradition is something very different from plain and simple attachment to a past that has disappeared; it is the complete opposite of reactionary distrust of all healthy progress. Its very name is synonymous with movement and advance . . . Tradition means a march forward, along a line of continuous development, both steady and alert, part of life itself . . . As its name indicates, it is the gift that passes from one generation to another, the torch that a runner hands on at each stage to the next member of the team in such a way that the race does not stop or slow down. Tradition and progress are so harmoniously integrated with one another that tradition without progress would contradict its very nature, while progress without tradition would be a wildcat enterprise, a leap in the dark.[1]

It was the opinion of C. S. Lewis, David Jones and a number of other writers who made up a distinctive school in recent English religious thought and literary criticism, that a 'break' in our tradition at some point in our recent history means that we are, whether we like it or not, living *après le déluge*, and now have to go round in the perpetual frame of mind of people in a disaster area who are reduced to salvaging what they can from their happier past.

I am quite sure that as far as the essential Christian tradition is concerned, they were mistaken. That tradition has never been broken; Christ has always been present and available to his people, and his people have always gathered round him so as to become the recognisable sign to the world of his continuing life. Culturally there have indeed been many breaks. But such breaks there must be. They are not disasters; they are the necessary crises of death and resurrection. The seed must fall into the ground and die. Every individual life knows such moments of trial and judgement; so do families within the Church; so does the Church itself. They come in order that life may continue; so that there may be resurrection; so that we may bear much fruit.

The fruit that we work and hope for in our present generation is the restoration and renewal of the Catholic Christian tradition in this country. We want to see an end of divisions and the flourishing of new and varied patterns of Christian life. It is the purpose of the Catholic Church, aware of its own past both as the recognised Church of the whole nation and, more recently, as a 'dissenting' church, to help all English Christians, 'established' and otherwise, of the present day to live together in Catholic communion. We must ensure that the witness of none of these communities is forgotten, but continues to make its own positive contribution to our life in Christ. Anglicans of all schools of thought, Presbyterians, Congregationalists, Baptists, Methodists, the Society of Friends and others must all find their true home in a united Church: one that in its

[1] Pope Pius XII, in an address delivered on 19 January 1944.

116

pilgrimage has forgotten nothing, but, unlike the *émigrès* of Revolutionary France, has learnt a great deal.

Hearing the Word

The most important part of the labour needed to achieve this will not be literary or ritual; it will be theological and devotional. It is from a united faith that a renewed experience of united prayer and united worship will come, and not *vice versa*. Obviously we cannot have the first without the second; but it is faith that provides our aim and our priority.

The liturgical movement of the twentieth century, which is above all a renewal of faith, has given to the Catholic Church not only the prime means of renewing its own life, but also a way of bringing divided traditions into unity. The theological understanding of Catholic worship, and the conciliar and post-conciliar decisions which have guided that worship, provide the necessary answer to the doubts and questions of the protesting Christians of the last four centuries, the remedy to the abuses which they feared, and the programme for a new, developing and enriching synthesis of all that we stand for and wish to promote in human society.

The joint Anglican/Catholic statements on worship, ministry, and authority indicate that this programme can indeed be realised. If this hope is to be brought to fruition, then a theory and practice of worship on the lines that follow will need to be commonly accepted.

The fundamental guiding principle is this: all worship must be understood as initiated by the living presence and activity of Christ, the Word of God. We begin by hearing the Word. This principle we hold in common with all other Christians. It must be made unmistakably clear that the Catholic Church believes and applies it faithfully. We stand by the expression of the Word in the past and by his continuing and contemporary effectiveness. He never ceases to build his Church and to make it an effective sign to the world.

To take an immediate practical example, this means that attention must be given to our use of the Lectionary, by which the Word of God has now been made more fully available to

117

us. The Jerusalem Bible is not suitable for public reading; it was not produced for that purpose. We need a version specially prepared for reading aloud in church, as they have in France. Readers must be properly trained; as much care needs to be given to this as we are already accustomed to giving to training altar servers.

The liturgical year must be used as the key to bible-reading and catechesis. The religion of the New Testament is a religion of the living Word of God, still active in his Church and making his influence felt throughout the days, weeks and seasons of the year.

Preaching must make the words of Scripture live for us today. It is the main responsibility of the ordained minister to communicate the Gospel; he must therefore know Scripture and be able to expound it, showing how the Word of God, who taught his disciples in Palestine and who was with the Church he sent out in the apostolic age, is still with his Church to continue the same mission. Preaching in the parish is not the same as catechetics; the head of the Christian community speaks to all of those for whom he is responsible, giving them something that each of them can reflect on in accordance with his personal situation, and also building up the community spirit through the expression of a shared obedience to the Word by which the world may be helped towards its salvation.

The meaning of sacrifice

Where the heart of our worship, the Mass, is concerned, a renewed understanding of the eucharistic sacrifice itself will both deepen our own spirituality and further the reconciliation of those Christians who are separated from us in their eucharistic faith and practice. One would not expect anything else. Renewal and unity will come not from any compromise or bargain — and certainly not from dropping the notion of sacrifice, as some would have us believe — but from a better understanding of what we have been given.

Sacrifice — *sacrificium* — *sacrum facere;* to offer sacrifice is to make sacred, to make holy. True holiness is moral obedience: the perfect love of God. Christ has expressed this

118

in a perfect human life: not some kind of substitute, ritual holiness, but real holiness.

The Mass is an act of sacrifice in this precise sense: the bread and the wine become Christ's body and blood, become Christ himself, the very Person who is Holiness itself. They are made sacred, made holy. In every Mass, Christ makes holy the means of his presence, the signs that express for us the extent of his obedience, showing that he lived out in reality the way of holiness we hear set out for us in Scripture.

The Mass becomes our sacrifice to the extent to which we allow it to make us holy. To be holy, we must hear the Word of God and keep it. And the first way of keeping it is keeping it in our hearts. This we do when we receive Holy Communion. We receive the Word of God himself and 'ponder on him in our hearts, with thanksgiving'.

The first aim of a liturgical movement directed towards gathering the English people into a shared life of worship must be the spread of a eucharistic devotion that has this New Testament understanding of sacrifice at its heart. It is an understanding that takes us away from all the controversies of the sixteenth century, still perpetuated by so many in our own times, and that satisfies both the doubts and objections of the Protestant Reformers and the teaching of the Council of Trent.

It is also entirely true to the Second Vatican Council, for one of the main achievements of the liturgical revision that the Council decreed has been to make clearer the unity of the whole Mass: the fact that there are not two parts, one more important than the other, but a single action, originating in the communication of God's Word and Spirit and culminating in the real presence of the Son of God and of his gathered Church.

The liturgical movement has often enough over the last two centuries been identified with the restoration or resuscitation of particular styles of architecture or music, or of a particular social order, or of the rituals of the past, thought of as more authentic because more primitive or more 'national' in spirit. It has sought to correct the exaggerations of Protestantism, or it has found inspiration in pastoral and missionary movements in other countries. We cannot now take any of these lines of action, which were too limited in their scope or too restricted in their sympathies. The liturgical movement must be guided not by immediate pressures, nor by incidental, subordinate concerns, but by a deeper understanding of what it is God is doing among us, in continuity with the experience of all preceding centuries. The objections that are being raised at present all stem from one or other of these limited presentations or alliances of the recent past; they have no basis in the tradition of the Church of the New Testament.

Our own tradition

How closely do these suggested guidelines follow Catholic tradition and our English Catholic tradition in particular?

'Adaptation' was of course the keynote set by St Gregory the Great for St Augustine's mission; and further back still we can recognise ourselves in the chapel of the Lullingstone Roman Villa or in the silver hoard of the fourth century found in 1975 at Water Newton in Cambridgeshire. The achievement of the later centuries still stands before our eyes in every city, town and village. But what of the time since the break-up of the sixteenth century? What line have we been taking since then?

As far as the use of the vernacular is concerned, one can recall the words of Henry Cole, Dean of St Paul's, spoken in Westminster Abbey on 31 March 1559. He told Bishop Jewel and his fellow churchmen that the use of Latin in the liturgy or communion under both kinds were not issues over which anyone should go into schism, and that the Mass could perfectly well be said in English. He suggested that a future Council of the Church could well be in favour of Jewel's demands.

The theology taught in the English College at Douai and presumably reproduced in many a sermon, catechism lesson and conversation in the late sixteenth and seventeenth centuries has an equally familiar ring.

Omnis ergo verbi Dei praedicatio est Dei circa nos visitatio, said Thomas Stapleton: 'Every preaching of the Word of God is a visitation of God in our midst'. Everything started from that effective preaching.

The Word is Christ himself: outside the scriptures, but not other than Christ. Today Christ and Christ alone is the sole foundation of the whole Christian religion which we are to teach, beyond which no other foundation can be laid.[2]

Authority, for Stapleton, meant above all the living Word of God, not to be identified simply and solely with the letter of scripture, but always present to guide the Church in its teaching and action. The Church is related to the Word as the visible and audible sign of his presence; not service only, but witness was its characteristic activity: *Non nudum ministerium habet Ecclesia, sed testimonium.*

Sacrifice and Real Presence

The patristic theology of the Euchaiist, which has nourished the liturgical revival of the twentieth century, was also the main inspiration of our sixteenth-century theologians in their debate with the reformers of the Elizabethan settlement and in their own sacramental theology and spirituality. In the early years of Elizabeth's reign controversy centred round Bishop Jewel's *Challenge* sermon and his *Apology of the Church of England,* regarded until Hooker as the standard exposition of the faith of the established church. Nicholas Sander, for example, set his reply in the context of the summing-up and renewal in Christ of the whole of creation, relying particularly on Paul, Irenaeus and Gregory of Nyssa.[3] Catholic faith in the sacramental body and blood of Christ corresponded to our faith in the restoration and renewal of the whole man, body and soul. In the new birth, Sander explained, both flesh and spirit will be recreated. The body will rise again, united with the soul. Accordingly, we believe

that not only our souls, but even the same flesh receives into it the benefits of Christ's passion, the sacraments which he gave to us, eating and drinking really under the forms of bread and wine the true substance of Christ's body and blood.

[2] Thomas Stapleton, *Opera Omnia,* 1620, I. 513D.
[3] See *The Supper of the Lord,* 1566.

121

The Church of England theologians maintained that

> Christ giveth to the body bread and wine, but to the soul
> he giveth by faith, spirit and understanding.

'Their spiritual eating', said Sander irenically, 'lacketh some
truth. How so? Because the whole man is not fed.' He quotes
Gregory of Nyssa as a witness to the sacramental realism of the
early Church:

> What medicine is this? None other beside that body which
> is declared to be above death, and the cause of our salvation.

This view of the eucharist corresponded both with a full
Christian anthropology and with the language of the Gospels,
with their references to growth, to the Word of God compared
to a seed, and to the leaven which transforms dough to bread:

> So that body, which is made immortal of God, entering our
> body doth transfer and change the whole into itself.

In the generations that followed, Richard Hooker and the
Caroline divines, and the Anglican theology which looked back
to their authority and inspiration, were much nearer to Nicholas
Sander than they were to Jewel.

Sander discussed the real presence without going into the
theology of sacrifice; for a treatment of this theme, one can
turn to Cardinal William Allen, whose lectures at the English
College in Douai give us the doctrine that was taught to the
clergy who were to return to work in England in Elizabethan
times.[4] Leo the Great (Sermon 7 *de Passione*) and Bede (*super
Marcum,* cap. 15) are his authorities when he comes to explain
how the relationship between the Last Supper and the Cross
makes clear to us in what way the death of Christ was a sacrifice:

> Not only did Christ truly and freely offer himself to death
> when he performed this sacrifice at the Last Supper, where he
> voluntarily bound himself to suffer on the Cross, where he

---

[4] Cardinal William Allen, *De Sacramentis in Genere, De Sacramento Eucharistiae, De Sacrificio Eucharistiae,* Antwerp, 1574. See pp. 541-2 and 551.

consecrated himself to the Lord; but he also freely laid down his Soul on the Cross itself; in which properly and correctly they hold the essence of these sacrifices to consist.

The death in isolation would not have been a spiritual sacrifice; to be that, it had to be accepted, chosen and willed by Christ as the completion of his consecration, his being set apart to do the will of God. It had to be expressly offered up as a supreme expression of his love for his heavenly Father and for mankind. The classic character of this understanding of the New Testament doctrine of sacrifice and its application to the Eucharist has been amply demonstrated in the twentieth century by Maurice de la Taille, and is given clear expression in the second eucharistic prayer now used as a result of the Vatican II reforms:

> Before he was given up to death,
> a death he freely accepted,
> he took bread and gave you thanks.

To explain the fact that the sacrifice of Christ consisted in his freely chosen self-giving, Allen referred to a passage from Gregory of Nyssa (*Oratio I de Resurrectione*) showing the interdependence of the Last Supper and the Cross:

> As a sacrifice, he offers himself an oblation for us at once Priest and Lamb, who takes away the sins of the world. But tell me, when did this happen? It happened when he gave his close circle of friends his body for food and his blood for drink. He who gives to his disciples his body to be eaten, clearly shows that the sacrifice of the Lamb is now perfect and complete.

At the Last Supper, Our Lord showed that he was giving himself to his disciples and for his disciples; his purpose was already made clear and at the same time made effective; it was brought to completion on the Cross, and is continued in the Eucharist, which shows for all time, as the Last Supper did once for the Apostles, the meaning of Christ's life, death and resurrection.

This is borne out in Allen's discussion of the Real Presence. He sets aside the theories of those scholastic theologians who tried to explain the link between the sacrifice of Calvary and the Eucharist by the similarity of the effects produced on the Cross and on the altar. In doing this, he rejected in advance those seventeenth-century theories that have often been attacked by Protestant controversialists, who hold them to be typically Catholic. In spite of all their ingenuity, Allen said, they put difficulties in the way of a proper understanding of the fundamental unity of Last Supper, Cross and Eucharist. It was much better to think, with the Fathers, in terms of the nature of the sacramental sign.

Under the Old Law, signs pointed to a reality other than themselves; but under the New Law, inaugurated by the Incarnation, God had become closer to us, and had established in the sacraments signs which themselves contained and conveyed God's grace, a real fore-taste of the ultimate reality which they represented:

> so that in the eucharist, whether you look at the substance of the Body or at the sacrificial action, there is not some sort of ordinary calling to mind by a simple external imitation, but a representation so definite and substantial that we may call it not a shadow, but a true image; ... that is how this Body of Christ is the figure of the Body existing naturally, and this sacrifice is the image of the sacrifice of the Cross.

All this took place, said Allen, *in mysterio*, not *'per aliquam externam repraesentationem aut ludicram similitudinem ac fictionem'*. He uses once again the language of the Fathers: of St Leo the Great, for instance, who reminded his congregation that we must all carry out in deeds what we celebrate in mystery (Sermon 70, 4; PL 54, 382b). And he is using a language which has become familiar to us in all our thinking about the liturgy in the twentieth century.

Allen's return to the Fathers gave to English Catholic theology an authenticity which makes it speak to us still in our own time. We must never allow ourselves to think of the English Catholic tradition as in some way extremist or eccentric. It stands in the main stream of Christian tradition; and it is this persistent faithfulness that makes it a real growing point for reconciliation and renewal today.

The story can be continued down to our own time. Catholicism in England was not an unbalanced, restricted or extreme form of Christianity; it clung to the central tradition and to the wholeness of the faith. *The Garden of the Soul* Catholic was taught by Bishop Challoner to keep in touch through the liturgy of the Church with the common life of the whole people of God. His *Meditations for Every Day of the Year* followed liturgical as well as catechetical lines. He expressed the relationship of principal celebrant and people in offering the sacrifice of the Mass in a way which anyone nourished on Vatican II will find familiar:

> For these ends both priest and people ought to offer up the sacrifice of the Mass: the priest as Christ's minister, and in his person; and the people by the hands of the priest, and both the one and the other by the hands of the great high-priest Jesus Christ. And with this offering of Christ's both the one and the other ought to make a total offering of themselves also by his hands, and in union with him.[5]

In the nineteenth and twentieth centuries, English Catholicism has not always been so faithful to its own sound tradition. Archaeological, aesthetic or devotional preoccupations have often prevailed over theological ones. Cardinal Wiseman, for instance, had a much less satisfactory understanding of the diverse functions and inter-relationship of priest and people in the Mass than did Bishop Challoner. Wiseman was enthusiastic in his commendation of liturgical prayer, in which, he said,

> All . . . become equally sharers, equally interested, in the holy exercise; and the attention is kept alive, or easily recovers itself. Surely this is a great advantage, and gives at once immense superiority to the ancient, over the modern, form of prayer.[6]

---

[5] See the Preface to the first, 1740, edition of *The Garden of the Soul*, and Donald Attwater's article on 'Bishop Challoner's Prayer Book' in *The Life of the Spirit*, X (1956), pp. 384-90.

[6] *Essays on Various Subjects*, pp. 387-8.

But priest and people were so sharply distinguished from one another in his mind that he did not see that this could be applied to the Mass:

> In the more solemn liturgy, or Mass, where the principal actor is the priest, having a ministry exclusively his, the rest must be content to join their prayers mentally with him, or rather with the sacred rite performed by him. And so in some other functions, wherein the priestly character alone has efficacy to act.[7]

I draw attention to this attitude of Wiseman's, so different in emphasis from that of Challoner, to show the crucial importance of a correct theological understanding of the liturgy and of the community of the Church; in his case the pastoral application of what was otherwise an excellent understanding of corporate worship was hindered by an inadequate doctrine of the ministry and of the Mass.

At a time when so many wanted to urge the claims of Catholicism on the English people in a Gothic or a Counter-Reformation dress, some however thought more deeply. Cardinal Newman was one; Edmund Bishop was another. Bishop welcomed Westminster Cathedral as a building that meant 'the end of that romanticism which has carried so many of us to "Rome" and a good many to "Romanism" '. He was thinking not so much of the architectural style as of the interior planning, which followed the pastoral and liturgical principles laid down by Cardinal Vaughan:

> A church of this type, with its exceptionally wide nave and view of the sanctuary therefrom, unimpeded by columns or screens, was without question that best suited to the congregational needs of a metropolitan cathedral, where, day by day, the Hours of the Church's office were to be solemnly sung, and her great liturgies enacted, in the sight as well as the hearing of the people.[8]

The last phrase of Cardinal Vaughan's programme betrays however the persistence of that mistaken notion that we found in

[7] *Ibid.*, p. 387.
[8] W. de l'Hopital, *Westminster Cathedral and its Architect*, 1919, 2 vols., I, p. 25.

Cardinal Wiseman: the idea that the liturgy of the Church is something to be enacted in the presence of the people, who are there to see and to hear, but not to be heard. This was the result of the 'Veuillotism' that Edmund Bishop strongly condemned for putting, as he said, 'a great gulf between clergy and laity: we are now suffering its deplorable consequences'.

Much of English liturgical thinking in the twentieth century has been dominated by the idea that it is, in the words of one writer, 'the ceremonial, decorative part of catholic worship, which touches our senses', or, in those of another, 'the organised way of expressing official relations between God and man'.[9] Westminster Cathedral, ready as it is in its superb planning for something better, has not yet been able to progress much beyond this, with the people as audience, the clergy as spectacle and the music as accompaniment. True revival can only come from a deep renewal of our corporate life, growing out of a theology of the liturgy which is richly available to us but which has hardly yet begun to impinge on missionary attitudes or pastoral practice.

If this is to come about, we shall need to study some of those authors, mostly continental, who can put flesh on the bare bones of conciliar and Roman documents. We shall also need to be more sensitive to the work of the Holy Spirit in the Church, as he helps us to worship with greater personal feeling and freedom and at the same time in due order, bringing the diversity of gifts, life-styles and forms of cultural expression together in the one body of the Church.

The twentieth century and after: Ronald Knox

And we can also, let it be said again, continue to draw on our own tradition. One of the great mistakes that people make nowadays is to try to do theology out of Vatican II documents and nothing else. The result is both thin and indigestible. The documents provide splendid guidelines, and we cannot do without them, any more than we can plan a railway journey without referring to the timetable. But nobody sits and reads the ABC all the way from London to Birmingham. Nobody, I suppose,

---

[9] See M. Richards, *The Liturgy in England*, 1966, pp. 33-4.

unless he is Ronald Knox — and he cultivated the train time-table as a form of relaxation from his other work.

Ronald Knox is the very man I want to recommend as a source of nourishment for our own spiritual life and for sermons. It is high time he began to emerge from the neglect that always seems to fall upon authors immediately after their death.

Look for instance, at *The Mass in Slow Motion*, published in 1948. It is a book of spiritual exegesis, told to children, not a tract. But somehow, without demanding or imposing anything, he managed to look ahead. After the Epistle, there are 'two bits of liturgy which were so obviously meant to be sung that they do not go naturally at Low Mass'. 'I always rather wish those secret prayers after the Offertory were said out loud, because they are so very attractive, some of them.' 'All through the prayers, as well as all through the Preface and most of the way through the Canon of the Mass, the priest holds his hands like that. I expect really he ought to be holding them wide out and high up, but nowadays the rubrics have reduced it to a mere gesture.'

Ronald Knox foresaw the changes and was ready for them. He also had a due sense of proportion about their importance. He dealt with the substance and heart of the liturgy, not with the accidental details. He glorified God by helping men to be holy. Ceremonies could wait.

He told his schoolgirl congregation that

In theory, you are all crowding on to the sanctuary, turning the priest's solitary dance into a tumultuous round-dance; all holding out pieces of bread and shouting, 'Father Knox! Father Knox! Do bless this one!'. That's what the Offertory really is; only you aren't actually expected to do quite that.

And there is a sermon preached at St Edmund's Ware in 1959 which says everything that needs to be said about our corporate offering in the Mass. Ronald Knox began with Ezechiel's vision of the renewed Temple and of the stream of life-giving water which flows from it, the stream which began as a tiny trickle and broadened out at once into a great river. He spoke of the easy way in which we slip into our cosy private thoughts at Mass, this 'half-hour in the day when we are guaran-

128

teed from interruption from other people', when we are alone with God.

But 'the Mass is not just that shallow trickle — you can hardly call it more — of your own pious thoughts, your own aspirations to be made one with Christ'.

> In a small country congregation, where the people are all neighbours and mostly related to one another, you do sometimes get the sense of the Mass as it ought to be, a family affair. One of the antiphons for Corpus Christi day tells us that the children of the Church ought to be like sturdy olive branches round the Lord's table, a reminiscence from that beautiful psalm which gives you such a glimpse of harmonious family life. The priest is the father of his congregation; not only in the sense that he adopts them at the font, not only in the sense that he corrects their faults in the confessional; he is the breadwinner, welcoming his children and dividing up their portions for them. A family meal is not meant to be like a cafeteria, where you sit reading your newspaper, and glaring at the other people; it is a common feast of unity, everybody conscious of a common relationship to their father and to one another. And when we go to Mass, although we don't need to be looking round and seeing what other people are wearing or wondering why they are late, we ought to be generally conscious of our fellow-worshippers as forming part of a unity, in which unity we and they as a family are approaching God.[10]

Father Philip Caraman has described Ronald Knox's sermons as 'perhaps the most impressive body of pastoral teaching of our time . . . Comparable only with Newman's Oxford sermons; yet more valuable because the idiom and message belonged to our own generation'.

Here is another quotation, on the theme of giving thanks:

> How strange, that when you read the ordinary kind of instruction you get about the Mass, so little is said about the primitive, this dominating aspect of it! You will be

[10] R. A. Knox, *University and Anglican Sermons*, edited by P. Caraman, SJ, Burns & Oates, 1963, p. 428.

told that in the Mass we offer praise to God; that is implied in all sacrifice. You will be told that in the Mass we offer reparation for our sins; we are not likely to forget that. You will be told that in the Mass we offer petition for our own needs and the needs of all Christians, living and dead; the very urgency of those needs is clamorous in our minds, threatens, almost to be a distraction. But how little they insist that at the Holy Eucharist we ought to be giving thanks to God, because that is what the word 'Eucharist' means! [11]

How much more joyous would this year's Jubilee Service in St Paul's have been if it had been a Eucharist! Our study, our planning and our work today are, when you come to think of it, devoted to that one end: that when the Golden Jubilee comes to be celebrated, it will be the Mass of Paul VI that will be offered in St Paul's and in every cathedral and church in the United Kingdom, united more securely than ever before, because of the presence everywhere of the united People of God.

November 1977

PRESSING ON

THE Lambretta on which I used to ply my way to seminary studies in Paris by way of Lydd and Le Touquet was christened by my family Rosinante; such was their teasing reaction to my quixotic voyaging in search of a single Church for England. Twenty years and five vehicles further on, has the scooter-borne dream grown more substantial?

The answer is, of course, yes, though plenty more driving still lies ahead. One reason for the affirmative reply — one of the most important reasons — is provided by the present development of public worship. In spite of all the criticism and the orchestrated woe, the progress that has undoubtedly been made should convince everyone concerned of the necessity of continuing, with still more care and determination, the work that has been so well begun.

[11] *Pastoral Sermons*, 1960, pp. 222-3.

The breakaway and break-up of the English Church both relate to a Book of Common Prayer. The revival and resurgence of the English Church will relate to another Book of Common Prayer. To Books of Common Prayer, in fact: the Lectionary, Office, Missal, Pontifical and Sacramentary as the Church now has them, as a result, not just of Vatican II, but of the years of long experience and of nineteenth- and twentieth-century study.

It would be a great mistake if the bishops were to doubt and hesitate because of the complaints and the campaigning. With the liturgy as we now have it, everything is available to meet the needs of Catholic worship: everything that we had previously, and a great deal more.

But it would also be a great mistake if we were to be allowed to continue much longer without a clear public understanding of the pastoral purpose of the bishops in fostering the liturgy of the revised books. We have the conciliar and post-conciliar documents and we have the writings and other activities of the experts, but the corporate significance of all this for us specifically in this country has not yet really been spelt out. It is not a matter of just saying 'This is what the Church wants now, so this is what we as faithful and obedient Catholics must do', though, too often, that is about the limit of what has been said and done. If our salvation depended simply on our obeying new liturgical rules from Rome, it could easily be achieved. Unfortunately, in great as in little matters, where our salvation is concerned, a modicum of personal effort is required.

It may be, of course, that the episcopal conference considers that discretion is the better part of valour and that the wisest policy at present is to watch benignly from on high while the readers and correspondents of *The Universe* and the *Catholic Herald* (to look no further) slog it out in the plain. If that is the case, one would hope that their arms are at least raised in pious supplication to the Lord for a happy outcome, and that some latter-day Aaron is at hand to make sure they stay up.

The fact of the matter is that very few of us are yet really aware of the recent changes in our circumstances that make our immediate responsibility far wider than perhaps we would like to think. It is not enough just to attempt to keep our own people happy. We shall not do even that unless we aim at doing a great deal more. The liturgy as we have it now is for

131

building a new people; it is an inheritance, certainly, but it is also an investment. Tradition runs forwards, not backwards. However inadequate our present achievement, it is at least a first step towards creating a way of worship for a Catholic Church of our own country that will cater for a great many more people than it does today. We can hope for reconciliation with the Church of England, which already uses the Lectionary, and in not a few places other books as well. We have a new expression of Christian faith in English that should take us far beyond the crude old pattern of dogmatic division. For all its faults, it is more than a start: it is a great advance. And even from the literary point of view, it is not as bad as all that. Much of the trouble originates in poverty of execution, not in the quality of the material; and that particular inadequacy was just as damaging to the liturgy of the past.

There is a certain sectarian selfishness in much of what is said in detraction of the post-conciliar liturgy. Added to that, many of us appear to be incapable of practising the faith unless it be against someone else; it used to be against Protestants, but now it is against some nefarious group or other of our fellow-Catholics. That school of thought always hears whatever the Pope says as a condemnation of some particular private *bête noire*.

Behind much of the rejection, there is also an old-fashioned attitude to the clergy: a resentment of the fact that they are now ceasing to act in a mechanical and impersonal way and are living more consciously and reflectively than before their particular vocation in the Church. Those who still want the clergy to be seen and not heard are among those who are nowadays most upset.

The libretto and music of future Catholic worship in these islands will certainly not spring fully armed from an episcopal mitre, not even one of those *chef-de-cuisine* ones they brought back from Vatican II. The necessary theological, literary and musical inspiration and creation will be found in many varied and possibly unexpected places. But building a worshipping people is undoubtedly an episcopal labour (cf. Rom 15:16). The bishops cannot expect the pilgrim Church to move in the right direction if they do not play their own distinctive part. In England and Wales, they must think not just of Catholics, but of all; not just of this generation, but of those to come. They must see to it that we become more interested in passing on the faith than in promoting our own preferences. It will be up to the next generation, not to us, to find the right words for their faith; and if we can manage to speak our faith today in our own words, however clumsily and awkwardly, then there will certainly be, after us, another, bigger, Christian generation.

January 1981

V

MINISTRY

THE PRIESTHOOD OF THE CLERGY

THE book the Church needs on the sacrament of Holy Order has yet to be written. The theologian who has the courage and stamina to read all that is being written about it, the patience to wait until his meditation has borne fruit, the deep understanding of the mission of Christ and of his Church which will equip him to see and state the full truth without false emphasis, and the knowledge of practical affairs and human limitations which will make him capable of writing for men who are not yet in heaven, such a theologian will lay the foundation of a vital sector of Church renewal, for lack of which we are at present labouring in the midst of great obscurity, tension and difficulty.

The Second Vatican Council appeared to be treating the presbyterate as a bit of an afterthought; whether such an impression is founded or not, it clearly cannot be given any lasting significance. The present outburst of writing about the priesthood is not so much a reaction to any particular inadequacy in the conciliar decrees as a movement of thought which had already started before the Council, which the Council drew upon and ratified to a certain extent, but which has not yet borne all its fruits. One of the most useful studies of the priesthood now in circulation is in fact the commentary on the decrees on the ministry, life and formation of priests which has been brought out by a group of French theologians in the *Unam Sanctam* series of studies on the Vatican II documents.[1] It is,

[1] *Les Prêtres: Formation, Ministère et Vie. Décrets Presbyterorum Ordinis et Optatam Totius.* Textes latins et traductions françaises. Préface par S. E. Mgr Marty (subsequently Archbishop of Paris, in succession to Cardinal Veuillot). Commentaires par J. Frisque, H. Denis, Y. Congar, C. Wiener, P. Colin, J. Lécuyer, H. le Sourd, A. Weers, E. Marcus. Sous la direction de J. Frisque et Y. Congar. Collection *Unam Sanctam*, 68. Cerf, 1968. (Referred to here as US 68.)

incidentally, one of the best of the series in which it appears, chiefly because of the direct and scholarly attention which it pays to the text which it is expounding.

Four of the principal themes and crucial affirmations set before us by the Council are at present attracting the attention of those who write about the work of the clergy:[2] the priesthood of Christ, communicated to all the baptised; the distinctive priesthood of the ministry or the hierarchy, different in essence, not simply in degree, from the priesthood of all the faithful, but nevertheless a part of that priesthood (LG n. 10); the grounding of the sacrament of Holy Order in the apostolic college and mission; and the unity of that sacrament, of which bishops receive the full grace and scope.

The Clergy

Before each of these themes is examined in turn, something should be said about the use of the term 'clergy'. 'Clergy' and 'laity' have come to be applied to distinct groups within the Church, but it must not be forgotten that in New Testament usage *cleros* (1 Pet 5:3) and *laos* (Lk 2:32; Rom 9:32; 2 Cor 6:14) both apply to the whole People of God, set apart for himself by his own special choice, and distinct from the nations of the world.[3] The use of *cleros* for the ministers of the Church and *laos* for all other members is found in 1 Clement (60:5), and this specialised use of the two terms has continued to the present day. This secondary usage which has grown up within the Church should not simply be dismissed as an aberrant return to the Old Testament dispensation.[4] Clearly,

---

[2] See, for example, de Bovis, A., 'Le presbytérat, sa nature et sa mission d'après le Concile du Vatican II', *Nouvelle Revue Théologique*, 89 (1967), pp. 1009-42 with an extensive bibliographical note); Dodd, W. H., 'Towards a Theology of Priesthood', *Theological Studies*, 28 (1967), pp. 683-705; Denis, H., 'La théologie du presbytérat de Trente à Vatican II', in US 68; Galot, J., 'Le sacerdoce dans la doctrine du Concile', NRTh, 88 (1966), pp. 1044-61; Myer, C. R., 'The Priesthood in our time', *American Ecclesiastical Review*, 156 (1967), pp. 73-90; Thomas, H., OSB, 'Le prêtre dans la pensée de Vatican II', *Questions liturgiques et paroissiales*, 1967, pp. 121-33.

[3] Congar, Y., *Lay People in the Church* (London, 1957), pp. 1-2.

[4] See I. de la Potterie, SJ, 'L'Origine et le sens primitif du mot "laïc" ', in the collection of essays which he published in conjunction with S. Lyonnet, SJ, *La Vie selon l'Esprit, condition du chrétien* (Cerf, 1965). *Cleros* could also be applied to groups other than the ministry. The early Church spoke of a *cleros tōn martyrōn*.

any situation in which the fundamental unity of the whole People of God, gathered together in Christ by the gift of the Holy Spirit, is obscured, is a false situation, a return to a pre-Christian state of affairs; and in the history of the Church men have often enough fallen into this way of thinking and acting. But if we dropped every Old Testament term which the New Testament uses and transforms on the ground that misunderstandings of this kind can arise, we should soon be without any Christian vocabulary at all. It is perfectly legitimate to use the term *cleros,* which designates the whole Church of God, also for those whom God calls to a particular function in his Church; it is in fact a name which constantly reminds them of those to whom they minister.[5] The use of any other term might well separate 'clergy' still more from 'laity'; these two terms define but do not distinguish, reminding us rather of the interdependence and fundamental unity of all who, in Christ, are members of the Church. This primary sacramental principle, whereby a part becomes an effective sign of the sanctification of the whole body, applies throughout the whole life and history of the Church.

If 'clergy' can still appropriately be used to designate those who are set apart for the service of the Church, the fact remains that we still need to clarify our minds about the principle on which they are chosen and the purpose of their existence as a distinct group with a particular function. Properly speaking, the clergy derive their origin from the apostolic calling and ministry, a calling and ministry which was accompanied by particular privileges in the case of those who first shared the ministry of Christ and first received the Holy Ghost, but which retains its essential characteristics at all times in the Church. It may well be that the inclusion in 'the clergy' of those who receive minor orders related to ritual functions has meant a narrowing of our conception of what it means to belong to the clergy. In the same way, the use of the tonsure ceremony may or may not be found to have obscured the true nature of clerical dedication. Such questions need detailed examination. But the main point to bear in mind for the moment is that the clergy are defined not by the first gesture which sets them apart (e.g.,

---

[5] See 1 Pet 5: 1-4; cf. Acts 1: 17; the Apostles each had a 'share' (*cleros*) in 'ministry' (*diakonia*).

the tonsure) but by the fullness of the Sacrament of Holy Order, the episcopate. At present, the body of clergy extends beyond those who have received the sacrament of Holy Order in whole or in part, to include those in training or under probation; whether this is to be done in future, and the way in which it should be done, is obviously open to discussion. The important point to remember is that the clergy exist for the total *cleros* (or *laos*) and are defined by the Sacrament of Holy Order.

The Priesthood of Christ

The distinctive priesthood of the clergy has been clearly situated by Vatican II within the priesthood which 'Christ the Lord, the High Priest chosen from among men' communicates to the whole Church. It should here be noted, once and for all, that we are concerned here with Christ as *Sacerdos* and the Christian people as *sacerdotes*.[6]

Christ is Priest by his entire life, divine and human. His whole being is made over, consecrated, to God. He is the loving Son of the Father, from all eternity and in his incarnate life in time. He abolished the ritual priesthood which could not bring to perfection the work of sanctification which it was striving to accomplish, by being on earth the perfect Man, at one with God, whose holiness consists in his total harmony with God, his total expression of God's purpose in creation. Priesthood is the loving praise and adoration of the Father which has been made visible to mankind in the life of Christ.

Christ's priesthood is offered to God for men. It is part of the perfection of his priesthood that this should be so. His love for God the Father is expressed in his saving purpose: he came to make men priests with him. As sons of God, restored to fellowship with him, they are part of the Son's own worship.

---

[6] The fact that priest, from *presbyter*, also stands for *sacerdos* has of course given rise to much confusion and controversy. Whether we should go back to 'presbyter' when we speak of ordained Catholic priests is a moot point. It is probably more important to clarify our ideas than to make edicts about vocabulary. Language does not change by official order. The fact that the term 'priest' (*presbyter*) has taken on a sacerdotal significance is entirely in accord with this particular function in the Church, provided we remember that we are speaking of the worship of the New Testament, and not any other form of sacerdotal activity, pagan or pre-Christian.

With him, they are totally priests, made capable through Christ of consecrating every part of their lives in real worship of the Father.

The priesthood of Christ is not a ritual priesthood, which could be confined to a particular part of his life; he is priest by his whole Person. In the same way, the priesthood of those who are in Christ is not a ritual, partial priesthood, but involves the whole person of those who are now made over to God.

The love of the Son for the Father, in which Christ's priesthood consists, was expressed by the mission on which he came among men, sent by the Father, by the task of Shepherd which he accepted, a task carried out as by one who comes to serve, not to have service done to him, and, finally and completely, by his death on the Cross, the act of perfect love by which both his Apostolic and his Pastoral office were brought to fulfilment.[7]

Now only he could die for men as their Saviour. But he could and did share with men his work as apostle and pastor. Except on the Cross, and in those times of prayer which marked the way to the Cross, Christ was not alone. From the beginning of his preaching the Gospel, he shared his service of mankind with other men. He gathered together the messianic people with the help of other men, to whom he gave the responsibility of continuing his work. There were to be in his Church men who receive from him and exercise in his name the apostolic and pastoral office which is his supremely and in the first place but which he does not exercise alone.

The Priesthood of the Ministry

It is at this point that we begin to see how the priesthood of the ministry or hierarchy is essentially different from the priesthood of the laity. Christ makes all men priests so that by their work in this world glory may be given to God. In Christ, they become living sacrifices, holy and acceptable to God. They do this, not separately and individually, but as a priestly people. And in order to make it possible for them to be living sacrifices

---

[7] 'And I, when I am lifted up from the earth, will draw all men unto myself' (Jn 12: 32).

and to live together as a priestly people in this way, Christ makes use of other men whom he chooses.

One cannot read a page of the New Testament without discovering that Christ's act of total consecration of this world to God involves such a union between himself and humanity that he has taken men out of their involvement in temporal occupations in order that the meaning of their existence — of the act whereby they glorify God — may be derived from his work on behalf of men rather than from the work which belongs to the ordinary business of living in this world. The fact that within the Church there are those who act as Christ's ministers on behalf of other men does not diminish the universal priesthood of all the faithful. The truth is quite the reverse: by continuing to make his own priesthood visible, audible, tangible and intelligible to the world through men whom he chooses and appoints for this work, Christ continues to make all men aware of what true worshippers are and capable of becoming true worshippers.

Because all those who are in the Church have been baptised into Christ, have died and risen with him, they can make their lives into acceptable acts of worship. Everything that they do, that they suffer, that they are, is made over to God. Through them and in them the work of this world becomes wholly God's work. The secular becomes the sacred. But the secular does not consecrate itself. God consecrates the world to himself, he makes men priests, by sending his Son and his Spirit and by sending men whose only meaning lies in the fact that they make him visible and that he acts through them in the service of the rest of mankind.

Without a common priesthood, God and the world would remain separate. Christ would have offered his worship to the world, but the world would have been untouched. Instead, we share his priesthood. And without a specialised priesthood, God and the world would be confused. That is why there are men in this world through whom God tells us who he is and leads us and the world back to himself. They exist for the sake of the common priesthood. Without their special witness to God's commitment to his world, men would not know how deeply they in their turn can and must commit themselves to work in his world so that all may be made over to him.

The choice and sending out of the Apostles established a ministry in the Church which gave men a way of worshipping God, of being priests, different from that of other men in the Church. It is not their being priests that makes them different, for all in the Church are priests. What makes them different is their ministerial function; they must worship God by serving his Church, by gathering all mankind into unity in Christ, so that they may become an offering pleasing to the Father. Most men in the Church are priests by making over this or that part of the world to God; some men in the Church are priests by being, purely and simply, a particular means by which God enters, redeems and transforms the world. One has constantly to remind oneself here of the general principle that God is not bound by his sacraments. Our Lord reminded the Apostles of this when he told them that he speaks to the world through children. But the fact remains that he did establish them as Apostles. The Sacrament of Holy Order, which flows out from (though it does not exclusively represent) the Apostolic function, is a distinct sacrament with its special responsibilities. The fact that God saves the world, and the world worships God, in other ways, does not do away with the fact that he brought into being this particular way of giving him glory and continues to call certain men to receive this particular consecration.

The Apostolic Mission

Vatican II has set all our thinking about the Sacrament of Holy Order firmly within the context of the Apostolic mission.[8] If we are to ask how the clergy are priests, we have to understand first of all how the Apostles were priests. In other words, we have to understand what work they had to do, what they had to be, in order to give glory to God. A verse from St Paul's epistle to the Romans, used in *Presbyterorum Ordinis* to describe the apostolic ministry, has caught the attention of a number of commentators.

[8] See H. Thomas, *art. cit.*, A. de Bovis, *art. cit.*, H. Denis in US 68, pp. 193-232; Y. Congar, ibid., pp. 241-242; C. Ernst, 'Priesthood and Ministry', *New Blackfriars*, 49 (1967), pp. 121-32; P. Grelot, R. Salaun and E. Marcus, works mentioned in reading-list; A. Manaranche, *Prêtres à la manière des apôtres*, Paris (1967).

Presbyters, in their own way, share in the function of the Apostles, being given grace from God to become ministers of Jesus Christ among the nations, *carrying out the sacred service of the Gospel, so that the offering of the nations may be made acceptable, sanctified by the Holy Spirit* (MLP, n. 2, scriptural reference in italics).

St Paul speaks of his ministry in terms of worship; by bringing the Gospel to the nations of the world, and making them capable of offering an acceptable sacrifice, he is himself giving worship to God. The priesthood of the Apostles consists in their mission in the service of the Gospel, a mission involving preaching and pastoral guidance, whereby the men and women to whom they are sent become in their turn worshippers acceptable to God. The fruits of the Apostles' work, offered by them to God, are those who are consecrated by the Gospel and the Spirit among the nations of the world.

Holy Order — One Sacrament

There is a sense in which the Apostles both are and stand for the whole Church, so that this apostolate is in fact passed on in one way or another to all, just as the Gospel priesthood is passed on to all. But they did at the same time exercise a specialised function within the Church, and we see them passing this on as they institute bishops, presbyters and deacons. It is this body of men that constitutes the Sacrament of Holy Order. This sacrament as a whole, with the diverse functions of its members, has its own work to do as a sign of God's presence and activity in the world. The presbyter and his particular priesthood cannot be understood without reference to the episcopate and the diaconate. All three must be taken together, and all three together must be seen as receiving and transmitting the responsibilities of the Apostles. Now although bishops, presbyters and deacons were in fact spoken of very much in the same context in the conciliar documents (see especially LG nn. 10 and 18-29), the very fact that there is a separate document on presbyters has, for all the good things in it, in fact given rise to a certain confusion which still persists. The bishops established their collegiate status and the laity were given special attention, so the presbyters had to come in somewhere as well, in order to receive a good deal of fatherly advice about their duties. But far greater clarification about the purpose and function of the Sacrament of Holy Order would have been achieved if we had had not one decree on the pastoral office of bishops and another on the priestly ministry and life, but a single decree on the pastoral office of the clergy, bishops, priests and deacons.

The reason why it is very difficult to distinguish *episcopoi* from *presbyteroi*, bishops from presbyters, in the New Testament, is the simple basic fact that there is in reality very little difference between them.[9] And bishops and presbyters are also deacons. The bishop has received the fullness of the sacrament, so that he is also presbyter and deacon; presbyters and deacons share to different degrees in the same sacrament. The monarchical episcopate should be made to mean what it says and nothing more. The bishop is the overseer of a kingdom of priests; and far from being a solitary ruler, he receives a sacrament which unites him with other men who, under his authority and guidance, share his responsibilities towards the same local worshipping community.[10]

Conclusion

This article has touched on a number of themes which at present are running through all study and discussion of the Christian ministry, in an attempt to answer the question which is still being asked in these post-conciliar years: 'If the laity are priests, what are we?' It has attempted to show that the person we describe at present as 'a Catholic priest' cannot be understood if we start simply from priests (presbyters) taken as a body; that one must look at the whole group, called, conveniently and appropriately, clergy; that this group is part of the mystery of Christ, the sacrament called Holy Order; and that it

9 'All priests, together with bishops, so share in the one and the same priesthood and ministry of Christ that *the very unity of their consecration and mission* requires their hierarchical communion with the order of bishops' (MLP n. 7). Italics mine.

10 See G. Rampaldi, SJ, 'Vescovo e Presbitero Profeti di Dio', *La Civiltà Cattolica*, May 1968 (2829), pp. 213-20, and 'Vescovo e Presbitero Ministri di Cristo nella Chiesa', ibid., June 1968 (2831), pp. 450-8.

originates in the group constituted by Christ and the Apostles and is best understood if we look at what the Apostles did rather than at what a *sacerdos* is.

But this group does have a sacerdotal function, essentially different from that exercised by those who are not members of it. We have seen already that it consists in being used by Christ to make his priesthood available to all men. We shall all be judged on our priesthood, on whether we have worshipped God by being Christian Prime Ministers or local councillors or miners or fathers of families or research chemists. The priesthood on which bishops, presbyters and deacons will be judged is their care of God's Church. And this priesthood is essentially eucharistic. The crown of all apostolic endeavour is the Eucharist celebrated by the Christian community, in union with their bishop, presbyters and deacons. Fr Congar has recently expressed some concern lest the centring of the Sacrament of Holy Order on the apostolate rather than on the Last Supper should lead to a depreciation of the sacerdotal aspect of the sacrament and to a false distinction between the man of mission and the man of cult.[11] What is necessary is not that we should depreciate the celebration of Mass in favour of preaching or pastoral care, but that instead of regarding the Mass as an isolated piece of ceremonial we should regard it as the crown of all 'apostolic', 'prophetic' and 'kingly' work. If, after Trent, we have tended to restrict and ritualise the Mass, confining the clergy to the sanctuary, we must not, after Vatican II, simply fall into the opposite error of throwing the clergy out of church. The clergy must celebrate the Eucharist in the context of St Paul's theology in Romans 15:16. There, the balance can be seen. They must teach, in order to celebrate properly, and they must be pastors, in order to celebrate properly. But only when they celebrate do they see why they do these things.

The worship of the New Testament is the worship of Christ. It is he who acts and who offers, showing the Father his love for men, showing to men his love for the Father. His ministers in eucharistic worship are only his ministers, and nothing more. They situate themselves within the saving work which is entirely his. Their priesthood lies in the sacramental work

[11] In US 68, pp. 241-9.

which he does through them; their own worship and holiness is found in their personal conformity with his work. Bishop, presbyter and deacon exist to celebrate the Eucharist. If they do not celebrate, they do nothing. When they do, they do everything. The Mass contains the whole worship of the New Testament. The priesthood of the clergy would be not more authentic if the clergy ceased to be 'men of cult'; it would simply cease to exist. Without the Eucharist, without the love of the Son for the Father in the Holy Spirit, of which they are the ministers and in which all things are summed up, they might be competent teachers and rulers, but they would not in Christ's name be leading men beyond themselves to the Father.

September 1968

FREE MEN PRAY

A MAN who can pray is a man who is free. His life is more than his work, his time-table, or his balance-sheet; he does not fit into the pattern made by social pressures; he controls his life, its strength, its content, and its aim.

Prayer is the discovery and release of ourselves through the discovery of other persons. It is therefore, in the first place and at all times, a continual, conscious openness to God, to the Father, Son and Holy Spirit who are that total openness and complete relationship on which the world of persons depends. It is the joy of being able to say 'you' to someone with whom we share complete confidence and trust. Only trust like that can free us. Only the fidelity of another person capturing and holding our trust can open us, can untie those energies which are wasted in self-protection, can break the hard shell which blocks our growth.

The world longs for this freedom. Only God can give it; he is the only one who is for ever faithful, for ever loving. He has proved this in the life of his Son. He has proved it in the lives of those who have received the Holy Spirit and who have therefore grown in love and faithfulness to the end. In every parish, in every street, there are men and women who now, because of God, fulfil themselves, being raised above the Adam and Eve of their broken past: they achieve the humanity to which they are called by the Father.

Bishops and priests must have this freedom. They are following a particular call from Christ as the only way for them of being free; and the condition of this gift is that it is used for Christ, to give freedom to others.

The freedom of a Christian man is experienced in a liberated heart, in a lightness of spirit which delights in the presence of God and the presence of others. A bishop or a priest is a man who knows this freedom and gives it effectively to the men and women whom he brings to the knowledge of their God. When he worships God with them, and lives his life with them and for them in full pastoral charity, his freedom lives and grows.

A priest without prayer is a man who is no longer free. He has lost the one whom he loves, the one who called him out from the closed circle of his own heart. The new liturgy — Mass, breviary, sacraments, every expression of our service dedicated in love — is the language of free people who live in the only atmosphere a priest can really breathe, and amongst whom he can relax and be at home. It is the language of Christ's Church; to speak it, the priest must live with Christ.

The future of the Church is with those for whom this personal love of our Lord is their cherished means of liberation. He gives the Spirit through whom, taken out of themselves, they are set free and related to the world. To pray is to listen to the Spirit in the Church so that he may be given to others.

The priesthood of Christ is identical with his humanity. The priesthood of the ministers of Christ makes them not functionaries, not clerks, but men. They are not men if they do not love. The celibate priest has given his whole life for love, and by love he will be judged. If he loves, then he will pray, for he cannot do without the company of the Beloved. A priest without that passion is no use to God or man. It is the men of prayer who will learn the new language, the new loving ways of the Bride. A love which does not change grows cold. A freedom which does not grow sinks into routine. A person who does not exercise his freedom by making new choices and decisions each day for God will soon find that he is a slave again. Today we are learning new words to express our devotion, and enlarging our scope through new freedoms; all this that Christ may be the centre of all men's hearts. 'Peter, do you love me?' is the question every priest must answer, every day.

November 1969

BAREFOOT IN THE PARK

IN Regent's Park the other day, I passed a young man with his girl friend who was carrying his sandals in his hand and walking barefoot round the rose garden. I was reminded of W. B. Yeats's friend Nettleship who was had up by a policeman for doing just the same thing in the same place:

> I was carrying my boots in my hand and he thought I was a burglar and even when I explained and gave him half-a-crown, he would not let me go till I had promised to put on my boots before I met the next policeman.

Where do priests' sympathies lie? With Yeats and Nettleship or with the policeman? Is their life a matter of

> Boots, boots, boots, boots
> Moving up and down again

or do they prefer to believe that

> Heaven is to tread unpaven ground?

Certainly one comes across priests who think that faithfulness to unchanging routine is the only safe way to salvation. But ordination and celibacy are supposed to open the way to spiritual freedom; they provide the means of change and transfiguration, and are not to be received as so much armour-plated double-glazing against the world which God creates.

Joy and Pleasure are our business as well as Justice and Peace. Perhaps the Roman Synod needs to think about the first as well as the second. In any case, the priest who does not welcome his free manner of life as a magnificent opportunity to do something for people, by helping them to escape from the prison structures confining their lives into the freedom of the Law of Christ, is in a pretty bad way.

No class of men is less encumbered than the Catholic clergy. All that frustrated talk about the institutional Church sounds like temper-tantrums and personal hang-ups, not the firm hold of order and reality which the Spirit of God provides. Christ and his apostles believed that the love of life today and tomorrow gave more certain enjoyment than the fear of death which urged on the frantic pleasures of the pagans. And that is why the world (and the Pharisees) so disliked them. The risen Christ has beaten Pan, Dionysus and all that lot at their own game.

If people dislike us today, is it for the same reason?

August 1971

DISORDER AND DISARRAY

ANYONE seeking to comprehend the problems of the changing Church of the twentieth century would be well advised to make a study of the blurred and erratic life-style (which may, indeed, amount to a crisis of identity) at present to be observed in the premises of ecclesiastical tailors and tradesmen. A well-known bookshop, for example, once a store of churchly respectability, now flaunts its presence on the street, flashing that dubious sign 'Books' over its doorway and enticing the customer within by means of a fine display of sensationally packaged paper-backs, sold by unisex assistants in jeans; the hard theological stuff can also be had, but only by pressing on through the front shop and climbing the stairs to the browsing sanctum reserved for the cognoscenti beyond.

But it is the tailors who have been the worst hit. In their ranks, dismayed confusion still prevails. The bookshop has at least pulled off a successful adaptation; religious business continues and even flourishes. At present, those who clothe the clergy still seem uncertain which way to turn, and until a Pierre Cardin for priests emerges to redirect the startled flock, market prospects look dim.

Take the Roman collar, for instance. A short while ago, it was the fixed rock which, if all else fluctuated, gave definition and clarity to the clerical image. It could be worn with a black suit of regulation cut, or it could be sported between a red moustache and Fair Isle pullover; it was there as the distinguishing mark of every Reverend from Paisley to the Pope. Now, even that, the last relic of Pius IX's post-1848 stand against civilisation, progress and the modern world, is being blown away by post-conciliar gales.

149

The extent of ecclesiastical disarray became clear for me recently as I tramped from one pious haberdashery to another in search of a plain black shirt to be worn with a plain white dog-collar. In the first one, a solitary assistant, salesman, fitter and cashier rolled into one, stood expectantly amid a motley collection of glass display cases, in which cassocks and chasubles which had hung for too long drooped forlornly in dusty folds. But he had no sale; the shirt required, he said, was not available; all he could offer was that awkward perspiration provoker, the stock.

At the next, brighter prospects; a wider selection of merchandise included 'The Curate's Convertible', a shirt with a collar into which a variety of neckwear could be inserted, from a blank celluloid visiting-card for formal occasions to a tie or even a scarf for off-duty moments. But such a shirt as I required was a monopoly product, made under patent, and that shop did not sell it.

Surely the third, a well-known, bow-fronted, highly respectable establishment close to the geographical heart of our National Church, would yield what I wanted. But as I approached, my heart sank. What had happened? Where once nothing but burses, vergers' staves, hassocks, prayer books, collecting bags, surplices and stoles had tastefully been displayed, bright socks and patterned shirts thrust themselves upon the eye, while above them rose a tailor's dummy formerly reserved for copes and decent Anglo-Saxon mitres; it was now barely covered in a string vest, the hemline of which was coyly raised to give full view of an Adam brief in jungle-green. Inside, where bishops and deans had once purchased their sober apparel from Anglican church wardens, a bewildered supernumerary, obviously dragged out of the accounts department, was trying to cope with the needs of two cloth-capped deacons from some remote dissenting chapel, who appeared to be in town for the Cup Final.

I fled. My sartorial problems will have to find some other solution. But what of the graver crisis of which these changes in fashion are a symptom? Clearly, the clergy do not know where in the world they stand. Officers or clowns? Gentry or just people? Makers of the news or media men? Slaves of the machine or holiday red-coats?

150

I once visited the training school of the Mission de France, where the educated sons of good bourgeois parents tried to turn themselves into apostles of the working class by wearing big boots and leather belts and neglecting to wash behind the ears. Needless to say, the French workers, well read and articulate as they are, just laughed at them.

You get the same reaction in the Underground, where a poster appealing for exact fares on London buses shows a classically well-meaning clergyman who proffers his 5p to the conductor as if he were distributing holy communion. The white expanse of his collar is a perfect place for scribbling a short reply. The last time I was on the Underground in similar garb, a drunken stranger shook me by the hand, protesting that he was as good a man as I. 'Nonsense', I said, 'you are as full of original sin as the rest of us.' I am not suggesting a swing from respectability to sackcloth nor, god forbid, to Carnaby Street; but now that Requiem Masses are said in purple or even white, we should surely take a less funereal view of our everyday garb.

The Times, 3 June 1972

OZONE AND THE CELIBATES

SEATED one day, like Martin Luther, in the *cabinet de toilette* of my seminary in Paris, I listened to two workmen installing an electrical ozone-making gadget on the ceiling. This useful apparatus, which crackled and emitted blue sparks when switched on, was supposed to freshen the air in that unwindowed place. Another one used to flicker and splutter in the roof of the chapel.

'A quoi ça sert, ce truc?' asked the young apprentice, for whom the fitting of *une machine à ozone* in a clerical gents was a new experience. 'Vous ne savez pas?' said the senior man, well used to wandering backstage in the ecclesiastical *milieu*. 'C'est pour leur célibat.'

A trade secret had been made known. The apprentice had that morning moved another step forward on his path of initiation. He now knew how that hard and mysterious saying in the Gospel according to St Matthew (19:10-12) was, in the twentieth century being fulfilled: his master had revealed the way by which, with the aid of modern technology, those men who 'make themselves eunuchs for the sake of the Kingdom of Heaven' go painlessly about their business.

He has no doubt, ever since, looked with sympathy as well as curiosity at the *abbés* and *curés* who cross his path. They are not as other men are; six years' exposure to blue sparks for a few necessary minutes a day have left them as impervious to the darts of Cupid as were, in England's Cheltenham, the Misses Beale and Buss.

In the Army, it was done, they said, by bromide in the tea: concealed dosing, provided by the RAMC and administered by the Catering Corps at the instigation of Whitehall, brought about by chemical means the moral transformation that the grace channelled down through the Chaplains' Department was powerless to procure.

Even without the popular legends of this kind about a variety of methods for the care and maintenance of masculine virginity, even supposing that the RC padre does it all by thought-taking and will-power, does he not appear to the troops and to the public at large an odd figure, keeping himself uncomfortably, by some cranky scheme of mental and physical hygiene, in a state of suspended animation?

Was not Charles Kingsley absolutely right about John Henry Newman and all those withdrawn Tractarians? The Victorian paterfamilias who approved Mr Punch's cartoons of Puseyite ritualists warned his daughters as they set out to tour the Continent that in the wicked city of Rome they would have to accustom themselves to the sight of celibacy being practised in the open streets. And whatever else he thinks about the Victorians, in this matter at any rate Ken Tynan must find himself forced to share their apprehensions and their distaste.

Funnily enough, Freud of all people has shown where they were wrong. In *Civilisation and its Discontents* he wrote of the way in which society oscillates between the cult of violence and the cult of sex, and foresaw something like the present outbreak of anti-puritanical erotic concern. A style of life which he approved (though he doubted its possibility) involves not comfort through the release of physical expression but its renunciation in favour of preoccupations involving other people's benefit. The energy devoted to seeking and maintaining sexual satisfaction can beneficially be expended on activities outside the self. The love practised by the celibate is the same as that which makes marriage possible: not the war of the sexes, but peace.

Christ, if cryptic, is on the whole a better guide than Freud; but Freud has been a better guide to Christ than many who think they speak for him and who really preach fear of the flesh, not its resurrection. If the devil is not to come back with reinforcements after being shown the door, someone else must take possession.

At a dinner party, a girl thought she might have embarrassed the priest across the table by saying 'eunuch' out loud. In an attempt to spare her blushes, he declared that he was one himself, but ignorance of St Matthew's text meant that the point was not taken. Since many, from Origen to the young electrician, have also got it wrong, the girl can be excused. Christ makes the aim both desirable and possible; Freud glimpsed it, uncovered many false trails and deceptive substitutes, but somehow missed the way.

Pills, protectives, prophylactics and probing do not produce the breakthrough to lovely goodness. The prescription for that is one cross, taken daily. The dose must not be exceeded; nor may it under any circumstances be self-inflicted. That is the way the damage is done; celibacy, after all, is supposed to be a way of getting better.

The Times, 29 July 1972

WHERE GROWTH BEGINS

A BATTERED hotel in a war-struck town, sanctuary and switch-board for the correspondents encamped there, rivals yet comrades, believing in spite of themselves in a truth which eludes them; here is one of the familiar symbols of our century.

It can stand for today's beleaguered Roman Catholic clergy, a mixed race of men with shared memories of six shut-in years neatly bracketed in their common past. The seminary — an institutional cross between prep school, Stalag, and green room — was designed to fix for life their attitude, and therefore the Church's attitude, to the broken world around them. Retreat givers used 'The Hidden Years' as their glib comparison, forgetting that Jesus stayed at home and worked. No seclusion for him in a levitical barrack-room; burial came, not at the outset of his career, but at the end.

'C'est là ton cimetière?' said the six-year-old daughter of my French friends as she looked in at the gloomy portal of my Parisian seminary. She spoke more truly than she knew. But seminaries, like cemeteries, are on the way out. Four hundred years of segregation, preserving a private church, winding up a mechanism that was meant to run for life, have now come to an end; Trent's counter-culture nurseries are closing down.

A new pattern of preparation for ministry is taking shape under the twin pressures of history and of faith.

History: there are no more younger sons and there are no more peasants. Feudalism and the Ancien Régime made the clergy an order within society, giving a place to those who were not going to get one by inheritance, and opening a career to the talents of local boys wanting to make good. After the Revolution, the Church of the nineteenth century tried to restore the pattern; where it still exists, it is an archaeological survival.

Faith: the shift in theological understanding is ultimately more important. The sacrament of Order had been built up, over the centuries, into a miniaturised circuit to be slotted in to the human mechanism of candidates for ordination, making them, at one fell swoop, and at the outset of their careers, embryonically capable of all the activities they had to deploy afterwards. If they came to be bishops, it was not clearly understood what they gained by it, apart from personal jurisdiction, with the consequent danger of drowning the Church in Canon Law; instead of serving the Word, bishops administered the Code.

Vatican II sorted out this particular tangle. Direct responsibility for mission and public service starts from the bishop, and members of the presbyterate, together with the deacons, share his work, communicating the Gospel and caring for the Christian people in a variety of ways.

The corporate unity of the Church is also better understood. The New Testament broke down all barriers between clergy and laity. The only inner distinction is the one between those who are chosen for special responsibility and those who are not. And here selection must be made from all members of the Church,

154

not from a particular caste, constituted at an early age. Access to the presbyterate and the episcopate should properly come from within the whole range of 'ministries'. One can prove oneself for receiving authority not just by keeping rules and passing examinations, but by successful management in any form of Christian life and service, including being faithful to one's wife and raising a family.

This does not mean that there will be no place for life-long service to the cause of religion, including the offering of a celibate life. This will go on. But the Church is now less anxious to make priests of the men who undertake a life under vows. There is no reason why someone who wants to work, for example, as a monk and a teacher, should necessarily be given the stan-dardised sacrament of Order, as if the only way of acquiring status in the Church were by way of receiving special powers by ritual means.

Seminaries should be 'seed-beds' for every form of Gospel service, not hot-houses for a segregated corps of janissaries. It should become possible for anyone to study for a time in one of the colleges providing training for ministry without head-ing immediately for ordination.

It is true that bands of beardless boys are still led on seminary visits, and 'vocations directors' fish among pious and potentially celibate youth instead of looking everywhere among competent adults for the Church's leaders.

But the death of the old 'clergy' is something for the fore-seeable future; not because the Church is in decline, but because it understands itself better than before. Being a practising Catholic once meant toeing a line laid down by a sacerdotal jack-of-all-trades on whose head all Church functions had been laid. The New Testament pattern of obedience to the Word of God is really rather different; something more like it is at present beginning to appear within the Catholic community.

The Times, 2 September 1972

MESSAGE RECEIVED — AND UNDERSTOOD?

AS every theological student knows, the Church is like the Army: one does not do much, but one does it early in the morn-ing. Accordingly, a friend of mine and I, the major portion of our day's work well behind us, were, in our Underground train, engaged in a conversation more lively than that of our fellow travellers, who were ensconced in meditation behind their newspapers as they moved towards the daily heat and burden.

We were discussing the advertisements displayed in the carriage as a handy focus for the roving eyes of face-to-face commuters; their literary interest seemed to us to have declined since the days of those historical jingles composed to leave readers with the conviction that there is no substitute for wool. But there was one limerick, which extolled the virtues of a London skating rink. A certain young lady had found its charms as a rendezvous so efficacious that she soon had her young man on ice.

Clearly, the *terminus ad quem* had controlled the whole effort of poetic creation; my companion suggested that the writer must have thought of the last line first and then worked like a black to thrash out the previous four.

As he spoke, the sedate reserve which had hitherto prevailed around us was shattered. A copy of *The Guardian* was lowered to reveal the face of a stern-looking gentleman with a big black beard who fixed the author of this apparently harmless statement with his glittering eye and administered an irate rebuke. 'You appear to be entirely unaware, sir, of the fact that you have just uttered an offensive remark, of a kind that should never have been heard in a public place.'

I sensed politely concealed amusement and unrestrained curiosity running through the minds of the phlegmatic occupants of our train; how were the chattering clergymen, so oddly wide awake at this morning hour, going to deal with this onslaught on their *bonhomie?* But my partner in the conversation was equal to the challenge. 'I am indeed unaware, sir, of the fact which you have so kindly brought to my notice. I am most grateful to you; thank you very much.' *The Guardian* was raised once again to hide the face of the censor, as we looked at one another, wondering what had set him off. Was he the author of the limerick? Did the expression 'to have someone on ice' convey some double meaning about which our Latin moral theology textbooks, for all their thoroughness *de sexto et nono*, had left us innocently ignorant?

As we left the train, my companion asked our interlocutor what the expression was which had called forth his rebuke. 'You should not have said "worked like a black", sir; had there been a coloured person on the train, he would undoubtedly have felt deeply insulted.'

So we were racists. These smug clergymen in their white collars and their black suits had in their vapid and obtrusive talk, unwittingly revealed the twisted thoughts which controlled their every action; their counter-colour plot, their priestcraft had successfully been detected and unmasked. Behind *The Guardian*, a vigilant defender of liberal values went on his way rejoicing.

As we returned to the surface, the *ésprit de l'escalator* played its usual game. We knew what we ought to have said. There were two possible retorts. The first was brief: 'Sir, you are right. I should have said "worked like a beaver" ', with a brisk tug at his big black beard. The other was longer and would have required one of those pregnant pauses in the tunnel for its delivery: 'You appear to be totally unaware, sir, of the fact that the expression "to work like a black" does not come from South Carolina, but from County Durham, where it was first applied to coal-miners in the eighteenth century. My great-great-grandfather worked underground, sir, for sixty years and I use the expression in pious honour of his memory. Good morning'.

An opportunity of using these replies will hardly occur again; but the encounter provokes reflection on the hazards of evangelism. At one time, it was the earnest Christian who did the Ancient Mariner act in railway carriages, seeking to argue unwary travellers into a state of salvation. Now it is the turn of the social reformer, waiting to pounce upon other men's casual infringements of the Race Relations Act. In neither case does any communication or exchange take place; an individual does his duty and is reassured, but he has neither delivered nor received a message. We need to hear as well as speak, change ourselves as well as change others. I wonder if the man with the beard, as he went up in the lift to his office, thought of anything else he might have said to the two chatty priests.

The Times, 24 February 1973

157

MINISTRY, SACRIFICE, CELIBACY AND THE FUTURE

THE flight from the priesthood and the decline in vocations, two of the most striking facts of Church life since Vatican II, have been and still are read by many as signs of disaster. We must hold the fort, we must bow our heads against the storm, waiting for better times when the Church we once knew can be restored: what other reaction can be expected of a faithful churchman in the midst of the present troubles, as damaging in their fearful scale as any of our past upheavals? If crumbs of comfort offer themselves in the shape of news of a reversal, here and there, of the downward trend in statistics of vocations, hopes of a reassuring return to the good old days are at once rekindled.

That is one way, and a not uncommon one, of understanding our contemporary crisis; but there is another way, one which has the merit of being constructive as well as hopeful, and which has solid grounds for its optimism in the movement of Catholic theology in the present century, in the crystallising, directive documents of Vatican II, in the further intense study and debate that has gone on in the Church since the Council and in the fresh apostolic and pastoral movements that are springing up everywhere. The Church is in the midst of a vast new missionary effort, far outstripping in its scope the expansion of the sixteenth and nineteenth centuries; we are undertaking new developments in our life which are aimed at the recuperation of all that was lost in the ages of Reformation, Revolution and Restoration, and, above all, at further deep advances in the Christian transformation of human society. Those times of apparent disaster in the past were times from which the Church has eventually learnt lessons about herself which must now pass into everyday behaviour and practice.

What follows is an attempt at a summary of the main theological affirmations about the ministry of the Church and about the meaning and function of the dedicated celibate life which emerge from the conciliar documents and the post-conciliar debate, together with some practical proposals which they make possible and which, I would argue, indicate sound lines for the future development of the Church's policy.

References to recent literature have deliberately been omitted, partly because of the vastness of the field, partly in order to make it clear that this is not yet another tentative, scholarly article, but a gathering together of what lies printed in many journals and books. If defence with text and authority in hand is needed or called for, it will be forthcoming. What is said here is being said and thought by many throughout the Church; it now appears in these pages in the hope that, sooner rather than later, notice and action will be taken.

(i) *The Ordained Ministry*

The fact that underlies a correct understanding of the nature and function of the ordained ministry is the summing-up and fulfilment by our Lord Jesus Christ of all prophecy, priesthood and kingship: in his Sonship, Divinity and perfect Humanity these separate Old Testament and universal roles have been fused for ever into one. What men have done in a specialised and sectional way in order to express and carry forward both their search for God and God's education of his creatures, has now been gathered together and carried out to perfection in the complete, integrated, wholeness which we see in the life of Christ. There is no need now for a return to a parcelling-out of man's religious activity, for in him these separated human functions, together with the still more fundamental separateness of secular and sacred, have been abolished. Perfect worship is now also perfect knowledge of the truth and perfect justice. In him, every act, every gesture, every word was holy, and at the same time was entirely normal and human: a real part of this world's life. All was prophetic, speaking of God, all was priestly, worshipping God, all was kingly, effectively manifesting the rule of God. There was no compartmentalised, ritual, 'sacred' part of his life: all was made over to God, and all was genuinely and utterly human.

Now this integrated wholeness, this restored humanity, is, under the New Covenant, being communicated to men and women. It was communicated first to Mary, Mother of God and Man, in whom woman takes her right place, through her obedience to the Word, in the plan of God and in the Communion of Saints; in the same way it is communicated to all

159

who by their obedience, live as members of his chosen family, the Church. It is a misunderstanding of the New Covenant to think that the old, specialised, separate roles of prophet, priest and king are to be re-introduced, as if Christ has not once and for all brought them into an indissoluble unity in his own life, given for us and now given to us. There are in the People of God no specialist priests, kings and prophets; all bear these titles, because all are in Christ. There are baptised Christians, confirmed Christians, ordained Christians; all bear a character, the character of Christ, and none of these is any more priest, prophet or king than anyone else, because all are equally members in Christ of the New Israel. There is no difference of degree in their priesthood, any more than in their status as prophets or rulers. The Apostles were rebuked when they asked about differences of degree. All have the fundamental holiness given them by Christ in baptism, which makes them, once and for all, New Testament priests, and on that basis they have to build if they are to become the complete persons, the other Christs, he wants them to be.

The 'essential difference' conferred by ordination is not a difference of degree within the general priesthood of all; it is a difference of representation, of function and of service. The ordained Christian has the responsibility and the duty of watching over and ministering to the Church; in virtue of his ordination, he has, in a special and unique way, the charge, received from Christ directly (the episcopate) or in a subordinate way (the presbyterate and the diaconate), of building up the People of God and guiding its work in this world.

The word 'priest' has taken on predominantly sacerdotal connotations, although it is, of course, derived from *presbyter* and is in its origin and in its essential meaning, no more (and no less) 'sacerdotal' than it is 'prophetic' and 'kingly'. It should retain all three meanings, since Christ exercised these three roles, fusing them once and for all into one. The bishop/presbyter/deacon is a minister of Christ whose concern it is to build up the Body of Christ, the People of God. It is as much a mistake to regard him above all as a *sacerdos* as it would be to think of him exclusively as a prophet or a king; it is also a mistake to think of him as a *sacerdos* in any sense in which the other members of the People of God are not equally *sacerdotes*. He is

160

a bishop/presbyter/deacon, and they are not; that is perfectly clear. And he exercises his Christian sacerdotal role in this way, while other members of the Church exercise it in other ways.

When the sixteenth-century Protestant reformers denied that the ordained ministers were priests (*sacerdotes*) in any sense that could be denied to other Christians, they were right; where they were wrong was in their denial of any sanctifying (or sacerdotal) role to them. This went along with their general theology of grace. The whole exercise of the ministry of the bishop/presbyter/deacon, in teaching, guiding and leading worship has a sanctifying effect, culminating in his sacramental and, above all, eucharistic activity; as servant of Christ the minister undoubtedly cooperates in our Lord's redemptive and sanctifying mission, and therefore is a *sacerdos*. But he is not simply a *sacerdos* in doing this; he is a Christian, in the full, rich meaning of that title. To limit the meaning of priest (*presbyter*) to a sacerdotal sense inevitably brings back into the current mentality and practice an idea of ministry which is pre-Christian, and less than Christian.

The bishop/presbyter/deacon is a minister of Christ, a minister of the Word, a servant of the Gospel, an overseer and elder of the Church, a steward of the mysteries of God, but not a *sacerdos* in any other than the general Christian sense. He is not a mediator adding anything to Christ's mediatorship. Ordination gives him a special place and special right to be heard, but it does not set him between God and anyone else. The Kingdom of Heaven is in the midst of us; Christ himself is in the midst of us, wherever two or three are gathered together; Christ is the mediator between bishop/presbyter/deacon and the world, between his minister and his people, and not the other way round.

The Sacrament of Holy Order confers upon the recipient the duty of representing Christ in the public service of his Church: he must teach, guide and lead worship in his name and to administer all forms of practical and material work in the service of mankind. The bishop sums up in his person all these functions, which he carries out, as a successor of the Apostles, in direct obedience to Christ and in communion with his fellow bishops. The presbyter has a share in the work of the bishop, in the same kind of supervisory capacity, but under his control

161

and direction. Because we have seen the presbyter as above all a *sacerdos,* in spite of the fact that specifically sacerdotal tasks form only a part of his role, we have regarded the celebration of the eucharist as his defining function, and the 'parish priest' as the typical presbyter. Now it is certainly true that the bishop, as president of the local community, has the celebration of the eucharist as his supreme task; but it is by no means the case that every presbyter should necessarily be given this particular role as his principal way of sharing in the work of the bishop. There are many ministerial roles which he can undertake; the presbyterate can well become much more flexible, much more varied, less stereotyped than it has been, along predominantly 'sacerdotal' lines. Not every presbyter needs to be empowered to preach, or to hear confessions, or to preside at the celebration of the eucharist; to be ordained presbyter is to be brought into the bishop's council as one of the governing and guiding body of the Church, bringing one's particular gifts and experience into the service of the Church in an official and publicly sanctioned way and being given whatever work the Church requires.

(ii) *Ministry and Sacrifice*

No one should imagine that it is being implied here that the ministry of the Catholic Church is not a 'sacrificing priesthood'. What is being put forward here is the suggestion that this whole notion of 'sacrificing priest' needs to be broadened and deepened if it is to be understood and lived in the true New Testament way. Sacrifice, consecration, making holy, being holy, in the New Testament sense, means conformity with God's truth, obedience to God's law, love of God himself. Holiness, truth, and justice are inseparably united in Christ. The sacrifice of the New Testament is not a ritual act but a real one: the actual handing-over of one's whole self to God.

For one reason and another, a one-sided stress on the sacerdotal, cultual aspect of sacrifice and of the bishop's and presbyter's role, and the almost entire effacement of the diaconate, has contributed to the comparative social and intellectual ineffectiveness of the ordained ministry, despite their dedication, in recent centuries. The 'clergy' were confined to the performance of ritual from which a true and profound Christian meaning could indeed be extracted, but to which there could also be attached a variety of beliefs of a sub-Christian and even anti-Christian kind. The 'priest' was seen as safeguarding a distinct sacred area within which men and women could indeed feel secure in their faith in Christ, but it was not sufficiently expected of him that he should communicate to them the truth by which they would be led to a fully human, rational and spiritual holiness, nor initiate the kind of social change which was needed to promote justice.

The ordained ministers of the Church were seen above all as set apart, trained in seminaries, and placed in parishes to 'say Mass'. Where they stepped out of this role and made their mark in the world of thought and discovery or worked for one or other form of social justice, this was thought of as something exceptional, outside what was customarily expected of 'priests'.

This has often enough meant that many laymen who fought for a more rational and more just human way of life found themselves apparently opposing the work of the Church, even though they were favourably disposed to the teachings of the Gospel and indeed drew their inspiration from it. A recovery of the true balance and breadth of the New Testament meaning of sacrifice — consecration in truth, in the Johannine phrase — will lead to a new recognition of the scope and significance of Christian faith, as it is recognised not as a superstitious belief in mere ritualism but a demand for a rigorous and rational attachment to facts and for the promotion of peace through justice.

This means that access to the episcopate/presbyterate/diaconate should in future be extended to all those who by their work as members of the Church in the world prove their spirit of sacrifice, their Christian commitment and competence, in every aspect of their life and work. The system of almost exclusive recruitment and ceremonial conferring of the presbyterate in comparative youth, inevitably leads to a 'ritualising' of the sacrament of order, which has given rise both to anti-clericalism and to a great deal of lay infantilism in the comprehension and practice of the faith. Men can easily be found who are competent to say Mass and to remain devotedly faithful to a regular round of standard duties; but if such men, and only they, are also expected to teach and to guide men in the ways of justice, the results can be disappointing and even disastrous.

It must not be imagined that this widening-out of our understanding of sacrifice will bring about a decline in the practice of eucharistic worship. The reverse will be the case; the rationalisation and 'de-ritualisation' essential to Christian sacrifice will mean that the Mass will be seen in its true significance, not as a substitute for knowledgeable, well-planned action in the world, not as an arbitrary duty to be performed so as to please an exacting God, but as the best means of acquiring a knowledge of true wisdom and of orienting ourselves correctly within social reality. Those who preside over the celebration of Mass will be those who, in all walks of life, have proved their readiness and ability to work out the practical meaning of Christian sacrifice.

(iii) Celibacy

For a man or a woman, to be unmarried is to be free for the service of the Kingdom of God. Freedom from family responsibilities leaves one able to concern oneself entirely with all the special work committed to the Church by Christ, and so to be a witness of the Incarnation and Resurrection, of the presence among us of the Kingdom. Celibacy is not in itself a higher or a lower state than marriage; as we have seen, this calculation of degrees is forbidden by the Gospel. When our Lord spoke of being a eunuch for the sake of the Kingdom of Heaven (Mt 19) he was saying that God's standards for human life, whether married or single (he was answering a question about *marriage*) necessarily make all those who accept them 'odd men out' in the eyes of the world.

Marriage itself is at the heart of the Gospel and it is quite wrong to envisage it as a second best as a way to salvation. Marriage makes lifelong and constant demands; it requires unceasing dedication, and is the normal means to maturity and to establishing a true relationship with other human beings.

The Church has always had to be on its guard against any misinterpretation of celibacy which would undermine the Christian conviction of the goodness of marriage and of the

164

transmission and continuation of human life. It now needs once again to examine the laws which guide its behaviour, so as to make sure that the proper meaning of both marriage and celibacy are set before the human race as a whole, to whom the Gospel is to be communicated. The slightest knowledge of Church history makes perfectly plain the fact that a true balance has always been difficult to achieve; the idea was current for centuries that there is some impurity attached to marriage and that those who celebrate the eucharist should be untouched by it, and we must make quite sure that such motives are not still lingering in our teaching and practice today.

The clearest way of making this plain would of course be to allow married men to celebrate the eucharist, to be bishops, presbyters and deacons. There could then be no doubt whatever about our view of marriage. And this 'clearest way' is the way laid down in the New Testament. The Pastoral Epistles do not simply 'allow' marriage for the ordained ministers of the Gospel; they list the successful achievement of a faithful marriage and a stable family as one of the positive qualifications in any candidate for public office. This is the case both because marriage itself is good and because any creation of a separate caste within the Church, on the lines of the tribe of Levi, from which posts of special responsibility are to be recruited, is excluded by the essential unity in Christ of all members of his Church. The clergy, the Lord's share, is, under the New Covenant, either the whole Church itself or a part of it assigned to the care of a particular minister. In other words, it is coterminous with the laity, the *laos*, the whole people of God, so that the term should not be restricted to the ministers as if they were a priesthood within the People on Old Testament lines.

This means that in the future the celibate state and the ordained ministry must be much more clearly distinguished. Celibacy is a special call to men or to women giving them freedom to serve Christ in his world in an infinite variety of ways. To imagine that for men, at any rate, it must almost automatically and exclusively be linked with the sacrament of Orders is in fact to restrict both celibacy and the sacrament in their significance and practice.

The sacrament of Orders, in its three-fold structure, is a consecration to public office in carrying on the Church's service of the Word of God and of mankind. It should be conferred upon anyone, single or married, who shows himself to be called to that office. To limit it to unmarried men is to narrow down its meaning and to suggest that only the unmarried can truly and fully understand the Word and take responsibility for administering the Church's life. This amounts in practice to a devaluation of marriage which in the light of all that has been written about that sacrament in recent years can no longer be sustained. The New Testament declared that the experience of marriage was part of the normal *curriculum vitae* before ordination, and if we are the New Israel, the New Testament Church, it is impossible to see why that New Testament teaching, so deeply in accord with the central facts and meaning of the Gospel, should be set aside.

At the same time, we need to recognise that the almost universal ordination to the presbyterate of men called to celibacy leads to an institutionalisation of that state which robs it of a great deal of its meaning. Celibacy, whether under vow or not, means freedom for the service of the Kingdom of God. But can it be said that the celibate clergy have made the best use of that freedom? Often enough they have been the most conservative of men, routine in their churchmanship and conforming in their social context. The Apostles needed the lesson which our Lord gave them when he said that a child can be his means of communication with mankind as well as his officially appointed channels, and the ordained ministers of the Church, whether single or married, still need the same perpetual reminder and stimulus, together with the practical help, given by those with greater freedom of movement and with fewer public ties. Celibacy must for men and women be a way of undertaking the whole diversity of ministries bestowed by the Holy Spirit upon his People.

(iv) What can be done

It is not enough simply to set out a few theological affirmations about the ministry in the Church and the purpose of celibacy without pointing to the practical action which can and should follow for the future good of the Church. It must be emphasised that these proposals are not simply dictated by expediency (the present shortage of clergy; a decline in moral standards) but by the continual necessity under which we stand of bringing the life of the Church into conformity with God's purpose as revealed in Christ. The changes should be made on the grounds that they represent a real deepening of our understanding of the Gospel. This will surprise no one with the slightest knowledge of Church history. Slavery; torture; war; the social order: these are only a few of the areas in which the teaching and practice of the Church have been very slow to catch up with the meaning of the message as it was first delivered.

To make these changes will not be a betrayal of the past or a judgement upon it; but we ourselves may well be judged if we fail to respond to the teaching which is now becoming so very clear.

1. The conferring of the sacrament of Holy Orders should be conformed as closely as possible to the actual running of the whole Church as a society founded by Christ. Those who prove themselves worthy of public office, married or unmarried, in whatever capacity, are the ones who should be chosen for ordination; as bishops/presbyters to concern themselves with the Church's teaching, the care of souls and the celebration of the Church's worship, and as deacons to look after the material administration of the Church. The more the whole body of the Church becomes worthy of its calling, the more it will become plain that every kind of Christian discipleship can be a way to this special, public, consecrated service.

2. Seminaries should be schools of ministry of every kind, not directly linked to the sacrament of ordination itself, but preparing men as disciples of Christ to serve him in whatever capacity they prove apt for, whether married or celibate. It should be quite normal for a Christian to enter such an institution for some part of his life, for the deeper spiritual and intellectual formation which he needs to train him for the practice of the Christian life in whatever capacity it may be.

3. The choice of a single, celibate life should be regarded as a means of putting oneself freely at the service of the Gospel as an effective sign of the presence in history of the eternal life of the Kingdom of Heaven. It should be undertaken for short, definite periods or for life; it should not be tied to the Sacrament

of Orders, but instead associated with all forms of ministry and with all the gifts of the Spirit, for the building up of the Body of Christ.

4. The sacrament of Holy Order should be received by both celibate and married; and ordination itself should not be a bar to marriage. That an ordained minister should undertake to live the sacrament of marriage should be understood as a true part of his dedication as a living sign of the relationship between God and his people.

5. In the present transitional phase there is bound to be some confusion, even some 'illegality', until the laws have caught up with the new doctrinal and pastoral situations. It would be impossible to plan in terms of allowing the present generation of priests to die out before new prescriptions, coming from on high, inaugurated a new state of affairs. The following proposals are both theologically acceptable and possible in practice:

(a) Priests who have married should be permitted to resume their pastoral work in one way or another, the customary doctrinal and moral standards being of course applied. Their training and experience as priests must not be lost to the Church; their help is essential in this transitional phase.

(b) Priests at present in the ministry should be permitted to marry and continue their work as priests.

(c) Married men capable of being given public office and ready for it should receive appropriate preparation and be ordained.

Proposals (a) and (b) may sound like a recommendation to break vows solemnly given. But the plain fact is that as far as the secular priesthood is concerned, obscurity has reigned over the 'law of celibacy'. Was it a matter of the Church only ordaining those who already felt themselves called to celibacy, or was it a matter of imposing a law on those who wished to enter the public ministry? Many writers would now wish to say 'the first', but the experience of very many, including the younger clergy, is more in line with the second account of the state of affairs. If there had been no such law, many of those wishing to be priests would have been only too glad to be married as well. They accepted celibacy for the sake of the priesthood. Now that the distinct meanings for the Church of these modes of consecration, the sacramental dedication for public office and the undertaking of an unmarried life, have been more clearly discerned, it is essential that new orientations should become possible.

In a similar way, many of those called to celibacy in the religious life have accepted ordination as part of a programme required of them without in fact being called to official public office of this kind. It should be possible for them to cease any purely 'ritual' exercise of the sacrament of Holy Order, and to limit themselves especially to that ministry to which they find themselves genuinely to be called.

Personal experience is by no means irrelevant to this issue. An awareness of the work done by many friends among the Anglican clergy, and by relatives of three generations who have been married and ordained ministers of the Church of England, underlies the conviction expressed in this article of the authentic and necessary place that married men have in the public service of the Church. Whether they work as pastors or as teachers, whether they spend all their lives in the ministry or come to it after a successful career in another field, when the children have grown up and are ready to start their own careers, the Anglican and Free Church clergy set a perfectly clear pattern for the universal practice of the Church in the future. It would be quite absurd for the Catholic Church to deny the value of this experience or to refuse to take it into its system. People talk of a 'Roman' rite with celibate clergy living beside an 'Anglican' rite in which the clergy are married, both in communion with Rome. But this would be to reduce Catholicism as we know it to sectarian status and hopelessly to divide what should be in every place a united local church.

The Catholic Church must, wherever it exists, act in terms of its own God-given nature. If it is part of its nature as a Church that its ministers should include married as well as unmarried men, as this article has set out to show, then it is unthinkable that any part of the Church should have a discipline radically different from any other part. This is a matter of the Church's basic nature, not a superficial matter of language, custom or etiquette.

The programme here proposed is no mere attempt to make the best of things, patching up the Church in the midst of crisis;

nor is it a contrived accommodation to the immediate needs and demands of ecumenism. It is forced upon us by the very nature of the Church itself, given to us by God. For that reason, the only valid and sure reason for action, it will lead us out of our present discontents and out of our disunity, into a new flowering and expansion of Christian faith and life.

January 1974

BEYOND PRIESTHOOD:
THE MINISTRY OF THE SPIRIT

Our sufficiency is from God, who has qualified us to be ministers of a new covenant, not of the letter, but of the Spirit; for the letter kills, but the Spirit gives life (2 Cor 3:1-11).

I PROPOSE in this article to continue the reflexion on the sacrament of Holy Order which I attempted to pursue in January. My purpose, once again, will be synthesis rather than analysis: an examination not of this or that set of texts, of this or that aspect of ministry, but of the main lines of the doctrine which seems to me to emerge from Scripture, from the mind of the Church as collected together and expressed at Vatican II, and from the detailed studies of theologians. A proper understanding of this sacrament is the key which, at the present time, will best open our minds to a full realisation of what the new dispensation in human affairs inaugurated by God the Father through the work of his Son and the gift of his Holy Spirit really entails, and most safely guide our practical policy in obedience to our mission.

It is necessary, once again, to begin from the fact that in the New Testament Our Lord brought in an understanding of human life and opened up possibilities for the human race which we are still only beginning to comprehend and to put into practice. One of the principal ways in which we can grasp what he did is through a realisation of his achievement in drawing together and blending in a single human life those ways of expressing God's relationship to men and the relationships of men one to

170

another which had been expressed in the Old Testament, as they have been in every human culture, through the distinct activities of prophecy, priesthood and kingship. These activities had been carried on, in the main, by specialist groups and individuals, although examples can, of course, be given of individuals who exercised more than one of them. In man's divided state, divided within himself and against his fellow men, this compartmentalisation expressed man's desire for perfection and his inability to attain it in more than a partial way, through ritual expression, through fragmentary vision of the truth, through moments of real moral goodness.

But when mankind's integrity was restored in Christ, who was one with God and was united within himself, and communicated directly and openly with his fellow men, these three separate activities, these three practical approaches to divinity and to humanity, were blended and fused inseparably in Sonship. A meditation on John 17 and on the Epistle to the Hebrews makes this dazzlingly clear. The efficacity of his work as Priest is the result of his perfect conformity with the New Law, not in a ritual, ceremonial or symbolic way, but in a real way, in every detail of his relationships with his Heavenly Father and with men and women, in that effective manifestation of the goodness of God which brought him to the Cross and to his final Triumph. This Priesthood was also Prophetic; every act and every word spoke of the true God; and it was Kingly, for by his service of God and Man he became Lord of all, reigning from the Cross.

We must therefore at all times now bear in mind the fact that prophecy, priesthood and kingship are preparatory, pre-Christian categories which Christ has united indivisibly and transcended in his Sonship. We need them if we are to grasp what it is that he has done and is doing for us; but we need constantly to beware of reducing Christ to the level of the Old Testament or of pagan religions, of diminishing him to one or other of these roles seen in an all-too-imperfect human way and, even more, of reducing these roles as exercised by his Church and within his Church to a status and function which is in fact sub-Christian. We have introduced kings, in Byzantium, in Royal Gallicanism, in the Bourbon states, in Anglicanism, who have stood in relation to the Church as kings did in relation to the People of God according to the Old Testament, not the New Testament, model; we have found prophets difficult people to handle, in a Church that was supposed to be of its very nature prophetic; and we have lived in practice an understanding of priesthood that had not caught up with the New Testament.

We have, of course, at all times and in all places, done the right thing as well! Progress in understanding does not mean rejecting the past, as so many unfortunately would have us believe; it means grasping the truth which tthe past and the present contain and allowing it to have an even greater control over our daily lives. To see it clearly, we need to see it in contrast with inadequate or false notions, notions which we may ourselves unwittingly still be accepting. We did not have to wait for Vatican II for an understanding of the Church to be available to those who looked for it; but Vatican II was necessary if that doctrine was to break through into the minds of all of us and set the Church more firmly and truly than ever on its course.

The doctrine of the Church given us by Vatican II showed us with great clarity the fundamental and all-embracing unity of all the faithful in Christ. What the first Epistle of St Peter, for example, tells us about God's merciful acceptance of all those who, without distinction, he has called into his People, a holy priesthood who now, in Christ, offer spiritual sacrifices to God, the Council has spelt out for us in chapter 2 of *Lumen Gentium*. The need for such a reminder has been abundantly brought out since that time; to many of the faithful, the idea that they were priests was unfamiliar, and they are still experiencing some difficulty in finding their balance in their new-found role.[1]

And for many of those who have received Holy Orders the idea has proved disturbing as well; if the laity were priests, then what were they? The Fathers of Vatican II foresaw the debates that would be stirred up and attempted to forestall them by insisting on the 'essential difference' between the common priest-

---

[1] The contribution by Emile-Joseph de Smedt, Bishop of Bruges, in *L'Eglise de Vatican II*, Cerf, 1966, II, pp. 411-24, on 'Le Sacerdoce des fidèles', is one of the best statements of this theme; Bishop de Smedt situates the ministerial priesthood within this context in a way that has been abundantly confirmed by scholarly investigation since that time.

hood and the ministerial or hierarchical priesthood (LG n. 10); but this 'essential difference' has not proved easy to discern.

It must be understood within the context of the general priesthood of all the faithful and not outside, over against, or beside it: that is abundantly clear. The difficulties which we have had arise out of the fact that we have used priesthood (*sacerdotium*) in both a general and in a specialised sense, and, furthermore, that the specialised sense has tended to exclude the general. There was an 'essential difference'; we called the ordained man a 'priest'; therefore others were not priests! Neither Vatican II nor subsequent discussion has really cleared up this question of terminology.

It is impossible to do justice to the New Testament, the whole dispensation under which we now live, unless we bear constantly in mind the new life that Christ has bestowed upon all those whom he has called into full membership of his Church on earth. 'If a man is in Christ, he is a new creature' (2 Cor 5:17); this applies to all of us. We share in the humanity of Christ as the adopted sons of God. This status can be described under one aspect as 'priesthood' (*sacerdotium*); we are able truly to worship God, to relate properly to him and to one another, to share in the universal mediation of Christ. But to be properly understood it must be seen as 'beyond priesthood', as consisting now in sonship, in which all partial approaches to God have been taken up and transformed. The worship we offer now is real worship, not substitute, ceremonial worship: the obedience to the New Law of God in our hearts, in every detail of our daily lives. It is the fullness of priesthood, and it is more than priesthood; the ways of communication are open once again, moral goodness is possible once again, a loving relationship is established once again.

Now within this life of the Body of Christ in which we all share, and in which all of us should think of ourselves as equally members of the one Body, there is an immense diversity of special gifts of the Spirit, in virtue of each of which it is granted to every one of us to carry out different forms of work and of service. In 1 Corinthians 12, St Paul set out both this doctrine of the unity and harmony of the Body and the doctrine of the diversity of gifts bestowed by the Holy Spirit. It is in this context that the sacrament of Holy Order must be situated if its 'essentially different' and particular character amid all the gifts of the Spirit in the one Body of Christ is to be properly discerned.

St Paul does not pick out the ordained ministry for special attention in this passage. We do, however, find it discussed in detail and with special emphasis in the Pastoral Epistles. It is a gift of the Spirit that Timothy has received by the laying on of hands (2 Tim 1:6-11), for the service of the Gospel in which Paul, too, is engaged (cf. Rom 15:16). In virtue of this gift, the responsibility of Timothy, as also of Titus, is the building-up of the Church in harmony and unity through the communication of the Word of God and the choice of reliable office-bearers in the community. This is their work as bishops (*episcopoi*); their close collaborators, in all work for the Word and the Church, are the presbyters and the deacons.

These references are simply the most well known; they provide a picture, furnished in fact in one way and another by the entire New Testament, of a variety of gifts in view of ministries of all kinds in the Church, and of this particular gift, which picks men out especially for oversight and service and which is designed for the maintenance of an ordered way of life, for the fostering of peace and the elimination of conflict in the Church of the New Testament which Christ brought into being. The Church, discerning in this gift a sacramental reality in the specialised sense, has therefore gone right to the heart of the matter in calling it the sacrament of Holy Order.

The greatness of the gift which God bestows in this sacrament goes far beyond prophecy, priesthood and kingship. This is the fundamental reason why the writings of the New Testament do not use the word *hiereus* (*sacerdos*) to describe it. To be a Christian is already very much more than to be a priest in that sense: it is to be restored and renewed in the fullness of humanity, it is to be a son and a friend of God. It includes priesthood but it has caught priesthood up together with all other incomplete and imperfect half-states and half-truths, brought them into a new synthesis and infinitely enhanced them all in the new communion with God, Father, Word and Spirit.

To be a Christian bishop/presbyter/deacon means that within this restored community, sharing, through adopted Sonship, in the perfect priestly worship offered by the Son to the Father, one has received the special and distinct responsibility of creating unity and harmony. The Spirit of God is a Spirit of reason, order and light: the reason which distinguishes so as to understand and so as to simplify; the order which makes sense of infinite diversity; the light which is a blending of every colour in the rainbow. This Spirit uses those whom he chooses to bring out and express this reason, order and light within the human family. That is why Spirit and Institution are inseparably one in the New Testament. And that is why the Catholic Church is unique among all human societies: it has its structure, its shape, its government, as they all do; but that government is the rule of the Holy Spirit, penetrating all from within and bringing all into one by an infinite variety of means.

Because this variety is meaningful, not chaotic, the Sacrament of Order can be understood as the key to all work of the Spirit in the world: diverse yet unified, its purpose is to make the Spirit's living, growing pattern visible among men.

In a sense, of course, and that the most fundamental one, all Christians, all Christian life, all sacraments, are one, essentially the same in Christ. But every individual is also unique; and every gift of the Spirit is unique and each sacrament has its unique role. Those who have received the Sacrament of Holy Order have, as no one else has in the Church, the task of ensuring the unity of the Spirit in the bond of peace, through the Word which has been entrusted to their unique guardianship, and through the oversight which they must exercise in the whole Church. Those who have received the Spirit of God will recognise in them the only true guides and shepherds of the family of God.

The difficulty which we are having at present over seeing this clearly lies above all in the restriction of the term *presbyter* in English, as in other languages, to the sacerdotal sense. Can it be denied that this restriction has in practice led to many confusions and to an inadequate appreciation of that quality of life which is the inheritance of every Christian? Can it be denied that the ordained minister has thought of himself as a one-man band, with the rest of the Church as his audience, while, if the musical metaphor be continued, he should by rights have thought of the Church (or his parish) as an orchestra, with himself holding responsibility as conductor: a musician among other musicians? Have we not thought of all apostolate as belonging to the hierarchy, with all lay apostles somehow sharing in it, of all priesthood as belonging to the ordained, with the laity participating in it in some sort of diluted way, of all *magisterium* as belonging to the bishops, with the rest of us as never anything but pupils?

Vatican II has changed all that, or will do, when it is assimilated and understood. In the People of God, common life in Christ means a sharing in the benefits of all his gifts; the Sacrament of Holy Order, a particular gift to individuals chosen by the Spirit, is uniquely responsible for the supervision of that sharing.

This will be seen most clearly if we look at the Mass, the centre, the focus and the heart of the entire work of the ordained minister. Here above all we understand and live out what it means to live beyond priesthood. Really present in every Mass is the person of Christ; this is a real, not merely a ritual presence, of a person who in reality, not merely in ritual, fulfilled the will of God. As Vatican II has taught us, he is present in the baptised whom he has called together, and indeed in all those who are beginning to listen to his call; he is present in his Word; he is present in his ministers; he is present in his Body and his Blood. This is the worship of one who is our High Priest because he is the Son of God; and in every person who represents him, every word which represents him, every particle of the Body and Blood which represent him, he is prophetic at the same time as he is priestly, he rules over us at the same time as he is prophet and priest.

To be the bishop, the presbyter or the deacon who gathers that assembly together, who preaches the Word by which it is called and which it must obey if it is to be Christian, who conveys to the people the Spirit of the Law by which it must be formed and possessed, this is already to live beyond priesthood, since it consists not in the execution of a ceremonial duty, but in the convocation of a genuine community to hear and do those things which make it real. To lead the prayer of that assembly in the worship of the Father as bishop or presbyter, pronouncing the words of Christ which accompany and express the real offering of his Body and Blood, the reality of the Word which gives all words their substance, this is supremely to live beyond priesthood, for as Christ's ministers we serve not sign and symbol alone but the living, factual truth for which they stand.

The reintroduction of the term *sacerdos* or the restriction of 'presbyter' to a sacerdotal sense has been an understandable development, but it has been misleading. It has meant that we have tended to take the part for the whole. The use of a specialised language, the codification of elaborate ceremonial, and other features of clerical life which went along with it, have also led to misinterpretation. The new stage in the history of worship which has just opened will give us a deeper understanding of the real situation. The ordained ministers do not stand between God and man; it is God made Man, whom they serve, who unites them with their fellow men. They are agents of unity, not by domination, not by power, but by service.

And that service, a higher gift than priesthood, involves the knowledge of the language of unity: it is a service of the Word. A higher gift than priesthood, it involves the proper management of human relations: it draws all men into conversation. If it were only priesthood, the clergy could be content with their churches and their rubrics, if people would pay them enough for their ceremonies to keep body and soul together. That is the priesthood which Napoleon wanted to restore after the Revolution; the priesthood desired by a people more attached to their church bells than to the practice of the Gospel.

Bishops, presbyters or deacons of Christ have received higher titles than that of priest, *sacerdos*, because in the whole body of restored humanity they are those whom God has seen to be and chosen to be most human; in a broken and fallen world, they can communicate, they can lead and they can help effectively through their involvement in all the difficulties, sufferings and struggles of mankind. They are servants of reality; bearing the character of Christ, they will not cling to forms and expressions which have had their day, lest they hold humanity back among those shades and shadows which at their worst led man astray after fantasies and false gods, and at their best only prefigured the truth which in God and in man we have now been given.

If the suggested outline of the doctrine of the ministry given here appears shocking or revolutionary to some, may it not be that we have been content with something less than the full truth? It is not just contemporary scholarship which leads one to think that it is true to the mind of the New Testament Church. In a small Austrian village in 1945, a British soldier discovered that the Catholic parish priest was called not the rector, or the priest, or the vicar, or the father, or the clergyman, but *der Geistlicher*, the man of the Spirit. What higher title can he be given, in the People whom God's Spirit has called together and sent into the world?

May 1974

THE PRIEST AND THE ARCHAEOLOGIST

ON 15 August this year, I found myself, as they say in France, near the town of Laon, perched on a hill-top suddenly rising out of the plain north of Rheims, and set out to find what its magnificently sited cathedral had to offer. But there were few people about. A notice informed me that one of that day's two Masses would be offered in an hour and a half's time. I departed, with the conviction that some other way of keeping the feast would be provided on the way. Leaving the town, I found where all the people were: at a market and fair at the foot of the hill. It was yet another example of the universal European problem: what to do with the splendid old churches now deserted by the population which once surrounded them; how to fit them out for worship now that so few come; how to keep them up when both religious and patriotic sentiment have deserted them.

My next port of call was an Iron Age dig a little farther south, where a godson was in the team from England uncovering enclosures and burial sites. But before I got there, passing through the village of Guignicourt, I saw a young man in a dark-brown suit, hardly the thing for comfort on that very hot day, walking along with (I supposed) his grandmother. They could only be going to Mass . . . the sound of the church bell, then more people, of all ages, then the village square and its Romanesque church, cleaned, bright, re-ordered with a central altar, and then the priest who pounced upon me and fitted me out at once for celebration. All very different from the chilly emptiness behind Laon's ramparts: a welcome, a part to play, prayers for England and England's Catholics, people who knew the words and music and responded to the leadership of their priest.

He told me later that he was one of a team belonging to that district; he had a labouring job, as part of their common effort to win over the workers. My hopes of barely an hour before were already fulfilled.

In the village where I stopped to enquire after the archaeologists, they were observing the holiday in another way, with all the movement and bustle of a cycle race. And it was not long before I was being shown charred bones and the meal offering in an Iron Age grave, and hearing how the traces on an aerial photograph had put the expedition in the way of making their find. Before Caesar and before Christ: on the feast of human fulfilment, this confrontation with every man's sadness and with every man's search for survival. Here was another congregation, smaller but almost as mixed as the one in the church at Mass. Their leader spoke of the many problems they had to tackle in their investigation: not just finding the spot, not just digging, but gaining the confidence and co-operation of local farmers, police and government officials, coping with clandestine, unscientific collectors, understanding the French mind in cafés and bars as well as in official hierarchies.

The patient search for men, B.C. and A.D., dead and alive, through manual labour, through measuring and digging and making plans: the priest and the archaeologist were at one. The celebrant of the feast of Man restored, Man at the highest point of his achievement, and the uncoverer of man's presence on the surface of the earth, still labouring, still unaware: were they separate? Many of those who work and search for men are still unaware of God; but how many of those who think they have faith, and therefore awareness, are ready to dig, with the discipline of science, as those students, young and old, were digging, with minute care, under the afternoon sun in an open field in France?

November 1974

ON NOT BEING AN ELITE

WE all know, in theory, that if we have the faith it is not due to any particular merit of our own. But we do not draw the necessary conclusion. Instead of remembering how unremarkable we are, we like to think that we have been brought into a superior and exclusive club. If we are not to be an élite in worldly sense, at least, we say, let us take pride in our heavenly selection.

There is plenty in the Gospels to show that this is an all-too-human misinterpretation of our status as members of Christ's Church. The Apostles got it wrong, so it is not surprising if we do. In the Church on earth, it is the many who are called. We are part of the common herd. That is what is so off-putting about the Church; our acceptance of membership shows that we are no better than anyone else. No better, for instance, than those conservatives / progressives / liberals / reactionaries/obscurantists/modernists with whom we disagree so profoundly; no better than those grubby, uncultured, neurotic and shifty-looking people with whom we find ourselves obliged to associate. We have to leave it until after the Final Judgement to find out if we are part of the few who are chosen; and if and when we do have that good fortune, we shall have to accept the fact that there will be no non-élite around the place to give us the pleasure of feeling superior.

Elitism is no part of being a Catholic. But just as it keeps people out of the Church, while they fondly imagine that they can find some wider viewpoint, or are already personally on a higher plane, so also it damages relationships and enterprises within the Church. It can affect the laity as well as the clergy, religious orders as well as the anti-clericals. There is nothing more opposed to the spirit of religion than the overweening conviction that one is part of the *avant-garde:* 'With my talents, do you imagine that I would have gone to a secular seminary?' But the only sound basis for entering or staying in the religious life is the conviction of St Gregory the Great that while there are many who can live a truly Christian life in the world, there are many others who can only manage to be saved before God if they abandon everything (*Epist.* III, 65): no élitism there. Laity, religious, ordained ministers: all must accept the Church together as equals. Those who define themselves over against the bishops, or lay-people, or other classes of the Church of whatever kind, are only ruling themselves off the field of play.

Supreme responsibility for seeing to it that the Church enjoys this family spirit rests with the bishops. They do not look after part of the Church, leaving the rest to others; everyone must look to them as the effective sign of our unity. Theories of the sacrament of Holy Order that leave the bishops out of the picture, or at any rate on the edge — and one does hear them put forward — cannot do justice to the reality that we have been given. To win the position due to them, the bishops certainly need to assert themselves more, to organise themselves better, and, above all, to teach. This last-mentioned, and most neglected, duty is in fact without any doubt at all their first and most important concern. It is what they were ordained for: to be servants of the Word of God. And it is up to the rest of us to allow them this rôle and to encourage them in it. Too many Catholic writers and talkers treat them as mere steerage passengers. We should all be better off if we let them (and made them) do their real job of work: that of being expert guides on a one-class cruise.

May 1977

PASTORAL: PASTORALE?

WORDS get over-used and eventually wear out; if we are not careful, 'pastoral' may become one of them. Tacked on to a Council or to a Congress or to a Commission, it gives it a gentle and an unaggressive air. Pastoral theology is not the same as dogmatic theology; the difference makes it seem unfit for the academic rough-and-tumble. A pastoral conference need not be taken very seriously, some would hold, because it does not legislate. Pastors differ from pontiffs, as fathers-in-God differ from prelates. Shepherds are known to be kind to their fellow-creatures, and stand for God's humanity as well as man's.

Before we let the word drift any further downhill into anodyne insignificance, it would be as well to remind ourselves that real shepherds do not in fact live the idyllic life dreamed up in the minds of city-dwellers who use the country as their playground. Shepherds have always led a lonely and dangerous life, far from the company of other men, the prey of brigands, scorned by those who stay at home as rough simpletons unpractised in the elementary civilities of town or village. They have to protect their flock; and they have to rule them as well, for sheep do not spontaneously congregate into a single, harmonious, co-operative unit, as many other creatures do. Wolves may hunt in packs, but sheep do not even graze together.

The shepherds of the Gospel are supposed to be more concerned with seeking out those who are lost than with looking after those who are safely in the sheep-fold; and they have to be fishermen as well, adding exposure on the sea to vulnerability on land, becoming hunters as well as herdsmen. The pastors of the Church are sent out to gather a flock together; they have to turn scattered individuals who have not found a place in the family of God into full members of his People.

Shepherding is not an occupation within which one can discern any particularly well-defined path to promotion; a shepherd gets about as far as he can pretty quickly and stays there for the rest of his life. And fishermen can hardly regard their trade as the best way towards ending up commanding a liner on a world cruise. An ecclesiastical career should be a contradiction in terms.

When the ways of the Church get too well trodden, it is time to move on. We should not be seeking familiar landscapes in the Catholic Church, but rather extending our boundaries into unexplored territory. There is too little expansion going on in this country at present, though the signs are that a new wave may just be about to run. Reformation and Counter-Reformation; Establishment and Dissent; Evangelical and Catholic: in English Christianity, these are party labels that bear no relation to the future of the Church. We are not here to adopt some inherited style or to take on a prefabricated personality. A whole historical cycle is now running out, and Christianity is in fact beginning all over again.

And the pastors of the Catholic Church have the first responsibility for making this new start. All they have to do is preach the Gospel as they have received it. Defending a minority position, safeguarding a particular community, keeping a cultural tradition intact: these preoccupations may have brought results in the past, but limiting ourselves to aims of this kind is no longer practical politics. What we are concerned with is creating a new community in this country, one more human, because Christian, than the collectivist state that so many either seek to hasten on or contemplate fearfully and helplessly as it advances. We are creating a new culture out of the many foreign ones that have moved into our midst as well as from the one that we have inherited. We are not just one group among many in a variegated crowd, but hold the key to the unity and harmony of all. English Catholicism is more English than the English and more Catholic than any other claimant. 'Pastoral', as a word, may have more muscle than some of its users suspect, and 'pastoral experience' is certainly to be had in more fields than one. The pastoral note of Milton's 'uncouth swain' beckoned us onwards. 'Tomorrow to fresh Woods and Pastures new': that sounds about right for any pastor.

December 1978

WE ARE ALL PROPHETS NOW

THE 'Now' of the title is the 'Now' of the New Testament: not the brash assertion of some 'post-conciliar' pundit, who can never affirm anything without first of all blackening his predecessors, but a statement of fact about the Church of Christ ever since the beginning. We are 'a chosen race, a royal priesthood, a holy nation, God's own people', precisely in order to 'proclaim the wonderful deeds' of him who called us out of darkness into light (1 Pet 1: 9). It is the whole people of God that is prophetic: that speaks of God to the world. There are no solitary prophets any more; all prophecy is summed up in Christ, and Christ speaks in and through his Church.

It is easy now to detect a false prophet; anyone who denies or who passes over in silence any part of the faith as the Church has received it, whatever his eloquence and scholarship, is a false prophet. Anyone who refuses to recognise the voice of the whole Church as the voice of the Holy Spirit, speaking today, and teaches his own Gospel, chosen from yesterday to suit his own purposes, is a false prophet. Anyone who thinks that prophecy can now declare anything new, unknown since the coming of Christ, is a false prophet.

The pastors of the Church should know that the world is anxious to turn them as individuals into prophets: to represent them as lonely figures, ahead of their time, men of heroic proportions who are too good for the Church for which they stand.

When their Church comes up to their level, say the spectators, we may think of joining it. Meanwhile, a good Pope or a good Cardinal can always be treated as an exception, whose light simply throws the Church into greater darkness.

But the true pastor always refers the world not to himself, but to the Word of God and to the Church that he gathers together. Christ does not communicate with the world apart from his Church; his purpose is to gather us all into the one Body, to bring us all as a single sacrifice into a perfect offering giving glory to his heavenly Father. His presence in his Church: that is his message and that is his purpose.

In the history of our country since the sixteenth century, that prophetic presence has always been among us. Many Christians, including the leaders of other churches, turn their eyes away from that fact. But English history would not have been the same without it; the Catholic presence was always there, to be accepted by some and to be rejected by most. That rejection formed the ultimate, the most profound motivation for much that has happened in English politics. It is always the same; you cannot be neutral where the Church is concerned, and even where it was not publicly admitted, fear of the Catholic presence on the horizon has always been a powerful force within the British way of life. The size of the Catholic minority was immaterial; it was not numbers that weighed in the balance, but the inescapable pressure of that unique source of energy, the Catholic Church itself.

At this moment, when public resistance is veering towards public acceptance, it would be a betrayal of our responsibility to Christ if we were to forget our prophetic role. Oppression can give the Church strength, as it has given the Church in Poland. When the hostility is withdrawn and people are asking instead for what we have to give, we must give them not some compromise solution, some watered-down message which we may mistakenly think will leave them happy but undisturbed. We must give them everything that has made us God's people, no more, no less. There is a limit to explanations and re-phrasing; our very human imperfection is itself part of the sign that we have to give to the world. It is because they expect perfection that people will not join the Church; our message is that they must identify themselves with imperfection, as God himself has done.

184

Prophecy does not consist only of passing on a message that we have learnt from others. It involves discernment of God's presence in the world as well. It is the prophetic task of the Church in Britain to see what God is doing and saying to us in the whole of our society. A Church that is only concerned with polemical self-defence may well fail to see where the Spirit is leading us. True apologetics is not a simple defence of what always has been; it is a demonstration of the way in which the finest of human aspirations find their fulfilment in the Gospel of Christ. As we study to see how man's new hopes, discoveries and plans can be illuminated by Christ, we ourselves will begin to see how much more Christ himself has to say to us than we had realised. Speaking for the Word still leads, as it always has done in the past, towards the Church's growth, in understanding as in numbers.

In Biblical scholarship, in philosophy, in the human sciences, in public health and welfare, in central and local government, in industry, in foreign policy, the Church in Britain must undergo a conversion from the defence of apparently sectarian positions to a new prophetic style of action that shows the Catholic faith to be the way ahead for the whole nation. Many individuals have been through that conversion and are already showing that they have understood what is needed; they need far greater backing. Many others still use the Church as if it were a private retreat, a chosen hobby, or perhaps even a particular distinction adding some special embellishment to their personality. If the situation is to be changed, the change will have come from the top. In a prophetic Church, it would be strange if the pastors were not prophets.

The key point at which the outward-growing dynamism of the Church needs to be applied is higher education. It touches every area of growth in our society; and it is there that the Catholics who are involved are given least support. Nowhere in the Catholic world are the pastors of the Church as little committed to the universities as they are in this country. The Polish Church has not made that mistake; spiritual strength cannot survive and grow without the strenuous exploitation of intellectual talents.

But it would be wrong to end on a carping note. What has happened within the Catholic Church in Britain over the last ten years has been enough to prove that we are indeed already a prophetic Church. We are too self-critical by half. The public exercise of a little more confidence would do us no harm at all. Do we realise how many doors there are just waiting to be opened? Even if some others are still bolted and barred, we have it on good authority, after all, that Hell's gates themselves must yield against us.

January 1979

SERVANTS OF THE WORD, SHEPHERDS OF THE PEOPLE

The Ordained Ministry after Trent and after Vatican II

WHAT can the teaching and experience of the Church tell us about the way in which we should understand and respond to the special gift of the Holy Spirit that we call the sacrament of Holy Orders? Since it was the decrees of the Council of Trent that dominated and guided our thought and practice until the Second Vatican Council, I shall begin there; and we may then be able to see in what way, if any, Vatican II has further enriched and redirected our attempts to comprehend and follow this particular vocation.

The first lesson of the Council of Trent is conveyed by the order in which it arranged its agenda. The Council's opening session was in December 1545; its next two working sessions concerned themselves with the way of life to be observed by those who had come to Trent, and with the proclamation of the Creed as 'the Shield against all heresies', all present being exhorted, in the words of the epistle to the Ephesians, to put on the whole armour of God, together with the sword of the Spirit, which is the Word of God (Eph 6:13-17). In the fourth session, the Council's first decree was concerned with the Gospel itself, 'which Our Lord Jesus Christ the Son of God first proclaimed with his own mouth and then commanded to be taught by the Apostles as source of all saving truth and moral order'. Trent thus began by referring itself to the living Gospel, understood as a spoken proclamation given by Christ himself and received by the Apostles, who handed it on by means of 'written books and unwritten traditions'. The unity of this source and its verbal, oral character must constantly be borne in mind; the Council went on to concern itself with the canon of Scripture as the received written mode of access to the Gospel, but the essential point not to be forgotten in all our thinking about what it said in this and in its later decrees is that the written Scripture depends upon prior oral proclamation, and that the Council's point of reference is the Word spoken by God in his Son, seen as the single, personal, living and active source of all revealed truth.

The next significant stage for our present enquiry came in the fifth session (June 1546), whose second decree made provision for reading the Scriptures and preaching the Gospel, which the ninth section declares to be the 'principal function of bishops' (*praecipuum episcoporum munus*). This theme was, incidentally, taken up again at the twenty-fourth session, in 1563, whose decree *de reformatione* speaks in its fourth canon of the function of preaching as the principal task of bishops (*Praedicationis munus, quod episcoporum praecipuum est*). At the sixth session, the second decree dealt with the responsibility that the bishops have for the pastoral care of those committed to their charge, and therefore with the necessity of living among them, and the various decrees *de reformatione* of the following sessions (each session was thus both dogmatic and practical) continued to spell out and regulate the pastoral duties of the bishops and their clergy among the laity.

The twelfth session of the Council in 1551, opened a series studying the sacraments, starting with the Eucharist. With the twenty-third session, held in July 1563, we arrive at the heart of our present concern: the sacrament of Order.

The first chapter of the text promulgated at this session is concerned to defend the existence of a new, visible and external priesthood (*sacerdotium*) of the New Testament, instituted by the Lord our Saviour to offer and administer the visible sacrifice of the Eucharist. In the fourth chapter it is declared that this distinct sacrament, conferred on some, not all, Christians (with a reference here to 1 Cor 12:28-29 and Eph 4:11), included bishops, established by the Holy Spirit to rule the Church of God, who were superior to presbyters (*presbyteris*). The decree speaks of the ordination of 'bishops, priests (*sacerdotum*) and other orders (*ceterorum ordinum*); the sixth canon attached to the decree declares that the hierarchy consists of bishops, presbyters and ministers (*constat ex episcopis, presbyteris et ministris*). Both the third and the sixth canons make it clear that episcopal ordination, understood as a sacrament, is necessary for constituting true ministers of the word of God and the sacraments (*ministros verbi Dei et sacramentorum*). Canon 14 of the second decree, *de reformatione*, of this session refers to the order of the presbyterate (*ad presbyteratus ordinem*).

The main lines of the teaching given to the Church on the sacrament of Holy Order may now be summarised. In the first place, the bishops understood themselves to be responsible for interpreting the Word of God, under whose sovereign rule they set themselves from the beginning of the Council. The bishop's principal duty, as they said several times, was proclaiming that Word. And in the second place, we have an emphasis on the visible priesthood (*sacerdotium*), instituted and ordained to offer the visible sacrifice of the Eucharist. The term describing those who were thus ordained was *sacerdotes*, priests, used as the equivalent of *presbyteri*, presbyters; it is also made clear, though with less emphasis, that bishops belong to this priesthood (*sacerdotium;* see Sess. XXIII, cc. I and IV). Trent makes it particularly clear that bishops preach the Word and rule the Church of God and that presbyters are priests (*sacerdotes*) who offer a visible sacrifice. This double emphasis was made necessary by the controversies of the time. What Trent left to be worked out later was the relationship between the episcopal duties of preaching the Word and governing the Church, and the act of offering the eucharistic sacrifice which, it was above all emphasised, was the prerogative of presbyters, whom the bishops had ordained as true *sacerdotes*.

The reform of the clergy set in motion by the Council of Trent will centre round these two distinct themes: the pastoral responsibility of the bishop and the sacerdotal character of the presbyterate (and thus also of the episcopate). This represents a continuation of the theology of the middle ages, which saw in the *sacerdotium* the seventh grade of the orders of the clergy and did not settle the question of the status of the episcopate. Did episcopacy simply add jurisdiction, with further dignity and responsibility, to priesthood, already received in its fullness by the presbyter, or was it a further sacramental order, distinct from priesthood? Trent inclined to the second view, without settling it, and post-Tridentine theologians, notably Bellarmine, will affirm the sacramental character of the episcopate.[1] The fact that the question was put in that way arose, of course, out of a concentration on the sacerdotal nature of the presbyterate; offering the sacrifice of the Mass was so clearly the supreme activity of the Church that it was difficult to see how exactly the sacrament of Order could be taken any further.

And so reform goes ahead along two distinct paths. The reform of the episcopate is inspired by the image of the Good Shepherd. The bishop is above all the devoted pastor of his flock. He must live among them, teach, guide and rule them; his love for them must drive him to minister to all their needs. The teaching and example of bishops like St Charles Borromeo, Bartholomew of the Martyrs, Archbishop of Braga, and St Francis de Sales produced a great revival of the true sense of the episcopate, which made the seventeenth century one of the most brilliant periods in the history of the Church. The benefice system and the linking of the upper clergy to the higher ranks of the social hierarchy continued to have their damaging effect. But there is no doubt of the extent to which bishops now concentrated their work as pastors and of the duties and manner of life that went with it, with corresponding results in the spiritual life of the whole church.[2]

Now clearly it would be quite wrong to say that the function of pastor and the pre-eminent duty of preaching which as we have seen dominated the thinking of the Council of Trent about the episcopate, was not passed on to the clergy under their charge. What was true of the bishops as pastors of the first rank was true also of the presbyters as pastors of the second rank. The exhortations given to the bishops by the spiritual

---

[1] For an examination of this topic as it was treated by sixteenth-century theologians before Trent, see J. P. Massaut, *Josse Clichtove, l'Humanisme et la Réforme du Clergé*, Paris, 1968, 2 vols. especially vol. II, pp. 47-65. For a more general discussion, see *Catholicisme*, IV, 801; Y. Congar, *Sainte Eglise*, Paris, 1963, 285; and O. Rousseau, 'La doctrine du ministère episcopal et ses vicissitudes dans l'église d'Occident', in *L'Episcopat et l'Eglise Universelle* (ed. Y. Congar and B-D. Dupuy), Paris, 1964, pp. 279-308.

[2] See Paul Broutin SJ, *La Réforme Pastorale en France au 17e Siècle*, Paris, 1956, 2 vols. and, for one particular diocese, R. Sauzet, *Les Visites Pastorales dans le diocèse de Chartres*, Rome, 1975.

writers of the time were given to their clergy also. The *Pastoral de Limoges*, published in 1694 by Michael Bourdon, vicar-general of the diocese of Limoges, in order to gather together the fruits of the pastoral experience gained in the renewal of that diocese over the whole seventeenth century, stresses the fact that preaching is the first responsibility of pastors, to be put before the administration of the sacraments, since the Council of Trent had declared it to be the principal duty of bishops, 'who are the first pastors'.[3] But only too often one reads that the clergy are reluctant to preach or incapable of preaching; it is difficult to get them to think in terms of the order of priority established by the Council. And it must also be said that the overwhelming emphasis of the advice given to the pastors of the second grade lay not on preaching the word but on the sacrifice of the Mass, and this fact we must now examine.

In the development of the theology and spirituality of the priesthood in the seventeenth century, Cardinal de Bérulle is a figure of outstanding importance through his influence on the French clergy and on seminary training, and thus on the outlook of clergy throughout the world right down to the present day. For the urgent restoration of the clerical state in the general decadence of his time, he sought above all to promote holiness: a holiness drawn from attention to the central activity of the priest, highlighted by Trent: offering the sacrifice of the Mass. Everything centred round this theme, and not round the first theme elaborated by Trent, the pastoral function of the bishop. For one thing, Bérulle, and those who followed him like Monsieur Olier and St Vincent de Paul, were not directly concerned with the holiness of bishops, any more than St Ignatius Loyola and the Jesuits had been. For another, so damaging was the practical effect of the long-standing theological distinction between the power of jurisdiction and the power of order, that men could very often be bishops and hold lesser benefices without being priests. Just as Constantine, for example, could in the fourth century be a Christian Emperor and call himself 'bishop for

---

3 'Il faut tomber d'accord que l'administration des sacrements est une fonction très noble et très sublime, puisque Dieu se sert de ces sacrés canaux pour faire découler la grâce dans les âmes. Mais on ne peut douter que la prédication lui soit préférable et qu'elle ne soit le principal emploi des pasteurs puisque le Concile de Trente et les autres qui ont suivi ont tous appelé ce sacré ministère le principal devoir des evêques qui sont les premiers pasteurs': quoted in Paul Broutin, *op. cit.*, p. 372.

those outside', while deferring baptism to the end of his life, so many in the seventeenth century who exercised authority as bishops or held other ecclesiastical offices, remained in minor orders, not being anxious to accept the obligation to holiness that ordination as a priest would require.

In order to reform the clergy in the way most obviously available to him, Cardinal de Bérulle wanted to train dedicated men who drew all their strength from the sacrifice of Christ. The Eucharist, gift of God to men, offering of men to God, was the extension of the Incarnation, the continuing means of our Redemption; the ordained minister, having the power to consecrate and offer the Body and Blood of Christ, was an instrument chosen by God to bring about the salvation of the world. The Cross was Christ's moment of total renunciation; a renunciation that was expected of the priest who represented him. A particular feature of Bérulle's spirituality, with far-reaching consequences for the French school, flowed from his teaching that in Christ the absence of human person, his humanity being rooted in the one Person of the Word, represented the perfection of renunciation and self-denial. The ordained priest, imitating Christ, must even abandon his selfhood and hence his own personality, to follow him. Cardinal de Bérulle's understanding of sacrifice as offering rather than immolation serves to correct the impression given by this teaching, but the often disastrous consequences of attempting to practise an apparently high ideal, with its mistaken metaphysical and theological basis, have more recently led us to search for a better understanding of the difference between the Creator and the creature, and of the Person of Christ, together with the effect of his Passion and Resurrection in our lives.

The worship of God in the Mass, and the guiding of souls to take part in that worship: that was how Bérulle presented the work of the ordained ministry, with immense benefits for the Church down to our own day. But now that the priesthood of the laity has been given its place by an ecumenical council, we have been forced to look more closely at his doctrine and to ask ourselves whether he really brought out the specific character conferred by ordination.[4]

---

[4] On the richness and strength of Cardinal de Bérulle's doctrine, as well as its limitations, see M. Dupuy, *Bérulle et le Sacerdoce*, Paris, 1969.

The work of Monsieur Olier clearly also needs examination in any study of the spirituality of the post-Tridentine priest. As the founder of the *Compagnie de Saint-Sulpice* he set going a tradition of priestly spirituality that has continued until our own times; the great crisis of the seminaries and priesthood in France indicates the contemporary running-out of that tradition.[5] In that crisis we are all involved; but I believe that we are now beginning to reach *terra firma* and that the basis of renewal is being found. Monsieur Olier's *Traité des Saints Ordres* (1675) epitomises the strength, as well as the limitations of that tradition. It is organised round the notion of the clerical state and the degrees by which the future priest is led to the service of the altar: the four minor orders, the sub-diaconate, diaconate, and priesthood. Rung by rung and rank by rank one climbs to the highest level of participation in the holiness of God:

> Tous les ordres dont vous avons parlé ne sont que le commencement des grands pouvoirs dont Jésus-Christ rend le prêtre et l'évêque participants dans son Eglise.[6]

But this is the only mention of the bishop in this section. Following the thought of Cardinal de Bérulle, Monsieur Olier is entirely concerned with the supreme power possessed by the priest of

[5] Paul Vigneron's *Histoire des Crises du Clergé Français Contemporain* (Paris, 1976) is a sombre statement, thoroughly documented, of the contemporary dropping-off and disarray of the clergy in France, characteristic of the difficulties and anxieties that have been felt almost everywhere. His book indicates the decline of the spirituality established in the seventeenth century and given a fresh but temporary impetus by two world wars, with its stress on the Cross and on sacrifice, but with the special functions of the ordained minister in the Church over-developed in one direction and very much under-developed in others. No one can doubt the centrality of sacrifice, in union with Christ, for every Christian. It should be remembered, however, that it was the Good *Shepherd* who 'gave his life for his sheep'; we should concentrate on working out the *pastoral* role of the ministerial priesthood, if those whom the Church calls to ordination are to see clearly and fully the precise way in which they are to give their lives.

For further information about the situation in France, and a more sober and encouraging appraisal, see Julien Potel, *Les Prêtres Séculiers en France. Evolution de 1965 à 1975*, and *Demain d'autres Prêtres? Leur Place et leur Rôles* (Paris, 1977). The review *Vocations* (Centre National de Vocations, 106, rue du Bac, 75341 Paris Cedex 07) should be read by anyone concerned to understand the depth of the present crisis and the solutions that are being found.

[6] *Oeuvres Complètes de M. Olier*, Paris, 1856, 657-8.

making Christ present on the altar and with the holiness which must correspond with it. The priest is the representative worshipper of God, reproducing on earth the hidden life of Christ in heaven; his state is assimilated to that of the religious orders, who, like the orders of angels in heaven, are dedicated to the glory of God in all things.

M. Olier has developed the one line of thought that offered itself to those seeking reform after Trent. Since he was not directly involved in the reformation of bishops, he concentrated on the second major theme; the priest at the altar, which he works out along the lines, long traditional, of the Church's thinking about the sacerdotal quality of the sacred ministry, together with the thinking about hierarchy made classic by the writings of the Pseudo-Dionysius. As in the case of Cardinal de Bérulle, the immense fruits of holiness produced in generations of priests by his exalted teaching and the dedication it inspired must not now conceal from us the restricted nature of the theological area within which he worked, its one-sidedness, even where the doctrine of the Council of Trent, with its renewal of episcopacy, is concerned, and the neo-platonism which gives it a cultural form which not only need not now be retained but which is positively at variance with the teachings and achievement of Christ.

This philosophical and cultural conditioning can be seen in his exegesis of 1 Peter 2:9. Writing of 'the Prelates of the Church' and of the clergy, he observes:

C'est ainsi que saint Pierre, comme l'héritier capital de Jésus-Christ, en parle lorsqu'il fait la description et le dénombrement des Ordres de son Royaume: *regale sacerdotium, gens sancta, populus acquisitionis;* dans le Royaume de l'Eglise, le royal sacerdoce qui réside en éminence en la personne des Evêques, *regale sacerdotium,* occupe le premier lieu; après, il met le saint clergé, le nommant *gens sancta,* personnes saintes et sacrées appliquées aux autels et au culte de Dieu; et enfin il décrit tout le corps des fidèles par ces paroles, *populus acquisitionis,* peuples acquis par Jésus-Christ . . .[7]

[7] J.-J. Olier, *Projet pour l'establissement d'un séminaire dans un diocèse* (1651) quoted in Paul Broutin sj, *op. cit.,* n. 2, II, p. 254.

He thus assigns to different 'orders' in the Church (altering the New Testament meaning of 'order') expressions that 1 Peter applies to the whole people of God indiscriminately; and to make *regale sacerdotium* come first and apply to the bishops, he is obliged to change the order of the words in the text, putting *regale sacerdotium* first instead of second (the Vulgate order, incidentally, is the same as the Greek).

The teaching of English Catholics

The English tradition of thought about the ordained ministry has for the last hundred and fifty years been dominated by a theology constructed on lines similar to those developed by the French school. Bishop Challoner clearly distinguished the roles of priest and people in the Eucharist, but he also had a strong sense of the unity of their action, saying that both offer together, 'by the hands of the great high priest Jesus Christ', so that it is possible that further study of pre-nineteenth century English Catholicism would reveal a line of thought foreshadowing the theology of the eucharistic community that has become familiar since Vatican II. But Cardinal Wiseman made a more sharp distinction, emphasising that in the Mass, as in some other functions, 'the priestly character alone has efficiency to act', and that 'the principal actor is the priest', while 'the rest must be content to join their prayers mentally with him'.[8] In *The Eternal Priesthood*, (1883), Cardinal Manning organised his thought about the ordained ministry entirely round the notion of priesthood:

> Whatsoever is true of the priesthood in itself is true both of Bishop and of priest. And in this we see why at first the names were for a while common and interchanged. The injunctions of Christian perfection given by St Paul to Timothy and to Titus were given to Bishop and to presbyter or priest alike.[9]

Now it is true, of course, that *episcopos* and *presbyteros* are used equivalently in the New Testament. But Manning does not

8 See Michael Richards, *The Liturgy in England*, 1966, pp. 11-21.
9 H. E. Manning, *The Eternal Priesthood*, 1883, p. 3.

notice that in adding those words 'or priest' he is making a crucial and unexamined shift of meaning, as theologians had done for centuries before him, right back to St John Chrysostom, from *presbyter*, to *sacerdos*, and hence to the subsuming of the role of the presbyter under the overall sacerdotal theme, with which we have become so familiar.

In the twentieth century, the extent to which this theme continued to dominate our thinking until the Second Vatican Council can best be seen in the revered Dr E. J. Mahoney's *The Secular Priesthood* (1929). The whole work is organised round the notion of priesthood as defined at the Council of Trent; Mahoney underlines the influence of the French School of the seventeenth century on English writers (p. 225). The consequence is that he is obliged to defend the idea that there exists 'a priestly body altogether distinct from the laity' (p. 17) and to regard 'the "pastoral office" of the priest' as something added to priesthood in certain cases, differentiating 'those priests to whom the care of souls has been committed from others whose vocation may be incompatible with the cares of a parish' (p. 44). In speaking of the sacrament of Holy Orders, he says that 'the word "order" means the harmonious relation between various things, the subordination of the lower to the higher', retaining the feudal note of 'rank' that for so long overlaid the Gospel emphasis on service and on the rejection by the Apostles of any idea of superior degree. He is involved in discussion of the relative dignity conferred by the religious life and by the secular priesthood, and the levels of sanctity to which one is obliged by these states of life. He finds it necessary to explain the use of the term 'secular' when applied to a particular group of priests and attempts to get rid of any pejorative sense that may be associated with it.

All of these problems have been set in a new light by Vatican II, so that Dr Mahoney's apologetic, learned and conscientious as it was, can now be seen to be a battle carried on in defence of false positions, of theories that only arose out of temporary solutions, devised under the pressure of alien cultural conditions or of the challenge of heresy.

This new perspective can be set out as follows.

In the first place, the Church as a whole must be envisaged as a priestly people. 1 Peter and the Epistle to the Hebrews make

195

it clear that all members of the Church, in virtue of their faith in Christ, expressed in baptism, share the priestly character. *Lumen Gentium* makes this fundamental fact the starting point of all our thinking about the relationships that are established among us in the Church. Instead of starting from the priesthood of the ordained ministry and then trying to work out how the laity have a share in this priesthood, in the way we have done since Trent,[10] the Council starts from the general priesthood and then goes on to treat the special ministerial priesthood in that context. And this is the essential order of things that must be followed if the full achievement of the New Testament is to be understood and appreciated.

Chapter II of *Lumen Gentium* makes it clear that within this general priesthood there exists a ministerial or hierarchical priesthood, different from that of other members of the Church in some essential way:

> *Sacerdotium autem commune fidelium et sacerdotium ministeriale sive hierarchicum, licet essentia, et non gradu tantum differant, ad invicem tamen ordinantur; unum enim et alterum suo peculiari modo de uno Christi sacerdotio participant* (n. 10).

This passage will repay close study: If the general category is priesthood, the essential difference of which the document speaks cannot also be priesthood: it must be designated by the adjectives which are used: *ministeriale sive hierarchicum*, ministerial or hierarchical. The notion of a difference of degree, so foreign to the New Testament, is set aside: *non gradu tantum*, not just a difference of degree, not a mere difference of degree.[11]

Ministry and *hierarchy* are thus the terms designating the essential character of this part of the one priesthood that Christ communicates to his people; and *hierarchy* cannot be given the sense of 'rank' which it has acquired over the centuries, but

---

10 For a classic statement of this line of thinking, see G. D. Smith, 'The Priesthood of the Laity', *The Clergy Review*, XXII (1942), pp. 1-11.

11 If the Council Fathers had wished to retain the notion of degree, they would have said 'non tantum gradu, sed etiam essentia'; by their manner of expression, they highlight *essentia* and set *gradus* aside. This point was missed by the 1974 Synod of Bishops when referring to this passage in the decree.

which is clearly set aside in the decree; it must be strictly interpreted in its literal meaning of 'principle of sanctification'.

Chapter III of *Lumen Gentium* then goes on to explain what this ministry is: 'The ministers, invested with sacred power, are at the service of their brethren' (n. 18). It is a ministry that began with the Apostles and was then conferred upon bishops, who shared it with their helpers the presbyters and deacons:

> *Episcopi igitur communitatis ministerium cum adjutoribus presbyteris et diaconis susceperunt* (n. 20).

The translation published by the Catholic Truth Society has 'priests' here for *presbyteri*; this obscures the deliberate choice of the term *presbyter* here by the Council, which avoided the word *sacerdos* in designating this ministry and carefully employed the New Testament expression. This concern for terminological exactitude can also be seen at work in the way that the words *clerus* and *sacerdos*, proposed to begin with, were set aside in the discussions that led up to the formulation of the decree *Presbyterorum Ordinis*, on the ministry of life not of 'the clergy' or of 'priests', but consciously and explicitly of *presbyters*.[12]

This decree develops in detail the theme which emerges from Chapter III of *Lumen Gentium* and which now sets the theology of the sacrament of Holy Order firmly on its true foundation: everything begins with the bishop. Presbyterate and diaconate must be seen as two distinct forms of participation in the one sacrament which the bishop receives in its fullness. No longer do we look on the priesthood as the fullness of the sacrament, with the consequence that episcopacy appears to add nothing except jurisdiction (and the consequence in practice, that men could exercise the functions of the episcopate and draw its revenues without receiving ordination). It is now abundantly clear that the ministry which constitutes the essential difference marking off the sacrament of Holy Order and making those who receive it a particular kind of priest, but not more priests than any others, is in the first place, and in its completeness, episcopacy. We need to under-

---

[12] A glance at the decrees and canons of Trent (see p. 239f. above) will show that this is no revolution but a careful use of traditional language.

stand what a bishop is first, and then, by derivation, we can understand what a presbyter is, and what a deacon is, in the service of Almighty God.

And to understand what a bishop is, we can go back once more to the Council of Trent. In what we are trying to establish about our ministry since Vatican II, there is no question of our rejecting anything that was said by Trent or any other Council. What we must do is collect all the elements together, and arrange them as accurately as possible, avoiding the distortions that have arisen from an emphasis on this or that aspect or from the retention of material that has no place in a true New Testament theology.

Servants and Shepherds

Trent, as we have seen, began its work by setting out the Church's responsibility to the Word of God, and said that 'preaching the Word' is the principal function (*praecipuum munus*) of the bishop; the Council also insisted on the primordial role of the bishop as pastor. And it is round these two themes, which are really one, that the theology of Holy Order must be organised, if we are to arrive at a true balance and completeness in understanding our ministry.

It cannot be of secondary significance to discover that Our Lord did not call his Apostles priests: he called them shepherds and fishermen. To establish the essential difference of the particular call that he gave them, he went back beyond the social categories of prophet, priest and king to an earlier stage in human history and to more fundamental and widespread human activities: the work of the pastor and the work of the hunter. He used the imagery of cultivation: the harvest of corn and the harvest of wine; and he used the imagery of the household: stewards and servants. The so-called 'High-Priestly Prayer' of John 17 does not use the language of priesthood directly, but goes beyond it, taking it up into categories that express the aims of priesthood, now achieved: unity, sharing, gift and possession. The consecration of the Apostles was to be a consecration 'in truth', brought about, that is to say, not by symbols and shadows, but by reality. The whole thrust of Old Testament thinking about sacrifice, from ritual to real moral obedience, is here brought to completion. By Christ's own consecration of himself in perfect obedience, dying, not in simulation and ceremony but in stark reality, not in a Temple within the City but on a cross outside the city — the very opposite of sanctuary as hitherto conceived and built — our own potentialities for obedience and worship are now made capable of realisation.

And the Apostles were sent out to bring this truth, this reality, to the world. That is why they called themselves 'Servants of the Word' and made that service their over-riding concern (Acts 6). They would be shepherds of Christ's flock, gathering together the new People of God, by communicating the truth to the world, by proclaiming the Word.

The instructions given to the next generation of those to whom charge of the Church was given, the bishops, presbyters and deacons spoken of in the Pastoral Epistles and in 1 Peter, do not speak of priesthood, but emphasise the qualities of character and the experience that will make a man capable of looking after a community and all its problems, shown in his ability to look after his own family, and stress the need for holding fast to the teaching that had been received:

> If you put these instructions before the brethren, you will be a good minister of Christ Jesus, nourished on the words of the faith and of the good doctrine which you have followed (1 Tim 4:6).

The controlling image is that of the Shepherd:

> Tend the flock of God that is in your charge, not by constraint but willingly, not for shameful gain but eagerly, not as domineering over those in your charge but being examples to the flock. And when the chief Shepherd is manifested you will obtain the unfading crown of glory (1 Pet 5:2-5).

'Those in your charge': these are the clergy, the *cleros*, who in the New Testament are the people of God entrusted to the pastors, not the pastors themselves. In an extraordinary reversal of roles, the pastors have taken over the term meant for the people. And this explains how the term 'secular' has been

199

wrongly applied; in reality it is the whole Church that is 'in the world', and not just the pastors, who are above all in the Church.

And so Vatican II has brought us full circle, not by denying Trent, but by returning to what was Trent's prime intuition, the central position of the bishop as pastor, with the service of the Word of God as his chief task. When the bishop or presbyter stand at the altar in the midst of the priestly People of God, their distinctive and particular role, the special charismatic gift that is theirs, is not that of priesthood, which, in Christ, they have shared with all the faithful since their baptism, but that of pastor: they and only they are responsible for this community which they call together by their proclamation of the Word of God and by their teaching. It is by their grasp and presentation of the truth that they provide the food by which their people are fed. Only the bishops have authority in the service of the Word to define it and declare its meaning. The Word is their means of consecrating the world, and so the Word, even before the people, is in their charge and care.

The Word is One

If this understanding of the ordained ministry is to be complete, the relationship of Word and Sacrament must also be put in its true perspective. Word and Sacrament are not two separate realities, working, so to speak, side by side. Bishops and presbyters are not given two responsibilities, for the Word and for the Sacraments, but one. The unity of Word and Sacrament can be grasped if we remember St Paul's phrase: the word of the cross (1 Cor 1:18). If the Cross is God's Word to the world, *a fortiori*, so is the Eucharist: God's Word is spoken supremely in our time and in our world by the Body and Blood of Christ. From its beginning to its heart and summit, the Eucharist is penetrated, activated, made effective, by the Word of God, calling us together, speaking to us through the others in whom he is present, addressing us in the words of Sacred Scripture, and, in today's words, through the one whom he has chosen to be his apostle, servant and pastor, and finally through the words by which he made known the very heart and meaning of his mission, becoming present for us in his

200

Body and Blood, the supreme expression of his mind and will, in which above all we have learnt that in God words and deeds are always one.

When we receive Holy Communion, unless we are coming in faith to receive Christ as God's Word, his message to us, his communication with us, we are unaware of what it is that we are doing. We must first listen to God's Word if we are to know whom we receive; we must assent to God's word, obeying his commandments, if our communion is to be true and holy.

I believe that this presentation of the Sacrament of Holy Order to be the one that emerges from the various texts both of Trent and Vatican II, both of which Councils set out, of course, to do justice to aspects of the teaching conveyed by the words of the New Testament documents. If it now appears that we have clung too one-sidedly to one element that goes to make up the New Testament ministry, that of priesthood, the reasons, cultural, philosophical and institutional, for this time-lag in understanding are not difficult to explain and can be paralleled over and over again for other aspects of Christian teaching. A synthesis built round the realities of apostolate, episcopacy and service will enable us to make sense of the New Testament evidence, to do justice to the full nature of the provision made by Christ for the continuation of his mission, and to order the life of the Church more adequately in the years that lie ahead.

Is it possible to pick out a dominant theme for our own ministry in this country at the present time? If we think of ourselves predominantly as dedicated to the service of the Word, then our minds and hearts must above all be concerned with truth, with the presentation of the Gospel as the message that brings order and meaning into the sphere of human knowledge and human life. We shall need to know the facts of our faith, understand them, and relate them to other fields of human enquiry. We shall need to think of that faith as addressed above all to those who do not believe; in the effort of communicating it to them, we shall discover its meaning more fully for ourselves. We shall need to be reconcilers of divided Christians, using the one and indivisible Word to bring those who are now separated into the one obedience of faith. And we shall need to concern ourselves with those who are least

201

able to cope in our society, with the weakest, wherever and whoever they are, since it is above all for them that the Gospel is Good News.

And in all this we must be thinking not of the past, not of defending our own tradition as a group within our society, but of the people of the future whom we shall make into the new People of God. For this is how St Paul summed up his own ministry, in the words that Vatican II chose as most clearly and fully expressive of the office of bishop, presbyter or deacon:

> I have written to you very boldly by way of reminder, because of the grace given to me by God to be a minister of Christ Jesus to the Gentiles in the sacred service of the Gospel of God, so that the offering of the nations may be acceptable, sanctified by the Holy Spirit (Rom 15:15-16).

To make all humanity into priests of God: that is the purpose for which some among his friends are called to be overseers, elders and servants, in the one Body of his priestly people.

July 1979

PIUS XII: A FORGOTTEN INITIATIVE?

SOON after taking over one of our longest-running parishes, a friend of mine announced to the congregation that the 'outdoor collection' would now be discontinued. The purpose for which it had been started — raising funds for new boilers — had been achieved, and he therefore felt it wrong to go on with it. This change of pastoral practice did not please two of the pillars of the parish, a couple who came to tell him that he would soon regret the day on which he had abandoned a custom faithfully and profitably observed by his predecessor over many years.

The following week they were back, full of apologies. 'We understand you now, Father', they said. 'We have remembered that before Father Y there was Father X, and he never had the outdoor collection; you are going back to what used to be the way in his time, so that's all right.'

Thirty years ago, encouraged by Pius XII, bishops in Europe started ordaining married men for the ministry of the Church.

Nineteen years ago, still before the Council, I visited in Copenhagen a married priest, a former Lutheran minister, who was able to report complete acceptance and an active apostolate in the parish where he was working. How is it that Pius XII's readiness to adapt the discipline of the Church to meet contemporary needs — so fruitful in many fields — has in this particular area, of such immediate pastoral concern, been forgotten?

Why can we not go back to the days before the Council, to Pius XII, and continue the work that he began? He was, of course, as in so much else, himself going to his own contemporaries and predecessors for inspiration, to customs still observed in many places, in communion with Rome as in separation, to the earliest days of the Church, and to the New Testament itself. The Pastoral Epistles — evidence ignored by Rome in recent documents — show beyond any shadow of doubt that the tradition of ordaining married men for the pastoral oversight and service of the Church is a more venerable one than that which has been in force more recently, of excluding them from that service.

It is Rome's way to say no to new ideas and initiatives until such time as they have been tried, tested and clarified and have proved their firm basis in the revealed truth of the Gospel. Then Rome changes, and proclaims that this is what we must all think and all do (and haven't we really been thinking and doing it all along . . .?). We have seen it over Church-State relations, over freedom of conscience, over ecumenism, over biblical and historical studies and over missionary policy, and we shall certainly see it again, in many other fields. It is a sensible way to conduct our affairs. None of us should expect immediate acceptance from our public, however genial or helpful our ideas; the fire of criticism, from superiors, from colleagues and from the world we hope to reach, is a trial from which no one is exempt. The more important the discovery or the principle at stake, the more rigorous and thorough must be the testing before it passes into general use.

The havoc and confusion of the last fourteen years have been no time in which to make so important a change in the administration of the Church as the general extension of the movement started by Pius XII a generation ago. We have, as a

203

result of the Council, been led to look more closely than ever before at the nature of the ordained ministry as brought into being by Christ. We needed to make sure that we understood properly the precise nature and scope of that particular ministry, among many others in the Church; we can now say that progress has indeed been made and that we have a firmer grasp of what we should be doing than we had at the time of the Council.

And we needed also to arrive at a better understanding of the gift and vocation of celibacy; there again, scripture scholars, theologians, spiritual teachers, psychologists, anthropologists, Church authorities (and practitioners!) have all had their word to say, to the clarification of our minds and the pacification of our hearts. As John Paul II has said, 'celibacy is a sign of freedom that exists for the sake of service'.

And to be such a sign it must be a reality. Where the reality is not there, where we have instead a dedicated bachelordom, a timid, touchy loneliness, an insecurity that seeks constantly for distraction and escape, then we have a sign that speaks of nothing but egotistical enslavement. Where we have public proclamations of principle and widespread flouting of it in practice, we have an alienating deceit.

The Pope has been quite right to insist in his letter for Maundy Thursday 1979 on the fact that no one can seriously claim nowadays that he only accepted celibacy because it was imposed by law on all candidates for ordination. Any religious superior or seminary rector, and any bishop accepting such a man, would have been guilty of neglecting his responsibility to see that no one who does not believe himself to be genuinely called to give up marriage for the sake of the Kingdom of God should be allowed to go forward.

The fact remains that whatever the spiritual guidance given and whatever the safeguards, that is how the regulations have been expressed: that if you want to be ordained, you must accept celibacy. The rules and procedures need to be changed. The call to celibacy for the sake of service comes first, and must be seen to come first. Well before any final decision about ordination, there should be a definite undertaking of the unmarried state, first temporary and then permanent. If the charism of celibacy is to be properly understood and practised, it must be shown to be quite distinct from ordination. It must be made absolutely clear that it is a matter of the Church choosing its ministers from among those who have already accepted their call to celibacy for the sake of service, and not of imposing celibacy on those who are or wish to be ordained. Priests who are not allowed to marry were a pagan invention. But those who give up marriage for the sake of the Kingdom are recognising the call of Christ: their vocation comes from the New Testament, not from paganism.

Christ, of course, gave no indication that all who accept that call were to be ordained. Nor did the early Church understand from him that those who were to be ordained had previously to set marriage aside. But the Church is today quite right to regard those who have entered into the freedom given by celibacy from the beginning of their adult life as particularly appropriate candidates for ordination. The priority must, however, be fairly and squarely seen to run in that order; the undertaking of celibacy must come first and come separately. It might well be appropriate also that the diaconate, now that the function of deacon is better understood and appreciated, should be very much more prolonged than it is at present. Simply laying hands on young men 'because parishes need them to say Mass' betrays almost total ignorance of the nature of the sacraments of the Eucharist and of Order.

While the Church must undoubtedly continue to recognise and to foster the charism of celibacy for both men and women, and to ordain for the pastoral ministry many of those who have received that call, it must also come to see in the fruits of dedication and service found among those who have received the sacrament of marriage proof of their suitability for ordination to the responsibility of caring for a part of Christ's people. A simple parallelism: celibacy for Orders, marriage for Matrimony, does not do justice to the New Testament demands; it is, let us face it, in flat contradiction to them.

And this principle must be recognised and applied everywhere in the Church, not only in one geographical or cultural area. To use the category of 'Latin Catholicism' in this context and to claim that a uniquely celibate clergy must be maintained because it is an unalienable part of Latin Catholic tradition is to appeal to a pastoral and missionary principle that was already being shown to be no longer workable or desirable before Vatican II.

The Catholic Church cannot be for ever tied to the administrative and spiritual tradition of any one of its parts, however important and venerable. We are now clearly committed to the authentic Catholic policy of promoting the unity and harmony of local churches, each one adapting its life in terms of the indigenous culture and creating new cultural, political and social patterns of its own: the People of God baptising and bringing into Christian communion the nations of the world. The future policy over the public service of the Church in Britain must be for the Catholic Church in Britain itself to decide. We are not a small sect, a particular 'tradition' concerned only with maintaining our identity by sticking to the letter of an administrative pattern imported from elsewhere. Such a policy will do for McDonald's or for Kentucky Fried Chicken, but it will not do for the Catholic Church. Paul VI already made it clear that if the hierarchy in this country were to decide to ordain married men, he would not stand in their way. Australia has made a start. The Cardinal Archbishop of Madrid has said that a start could well be made in Spain before long. How much longer will we wait?

The significance of such a move for Christian unity in these islands is particularly obvious. If we are not going to accept married men into the ministry, then we might as well abandon all our ecumenical struggles. If the Church throughout the world has for ever set its face against ordaining married men for pastoral care, then the Secretariat for Unity must clearly close its doors.

To have fathers of families who have earned their place in the presbyterium of the diocese by the example of their lives, by their professional competence and by their dedication to the service of Christ in his truth and in his people, working alongside those who have followed their call to give up family life for the same dedication would in no way diminish the strength of the celibate vocation. Far from it; it would help to clarify its specific purpose, making those who have accepted it more aware of what they are about and more determined to persevere.

Many of the arguments for a celibate priesthood are based on economics and politics — finance and control — rather than a true discernment of the nature of ministry. We now have ways of safeguarding our property which makes this particular device unnecessary. Where organisational flexibility and freedom are at stake, the arguments go both ways; there are dedicated married couples ready to go anywhere and do anything in the service of the Lord and there are encrusted individuals who create problems for the Church that only death will solve.

When it comes to martyrdom, even the facts tell the same story. Franz Jägerstatter was a married sacristan; his parish priest stayed at home with his housekeeper.

The fundamental argument does not however spring from ecumenism or from convenience. Nor does it arise simply from our present urgent need to find men for hundreds of empty parishes and thousands of under-staffed ones. The significance of the present situation is that it has forced us to think harder than ever before. It has brought us to the realisation that if the apostolic church chose married men for its bishops, presbyters and deacons, they, who had the mind of Christ, cannot have been far wrong. For that reason, and for that reason alone, the Church everywhere must in the twentieth century begin once again to look among dedicated married men as well as among the unmarried for its ordained ministry. Slowly but surely the change can come. Because it is needed. And because it is right.

August 1979

THE KAPORAL

A NORMAL part of a priest's vocational and personal routine is (or should be) going to Mass as a member of the congregation. It provides a check for our own competence as well as new ideas for our own parishes. We see ourselves as others see us: always a salutary experience, though we do not always remember the warnings we receive.

At Mass the other day, I began to wonder, as I have done from time to time before, how it is that attitudes to our public that would in any other way of life bring unemployment before the year was out do not appear to disturb, let alone to damage, a priest's serenely secure expectancy of three square meals a day.

207

The repeated snapping of the fingers at the servers, as if they were puppy dogs being brought to heel; the prolonged blowing of the nose before giving out the notices, as if to say 'You can wait till I am ready'; the hectoring displeasure vented upon the congregation for failing to buy more than four of the twenty diocesan yearbooks so kindly ordered for them, at episcopal behest, at the beginning of the year; the giving out of a communion plate to be passed from hand to hand so as to discourage receiving communion in any other than the old way: what was wrong with the man, that he should treat his people with such domineering disrespect?

St Peter was already warning his fellow-presbyters against faults of this kind: it would be naïve to be scandalised. The congregation's patience, Sunday after Sunday, stems from charity, not from uncritical acceptance. They have better things to do than to dwell on such faults. But faults they are; and they indicate a set of mind that goes far to explain the malaise of many of the clergy, indicating the point of friction, the operating fault that must be cleared if easy working is to be ensured.

Ordination can easily be thought of as conferring rank, privilege and private rights. It is only to be expected that anyone who was ordained on those terms should nowadays feel himself threatened; it shows that the Church is effectively recalling Our Lord's own attitude to his apostles when they themselves put forward such ideas, and is setting before us the better way, the one that has been handed down from the beginning, the one which human weakness so easily forgets.

A priest who has it in the forefront of his mind that he holds special powers, to be safeguarded as his alone, does not really understand either the true nature of the sacraments or his relationships with other members of the Church. Now that so much is being shared among us all, he is bound to be afflicted by anxiety, losing confidence and becoming defensive of the shrinking area that still appears to be left to him. And by the same token, a priest who relies on his uniform to win him at any rate external signs of respect and to enable him to perform the routine duties that are his stock-in-trade, is bound to feel uncomfortable in a world that, having seen all too clearly how uniforms can be misused, has turned so strongly against them.

We can find our way out of such insecurity simply by remembering that we are, after all, in the first place, and fundamentally, Christians. It is only because a man showed signs of being a Christian that the Church could make him into a sign of its mission and purpose: that the bishop could give him a share in the special service of the Word of God that makes him responsible for calling together and guiding God's family. He must continually reject the search for power and think instead of passing on to others everything that he has received. He is not so much a line of force, as a channel of grace.

I am not forgetting the power of God: our redemption by the power of Christ's death and resurrection, our new life in the power of the Spirit. But his power works through human weakness, through handing on to others, not through holding fast for ourselves, through having in order to give, not in order to feel safe in our possessions.

Our training and our thinking and our fundamental selfishness have turned many of us priests into one-man bands, playing to a public whose only active role was putting a penny in the hat stretched out to them. Now that the orchestra is taking due possession of the instruments, we should not be feeling bereft, for we are needed and challenged in our real, essential calling: gathering together in order and harmony throughout the world the great symphony of God's praise.

March 1981

VI
TEACHING

211

FOUR MISTAKES

FOUR fundamental errors of principle are putting the contemporary catechetical movement in this country in danger. Although a great deal of devoted, strenuous and highly competent work is being put into the renewal of religious education, there are signs of strain in the teaching world and also indications that an inadequate foundation for the future is at present being laid.

The first mistake lies in the view now taken of the past. Lecturers on catechetics are all too often much more fluent and forceful in their condemnation of what was being done up to a year or two ago than they are in making positive statements about what should be done now and in the future. This approach is also found in the classroom. Happily it can now be said that the *sensus fidelium parvulorum* is beginning to make itself felt, so that the question is constantly being asked, 'Teacher, if what we were told last year is a lot of nonsense, how do we know that next year's teacher won't tell us that your lessons are a lot of nonsense too?'

The second mistake is the neglect of what may be called supernatural psychology. The teacher should always bear in mind that he is subordinate to the inner teacher, the Holy Spirit, and that he is trying to stir and strengthen the gifts of faith, hope and charity which God puts in the soul of every child. Great good is being done by the deeper study of educational psychology, but one is sometimes given the impression that a better use of psychological science will necessarily result in stronger perseverance in the faith. It is on that account suggested, for example, that with good teaching at the primary stage Catholic secondary schools will no longer be needed. This sounds alarmingly like indoctrination. The Catholic Church is concerned with education at every stage from the cradle to the grave. This does not mean that we expect from

212

any of our teaching institutions a hundred per cent supply of practising Catholics. If we did get these results we might indeed suspect that something had gone wrong.

This leads on to the third mistake, which is forgetfulness of the parable of the Sower. Historical and contemporary sociology simply confirm the statistics given in that parable. Tables of figures should never be interpreted in the light of the presupposition of the Catholic Golden Age, a myth banished long ago by serious historians. We cannot expect to do better than the Gospel originally promised.

The fourth mistake involves the tying of catechesis to theological theories. While it is clear that the catechist must have a coherent theology, he must beware of putting across particular theologies as if they were absolute and complete statements of Catholic faith. It is the catechist's job to give his pupil the freedom of the Church, While the salvation history approach is fundamental in catechesis, it must not rule out proper reference to the eternal, non-historical, mystery of God. The salvific events of our history are also signs by which God reveals to us his inner nature. It is true to say that the only God we know is the God who is with us; it is also true to say that the only God we know is the God who is not with us.

One of the reasons why we have become involved in these difficulties has been the absence of a serious institution for theological teaching and research in relationship to which our catechetical work could be situated. Catechists have felt themselves obliged to revise our theology as well as our teaching methods, and the burden has been too much for them. It is, above all, on educational method that their reflexion should centre itself, and they should see their work as part of the programme of the Church for Christian education as a whole.

It is also vital that the adult catechumenate as envisaged by the Vatican Council should be properly developed in every urban area. Our methods of instructing converts are far too haphazard and individualistic.

Finally, three classics should be required reading for every catechist: St Augustine's *On Christian Doctrine, Manual of Faith, Hope and Charity,* and *On Catechising the Simple* are full of theological and practical common sense, providing the sort of groundwork which is still needed by every teacher of the Gospel.

August 1967

213

CATECHETICS AND THE MAGISTERIUM

CATECHETICS continues to be a centre of controversy, with attempts at reassurance on the part of those most deeply involved still being met with expressions of dissatisfaction from teachers, parents and a number of people more generally concerned with the defence of the Catholic faith in modern society. It may be worthwhile attempting to recall a number of general truths about the teaching of the Church which do not always appear to be borne in mind in these debates.

The teaching of the Church is given with divine authority and guarantee; this fact underlies the conviction with which it is proclaimed and the certainty with which it is believed. It is also the fundamental principle which makes possible a scientific theology, which gives full scope to rational enquiry and is fully aware of the varying degrees of definitiveness and clarity with which theological affirmations have been made and can be made by the Church. Some of those who are particularly worried at the moment seem to be unaware of this, and do not realise that whenever theology has been most scientific and most deferential towards the magisterium it has always by the same token been particularly aware of the nuances involved in utterances about the content of faith. And on the other hand, those wishing to emphasise variety and diversity at the present time do not always sufficiently recognise the importance of there being a detached scientific theology, interested only in establishing what is or is not of faith without having immediate pastoral and missionary problems in mind. For human progress, pure theology is as essential as pure research in the field of the natural sciences.

Theology of this kind is an activity carried on by minds informed by the full scope of the faith. Catechetics is an activity aimed at forming those minds. It presumes an attitude of faith and seeks to build it up correctly. It is therefore concerned with religious education at every level, and with the variety of methods by which this is achieved. It is possible that it has in recent years become confused with the pursuit and construction of scientific theology, concentrating on teaching a particular theology of its own, with a strong emphasis on salvation history, and not concerning itself sufficiently with method and with preparing minds to reflect responsibly on the reasons for which we believe and on the doctrinal content and practical application of the Gospel. Catechetics does not have to re-write theology, still less reconstruct the faith, to be effective. It presumes, of course, a serious biblical, historical and theological formation, but as an art and as a science it is something distinct from the proper study of these areas of knowledge. It must not become a process of indoctrination in an ideology and it must emphasise at the appropriate times both the historical, imaginative and practical aspects of Christian belief and the rational and loving contemplation of the timeless and eternal God to whom our life is leading us.

There has been an immense gain in the swing away from a catechetics which seemed to mean the pumping of speculative theology of the scientific kind to which I have first referred into minds which were unready for it. But this has meant a decline in the use of the memory in religious education and here, per- haps, a mistake has been made. We should not abandon mem- ory work simply because the old catechism was too abstract; we should give the memory the right kind of literary, imagina- tive and factual material on which to feed itself. With this kind of education as a basis, catechetics can then go on to include at the sixth form and adult stages a proper encouragement to reflect in a critical and philosophical way about our beliefs.

There is a third level of Christian education which can per- haps be discussed in more detail on another occasion, but which should be mentioned here in order to situate catechetics in relationship to its other neighbour. As well as being distin- guished from scientific theology, it should also be differentiated from the proclamation of the faith to those who do not at present believe. Catechesis and kerygma are not the same thing. There has also been a confusion in the past between kerygma and speculative theology. We have spent too much time defending every aspect of a developed theology to audiences who were quite unprepared for it. We need to think much more about the essential heart of the faith and the way in which this can be expressed to those who must see the faith as a whole, as some- thing at once simple and sufficient for a lifetime, so that they can make the necessary assent of mind and will by which the first all-important and all-involving step is taken on the path of the Gospel.

May 1971

215

A VOICE FROM THE PAST

'CATECHETICS continues to be a centre of controversy' was the opening sentence of the editorial in May 1971. I make no apology for returning yet again to this vital subject.

Even though many priests and teachers used the 'penny' catechism in the instruction of children and converts until comparatively recently, dissatisfaction with its language, its presentation, its order, its emphasis, was frequently voiced over the last half-century by almost all sections of the Catholic community. As long ago as 1930 Canon Drinkwater was expressing grave misgivings over the use of the catechism in school.

An attempt was made from time to time to improve it. One remembers, for example, Cardinal Heenan's simplification of the early 1960s: an attempt that, for some reason, was stillborn. Perhaps it was even then realised that simply to remove difficult phrases would not convert a text projecting such a diminished view of God and man and life into one which would convey something of the joy and spontaneity of the Christian's living relationship with the living God.

It seems incredible therefore that this catechism, to all intents and purposes identical with one last revised almost a hundred years ago, is now republished by the Catholic Truth Society, 'Approved by the Archbishops and Bishops of England and Wales and directed to be used in all their Dioceses'. The handout issued by the CTS states that the catechism is issued with 'the minimum of alteration to bring it up to date'.

Notices were sent to many, if not all, our schools. Teachers are very naturally confused. Many of them had come to accept the advice of their Diocesan Catechetical Centres that the best type of 'catechism' is one devised by the teacher, one specially tailored to meet the needs and ability of a particular set of children. Moreover, when the teachers opened this 'up to date' catechism they found absolutely nothing of the advances made by the two Popes and the assembled Fathers of the Second Vatican Council. (For that matter, Leo XIII's *Rerum Novarum*, Pius XII's *Mediator Dei* and *Mystici Corporis* are ignored.) Not a hint that our understanding of the Sacraments and liturgy has been greatly enriched. Not a word about our closer relationship with other Christian bodies. Still the same old archaisms ('What is the duty of masters and mistresses and other superiors?'); still the same two questions disposing of the whole mystery of the Resurrection; the emphasis throughout on 'what must I do' and hardly a word to describe what God has done for us, a myopic view indeed of God's love for men; still the same legalistic, triumphalistic, impersonal understanding of religion. Can the bishops of our country be serious in wanting this gravely deficient account of our Faith to be a guideline for Catholics, adults or children?

One might also ask why the Diocesan Directors of Catechetics were not consulted before the publication of the catechism. It appears that they were as surprised at its publication as the teachers. It will be for them to clear up the resulting confusion and explain that the bishops simply cannot intend children and adults to be deprived of the vision implicit in the developing doctrine of Vatican II.

The instigators of this reprinting and the revisers of the text would no doubt be the first to affirm their loyalty to Rome. And yet the advice of the Directory of Catechetics published by the Congregation for the Clergy (11 April 1971) is strangely ignored: 'Educated Christians today experience difficulty in talking about their Faith, which they believe is too bound up with obsolete formulas or with Western culture. They seek a new way of expressing religious truth, a way more in harmony with the manner in which men live and speak today, which will make it possible for faith to throw light on the real problems of contemporary man and to address itself to every culture' (par. 8). The document also makes it quite clear that doctrinal formulations must be accommodated to the capacity of those being catechised.

This affair provides another example of the recurrent lack of communication between the bishops and their officers, between hierarchy and people.

November 1971

217

THOUGHTS UPON FAITH IN A TIME OF CATECHETICAL CONTROVERSY

FAITH never stands still. Faith is the presistent following of God wherever he leads us, through all the shocks, disappointments and rewards of life. It does not depend upon health or success or fruition; it lasts through sickness and obscurity and it is our support at the time of death. It gives us enough encouragement to keep going, but never so much that we think we have arrived.

Faith is not the answer to all our problems. It supplies the materials and the atmosphere in which problems can be solved, but it does not do for us what we can and must do for ourselves. It gives the patience and security needed to live through times when the ordinary props of life have been removed: when a man loses his job, when a woman's husband leaves her, when incurable disease strikes in the freshness of youth. It supplies the flexibility of mind and the courage needed to respond to these challenges and not to be beaten down by them. And if it does these things, then post-conciliar re-education is not much to ask of professional men of faith.

Faith believes in the Church as God makes it, not as man has made it: in Christ the Head of the Church, in the Holy Spirit who lives in Christ and in us, and in the simple patterns of life which express our being in Christ and our life in the Spirit.

Men believe in the human Church rather than in God when they can only 'hold on to the faith' by living in the past: when instead of testing all things by the light of faith to discover the good that is in them, they either fail to discern anything new or else reject what they see as passing fashion, jargon without meaning or crazy novelty.

Faith is clear-eyed. It does not live in a state of fret, depression, ill-temper, suspicion, uneasy self-defence, anger, anxiety or brash contempt. It does not bang doors or make accusations. It speaks the persuasive language of reasonableness, not the factious rhetoric of the reformer or the slick repartee of the salesman whose product and whose firm must never be faulted.

When instead of faith we have a reforming ideology or else excuses and self-justification, then things have gone very wrong. In teaching the faith, for example . . .

May 1972

RECEIVING THE WORD

IN the churches visited this summer, it was the space behind the high altar in St Peter's, Rome, that most effectively invited people to pray. There, more than anywhere else, beneath Bernini's *cathedra Petri* and the Dove, they obviously found quiet and inspiration. For the Church today, this sets the pattern: the deep refreshment to be drawn from the Word of God proclaimed and from the Spirit.

There is no faith without hearing, no light for the mind without listening. God waits on our attention, and when it is given, gently leads our understanding forward. However ready our hearts, we are slow to learn. There is so much to absorb, so much to transpose into everyday habits and actions.

We do not truly understand the Church unless we realise that it is continually receiving and responding to the Word and the Spirit. The Gospels and the other New Testament writings were themselves in this way received by the Church; reception, guided by the Spirit, was active as well as passive; it ended in the judgement by which the canon of scripture was settled, but the labour of comprehension has still not come to an end. The early Councils also had to be sifted and received by the Church; their authority was only recognised and granted after they had taken place, and their precise bearing and significance are still under constant consideration.

The Church lives by the turmoil of debate. The Word divides, the Spirit brings turbulence. Peace in this world is only found at the heart of a storm. Receiving the words of Christ in the Church that he teaches always means effort, struggle and change.

Ex sese, non autem ex consensu Ecclesiae. Peter does not need our consent or our ratification when he speaks words that unfailingly bind the Church of which Christ has made him the shepherd and servant. But it remains for the Church to receive his words, to read them in context, to make them part of its mind, to reflect upon them and to push forward its understanding. Towards the teaching of the Church, expressed in its various ways with their varying degrees of authority, two attitudes deny both faith and reason: rejection and unthinking acceptance. The Church always, in due time, takes another way. Pius IX needed Dupanloup, Vatican I needed the German bishops, to get their meaning across.

Fides est cum assensu cogitare. Assent and thought are required in the reception of doctrine that is the formative activity of the Church. Where that reception is not going on, the Church cannot exist. To emphasise the need for it is not to deny the authority of the Church; on the contrary, it indicates that the Church's authority is being taken seriously.

Popes and Councils exist to give us something to work on. Determining and acknowledging the authority of their documents is only the first part of the study that is called for; the more important labour of discovering their meaning lies ahead. We are still examining the decrees of the Council of Trent and correcting certain hasty and one-sided interpretations that have been current since the sixteenth century, with results that have perpetuated old obstacles or set up new ones in the way of Christian mission and unity.

This active reception of doctrine within the communion of the Catholic Church is the only approach to Christian truth that meets scientific standards. It makes possible the progressive investigation, comprehension and development of doctrine. Without the constant interplay of defining authority, pastoral practice, missionary dialogue and scholarly study, Christianity would be no more than the respectful reminiscence of things past or an unending parade of contemporary private opinion. Without reference to the decisive action of other minds appointed and guided by the Holy Spirit in the Church, the work of theologians would simply represent the swing of emphasis from one momentarily dominant school of thought to another, without the possibility of ever arriving at conclusions on which Christians could rely. Illustrations of this have never been wanting in this country.

Those who want to use the Christian religion as social cement, from the somewhat bewildered Emperor Constantine to the traditionalists of today, are always disappointed when they find that it does not work that way. Seeds shatter concrete. The Church is not for trimmings either. The Pope cannot be an honorary president of Christendom, because he deals with people and with a living faith. Honorary prime ministers, honorary train-drivers, honorary trade union officials, honorary parents, honorary ship's captains are just as unthinkable. In a society held together by real teaching that is being absorbed by real minds, a real authority is needed. The Papacy is not only the ultimate institutional safeguard of freedom of conscience; it is the ultimate guarantee that the investigation of matters purporting to be revealed by God will not be a waste of intellectual effort.

But when it comes to assuring our own future, then the keyes are in our own hands. The reception of doctrine is no new-fangled theory aimed at circumventing authority; it is purely and simply the act of faith by which we are saved.

October 1977

PASTORS AND TEACHERS

EVER since a Danish Dominican friend of mine gave me a glowing report of the work of Fr Jérome Hamer, one of his lecturers at Le Saulchoir, I have entertained respectful and kindly thoughts of the Frenchman who is now Archbishop Hamer, Secretary of the Sacred Congregation for the Doctrine of the Faith. In 1962, he published *The Church is a Communion,* a key study of one of the master themes of Vatican II. His book on Karl Barth established him, also before the Council, as one of those best qualified for ecumenical dialogue and reconciliation. His admirable address to a meeting of bishops in Washington on 12 November 1978, on the theme 'What is a Bishop For?' shows that he is as well-informed, as precise, as constructive and as invigorating a man as ever.

In the final paragraphs of this address, for example, he points out that while a university, for all its concern with teaching, may well be presided over at times by 'a politician, an administrator, a banker or even a general', because of organi-

CARDINAL
1985
RELIGIOUS
+ SECULAR
INSTITUTES

221

sational needs that bring political questions into the foreground the same can never be said of a diocese.

> Whatever the circumstances may be, organisation can never override the primary and permanent task of evangelisation. All others are subordinated to this principal aim, including organisation, the importance of which must, nevertheless, be admitted. Always and everywhere the preaching of the Gospel will be imposed on the bishop, not only as a personal duty, but as the first of his duties.

There was a time when very few people expected a bishop to be primarily a teacher. Now that we are so constantly being reminded that teaching is his principal concern, and with appointments more accurately reflecting the mind of the Church in this matter, it was to be expected that tensions would arise of the kind that have recently been in the public eye.

It is certainly not the function or the intention of the *Review* to take sides in the present debate.[1] We have for quite a number of years now provided a means of expression for all points of view within the Church and of communication with other religions and philosophical traditions, and that will continue to be our policy. But it may be worth while offering some suggestions about the way in which the administration of the Church and the activity of all those who study and teach may be made to function more harmoniously and be seen, at any rate in the eyes of our friendly critics, to be more fully in accord with the workings of Christian revelation than they appear at present.

The strictures of the letter in *The Times* from the eighty-three theologians on 1 December 1979 on the enquiry into the writings of Fr Schillebeeckx — its secrecy, the fact that it made no distinction between the responsibilities of theologians and those of the Church's pastors, and its inconsistency with fundamental human rights — did not attract as much sympathetic support in the correspondence columns as the signatories perhaps expected. Its second and third counts may reasonably be considered off target. Just as it is the first responsibility of the

---

[1] See p. 321, entries for 13-14 and 18 December 1979.

pastors of the Church to teach, so it is the first responsibility of the teachers of the Church to be pastors. Any attempt to make a radical distinction between their roles must be resisted in the name of the most fundamental principles of the Christian religion itself. For the same reasons, it is also quite wrong to say that the bishops must be conservative, while the academic theologians must be exploratory and progressive. That would be to set up a permanent source of tension in the life of the Church and to relegate the supreme authorities to a nursemaiding role which they should rightly reject out of hand.

As Archbishop Hamer says in his address to the American bishops, 'A theologian is above all a believer'. His situation is exactly the same as that of the rest of us in the Church. It is only through his life in the contemporary Church that he finds Christ, and seeks to understand and to obey him. His efforts to express his faith must take the form of a conversation with the rest of us. No artist, no thinker, no poet, no scientist, is exempt from this; he has to communicate with his fellow human beings, putting up with incomprehension at times as well as deriving satisfaction from the welcome he receives. This is true of every form of human enquiry; and in the Church which is essentially communion, communication is found and lived at its greatest intensity.

Lack of communication with fellow-members of the Church — not only with Rome, but with his fellow scholars, many of whom found his work seriously wanting — is the most obvious fault in the public behaviour of Fr Hans Küng. For this reason, it is difficult to see what other steps Rome and the German bishops could have taken. It is however unfortunate that the bone of contention which the documents in the case made most obvious should be the doctrine of infallibility. A far more serious flaw than this, undermining the value of most of what he has written, is his understanding of the work of God's grace. It is the nature of the life of the ordinary individual Christian that is the essential issue here, not clerical authority.

The Church's institutions will never be perfect, whatever passionate intellectuals may desire or say. But that also means that there will always be room for improvement. The Congregation for the Doctrine of the Faith will need to prove that its secrecy is no more harmful to public order than that of our

Privy Council. To do that, it needs an executive arm as well as a judiciary. In other words, its principal function must be that which its Secretary urges on all the bishops: to teach.

The good teacher knows how to encourage as well as to warn, to give good marks as well as bad. We shall listen to Rome still more readily if its congregations can take to heart the bracing comment of the poet Roy Campbell:

> They use the snaffle and the curb all right,
> But where's the bloody horse?

March 1980

THEOLOGY AND THE PARISH

A PARTICULAR weakness of English Catholic life at this moment is the absence of any serious sustained writing on the intellectual content of the Christian faith. Some of those who established our reputation for being able to provide a coherent and systematic body of thought worthy of the attention of alert and able minds, are still with us. But it is not yet clear whether they have any successors: whether another generation of thinkers capable of sustained and persistent work, undistracted by ephemeral controversy, is ready to devote themselves to demonstrating the solidity and exploring the riches of Christian belief and experience.

It is sometimes suggested that *The Clergy Review* should leave such preoccupations as those just set down to others; that they are not the affair of the parish clergy, simple men looking after simple people, and that they should be regarded as the special responsibility of intellectuals, of those few people who are interested in speculation and argument and who actually prefer reading and thinking to other pursuits of a more ordinarily human kind.

But a division of labour of this kind would be a serious mistake in pastoral method. The presbytery, not the monastery or the lecture room, is the focal point of communication and organisation for the whole apostolate. In every centre of population, there is an intellectual battle to be fought. There are universities, there are adult education colleges, there are schools, there are the competing religious sects each with their arguments and counter-arguments: every parish should be aware of the places where enquiry and teaching are going on and capable not just of meeting local needs but of stimulating and satisfying the desire to know and to study the teaching of Christ and his church.

It is all too easy for priests to fall into the routine of saying Mass and making the sacraments available and to neglect the constant need to fill these regular activities with a teaching that is kept fresh and adapted to local and personal concerns. Teaching — getting the Gospel across — is the characteristic responsibility of the priest, without which everything else loses its point and its effectiveness.

It would be a betrayal of Catholic ideas if they were confined to the pages of books and to academic debate and were not given shape in local Catholic communities. Retreat centres, convents, monasteries, chaplaincies and teaching institutions of all kinds only exist in order to service the Body of Christ, which must live not just in artificial environments of this kind but in the organic, living context of complete human societies. That is why *The Clergy Review* insists so much on bringing the university world into close contact with practical parish life, and on supplying all those who live and work in parish surroundings with the coherently thought-out results of specialist study, so that they may be equipped to deal with problems which sooner or later will crop up in the homes and families with which they are directly concerned.

At the same time, it is the particular responsibility of the clergy, of those who are ordained to be servants of the Word of God, to see that the life of the Church is not directed by opinion, by sociological, financial and political pressure or by human interest, but is kept on a true path by considerations derived above all from its faith. Theology tells us who we are; it helps us to know God's revealed purpose and achievement. We are only too well aware of our inadequacies, our weakness under stress, our failures; if we are to rise above them and find our way, we need the vision which it is the work of the theologian to provide.

In the 1980s, it will be the particular preoccupation of any theologian worthy of his salt to take the expression of Catholic faith in English far beyond the old exchanges of Protestant and Catholic, beyond even the ecumenical pacification that we have reached, and to articulate for us an understanding which speaks for a generation that thinks in terms of the world scientific community and of the world religious community. Catholicism must be shown to meet the demands of minds that having encompassed the earth in search for truth find that the ultimate solution of their problems still escapes them. It must not appear to be a substitute for thought, but a true stimulus and nourishment for thought: a faith driving us to seek understanding not just of itself but of all that there is.

A parish priest whose horizon is his parish has ceased to be a real priest. A priest's work consists of opening doors; in every place, a Catholic parish should be a gateway to being at home in God's world.

November 1980

VII

THE ROAD TO UNITY

ECUMENISM AND THE ESTABLISHMENT

ONE does not need a very profound acquaintance with human nature to realise that ecumenism, that apparently most idealistic of activities, can be pursued for a variety of motives, some of which, by their place in the mixture, are bound to impede the attainment of the aim in view. To work for Christian unity may represent the postponement of a personal decision about the nature of unity itself; it may stem from a dislike of ever having to disagree with anyone; or it may be an attempt to inject new life and significance into an ecclesiastical tradition which is in fact beyond repair.

Ecumenical endeavours have a long history, and results so far hardly measure up to the effort involved. Should not ecumenists begin by taking the Church as given and working from there, instead of regarding disunity as the primary datum and attempting to do something about it in the light of some blue-printed but as yet unfulfilled master plan? The Catholic answer to this question is so well known that we do not need to put it forward very much these days, and are able to take it as read in all discussions in favour of unity.

For the sake of ecumenism, we have adjusted our way of life quite considerably in recent years, and have listened to the criticisms and complaints of others. It should not, therefore, be misconstrued as elder-brotherism if we ask that the Church of England should do something explicit and positive by way of a move in our direction. We are encouraged to ask this by the fact that many Anglicans in important positions recognise that their Church has not as yet committed itself to renewal to anything like the same extent as we have done.

The principal issue here is the continuation of the Estabishment in its present form, since, as long as it lasts, unity will be impossible. The stumbling-block is not the choice of bishops by the Crown; it is quite conceivable that the State should retain a working arrangement with a future united Church in England for making appointments, if some collaboration of this kind were needed to satisfy public opinion, although in fact Catholic and Protestant thought is less and less well disposed towards the setting-up of political links of this kind, which are a hindrance to the Church's responsible action as critic and reformer of society.

The real problem here is the inability of the Church of England within its present constitution to pronounce for its own members on doctrine and on liturgy. Until it can speak for itself with authority on these matters, it will not be able to take the necessary steps to make intercommunion possible with ourselves. Decisions on our side making clear what conditions we regard as necessary for communion can only make our own altars more or less 'open' to other Christians. Genuine intercommunion requires decisions from two or more parties. Is it conceivable that the Anglican Church, as things are at present, could make a declaration committing itself to Catholic belief in the Eucharist and in its significance for the assent of faith and for ecclesial reality which would be sufficiently binding to make intercommunion possible?

The answer would be Yes, if the link with Parliament could be removed. While that link remains, the decision could and would be contested. The impossibility of bringing the controversy to a satisfactory conclusion within the Parliamentary framework means that the Church of England would in fact shrink from entering on a public controversy of this kind.

A decision to ask Parliament to give the Church of England freedom to be its own master in doctrine and liturgy would be the best evidence from their side of a firm intention to seek unity. It is quite certain that were Anglicans to agree to make this request, Parliament would grant it. What good reason can there possibly be for any delay?

February 1973

AUTHORITY: CONSENSUS, NO;
CONVERGENCE, YES

I REMEMBER once sitting in the Station Hotel in York at the time of an Anglican diocesan conference. One heard snatches of clerical tea-time conversation drifting across the room: the older groups were discussing finance, and the younger ones authority. Age and experience instil a sense of priorities, as the parish priest might say; or was it that in those days authority could still be treated as an academic subject, a topic of conversation peculiarly suited to those who were hardly weaned from their books, with ordination just behind them?

Whatever the answer appropriate to those days, authority cannot any longer be treated as a subject to be studied once and then taken for granted. In law, government, education, morals as in church affairs, it is sought for and not found; 'Because I say so', is no longer a sufficient answer for anyone, even if the 'I' is the Church or the British Constitution and way of life.

The Agreed Statement on Authority in the Church from the Anglican/Roman Catholic International Commission must be read in the context of this contemporary search for a renewed grasp of the fundamental principles of civilised living. It is not just a matter of two churches agreeing to live in greater harmony or even to arrange a merger. What is at stake is our understanding of the whys and wherefores of the Christian religion: the strengthening of conviction, the clarifying of intelligence, the readiness and completeness of obedience. Can eighteen good men and true, the best that their respective churches could find, give us such a lead that we shall feel bound to follow, so as to establish a single communion where at present there are two and to make our common faith more clearly recognisable as the unique source of human fulfilment?

Ten years have gone by since the first preparatory meeting at Gazzada in Northern Italy. Two documents have so far been published, on the Eucharist and on Ministry. Neither of these has yet been given any kind of officially accepted status, but both of them have been welcomed by Catholic theologians as statements which reveal much more common ground than we have shared in the past and at the same time adequately represent our own faith, when read in the context of the relevant documents of the Church.

The question in everybody's mind was: will the third document, on Authority, enable us to say that both sides accept that context? If we cannot agree on the sources to which the first two agreed statements refer, then we have achieved nothing more than a temporary fellow-feeling among theologians under the pressure of passing fashion. If we are to be one in faith, and not simply in theology, then we must come to the same understanding of the way in which that faith is called into being, nourished and maintained. Does this new document enable us to say that this point has been reached by this highly equipped, well run-in team of front-line researchers? Has the breakthrough been made?

The answer is 'Not Yet'. The statement speaks of a consensus; this may indeed have been reached by the commission members themselves at their Venice meeting, though it is notable that for the first time they found it necessary to list four difficulties felt especially by Anglican members and not yet satisfactorily resolved for them by Catholic scholars. But it will not receive the same degree of support from Catholic theologians as did the other two documents, and so cannot be said to represent a consensus of a wider kind. 'Convergence', a word used three times in the penultimate paragraph, in which the word 'consensus' does not, incidentally, appear, would be much nearer the mark. Since that convergence includes some affirmations which, from the Anglican side, are both striking and generous, it is not by any means negligible, and is in fact full of promise for the future. But in various important respects the document is less satisfactory than its predecessors and is disappointingly less *au fait* with current theological progress outside the Commission.

The Preface, signed by the two Co-Chairmen, Bishop Clark and Bishop McAdoo, speaks of the distinction between the 'ideal' and 'the actual' as being an important one for the reading of the document and for an understanding of its method. Christ willed 'the ideal of the Church' and the Church 'has often failed to achieve this ideal'. One finds the Commission here falling at the outset into one of the oldest blunders in the ecumenical business. 'Ideal' and 'actual' are not terms that can be used appropriately of the Church of the New Testament. The whole point of Christ's work was that the ideal *was* the actual: that he established the Church, with all its human imperfections, as a permanent basis, and that it was precisely in the 'actual' Church that one found the 'ideal'. He did not give the Apostles a blueprint, telling them to get on with building according to a theoretical, drawing-board pattern. He gave them the Church itself and told them to go on building; the pattern would emerge later. The 'ideal' and 'actual' distinction has been responsible for most of the separations and divisions in the history of the Church and it is hardly likely to help us to bridge them today.

The second flaw in the general tenor of the document is its subjectivity. One misses a sense of the given, of the objective facts which it must be the purpose of any scientific enquiry to discover. Much is said of the process by which discovery is made; less is affirmed about the way in which the finds got there in the first place. The first paragraph of the Introduction starts out by speaking of 'The Confession of Christ as Lord', and so of man's response; in a document on authority, it would have been more appropriate to start from the initiative of God: The Revelation of Christ as Lord. We need to know clearly who the author was in the first place, and just how authoritative he is.

The third weakness consists in the apparent reluctance of the document to say anything of the direct relationship of the Church and its authority with the historic Christ. We are told that, through the work of the Spirit, the apostolic community 'came to recognise in the words and deeds of Jesus, the saving activity of God' and 'transmitted what they had heard and seen', but an essential step before that transmission is omitted, one that St Irenaeus, for example, the first great exponent of authority in the Church, is careful to include: the handing-on by Jesus himself of his message to the community which he had brought into being and which was in fact inseparable from that message: its living expression, the New Covenant now consummated between God and man. The Church was not an after-thought, not even an after-thought of the Holy Spirit; it was brought into existence by the Word. Indeed, if we follow the Acts of the Apostles, it was that Word.

In paragraphs 5 and 6, the historic and functional link of the bishops with the apostolic college is similarly omitted. Their responsibility is not simply one of 'general oversight', discernment', and 'giving authentic expression'; as successors of the apostles, they safeguard the faith once delivered. To 'preserve the integrity of the *koinonia*' they are in the first place and above all servants of the Word of God, of the message from the preaching of which the community comes into being. One cannot say that a text in which this aspect of the bishops' rôle does not clearly emerge adequately represents the essentials of Catholic faith: no consensus here.

In section III, 'Authority in the Communion of the Churches', the ticklish problem of the Papacy is dealt with by starting from local churches and then working towards the universal *koinonia*. The explanations given of the historical development whereby the see of Rome 'eventually became the principal centre in matters concerning the Church universal' will do a great deal to clear away misconceptions; but the co-existence, so to speak, of local and universal church is not brought out sufficiently clearly. The first local church was, after all, also the universal Church; the Church was already universal on the day of Pentecost. Although strictly speaking a local council, the Council of Jerusalem can also be regarded as universal, given the bearing of its decision; and it is significant that Peter was there. These points are obscured in what is said of the Council of Jerusalem in paragraph 9. It is not enough to say, as in paragraph 11, that 'the purpose of *koinonia* is the realisation of the will of Christ', expressed in John 17; the *koinonia* is that realisation; the purpose cannot be brought to fulfilment unless its achievement has already begun. For that reason, bishops do more than 'seek the fulfilment of the will of Christ' (n. 9); they obey, and call upon others to obey, the already present, effective expression of that will.

Section IV, 'Authority in Matters of Faith', is very much the best part of the document; the apparent shying away from infallibility is repaired in Section V, where we are told that decisions of ecumenical councils on fundamental matters of faith 'exclude what is erroneous', and are 'protected from error'.

Matters Arising

When we reach Section VI, on 'Problems and Prospects', we are brought up rather sharply against some areas of incom-

233

prehension that do not so much undermine what has been said before — in which there is so much cause for gratitude and, indeed, rejoicing — as make one think how much better the document could so easily have been. This section lists four problems still to be resolved. The first concerns the use of the Petrine texts in Scripture to support Roman claims. Here we are left with the vague statement, astonishing in its feebleness, that 'many Roman Catholic scholars do not now feel it necessary to stand by former exegesis of these texts in every respect'. The Commission presents the whole thing in terms of the long out-moded style of partisan controversy and appears to be unaware of the long ecumenical investigation of this subject from Oscar Cullmann and Otto Karrer down to the Lutheran-Catholic discussions of the present day. They should have shown themselves in touch with the far wider and deeper vision now available of this theme, quite different from the view arising out of the old polemics — which sees the rock-principle as inherent in the entire tissue, flesh and bone, of the Church. It is a principle of faith before it is a principle of government, and it is only a principle of government because it is a principle of faith. It controls the micro-organism in the Church in the same way as it controls the macro-organism of the Church, and it is precisely for this reason that the Church holds together with such firmness. Certainly, we have abandoned much of former exegesis; but we have done this in favour of much better exegesis, putting the whole thing on a sounder footing, and this the Statement fails to reflect. It speaks at one point (n. 12) of explaining the importance of the Bishop of Rome 'by analogy with the position of Peter among the apostles', but this suggests that two distinct realities are involved, comparable with one another, and overlooks the essential continuity of function in the one community.

The second problem arises over the use of the language of 'divine right' of the successors of Peter; here some Anglicans feel that they are being unchurched by the papal claims. This question was so thoroughly gone into at Vatican II and has been so much discussed since, that one is bound to feel that the area of incomprehension is still disappointingly vast. What appears to be lacking here is a sense of the universal Church: catholicity is necessarily expressed by actual communion with the Church throughout the world, including, as the document says, the bishop of Rome with his universal primacy 'as part of God's design for the universal *koinonia*, and cannot be sufficiently expressed by the possession of 'catholic attributes' by a local church that is out of communion.

The third difficulty concerns Papal infallibility (as distinct from the infallibility of the Church, which seems to be acceptable). And this, of course, leads on to the Marian dogmas . . . The fourth difficulty is the Papal claim to universal immediate jurisdiction; the document makes a couple of suggestions that may in due course resolve this one.

In the first two Agreed Statements, one felt that one was reading the work of theologians who, working together, had produced new insights and a fresh synthesis from which all could profit. In this one, the strong impression is given of a Catholic team working hard (too hard?) to answer the questions and meet the objections of an Anglican one. This impression is strengthened by the reference in the Preface to the fact that 'we have not been able to resolve some of the difficulties of Anglicans concerning Roman Catholic belief relating to the office of the bishop of Rome'.

If more attention had been given to the real 'Authority in the Church', that is to say to the Word of God himself and to the manner of his presence with his Church for all time, instead of to the many kinds of subordinate authority, the Commission would have got much further forward. For the Church is not held together by these subordinate authorities, in whom, as in the ordinary members of the Church, we will never find perfection. The search for a perfect theology, for perfect popes and bishops, for perfect organisation, for overwhelmingly visible holiness, keeps many out of the Church, as it has led many out in the past. But the whole point of the Church is that those things are not to be found there; perfection is found in God alone, and to join his Church is to line oneself up with human sin. That is what he did himself; besides being the only motive strong enough to bring us into his Church, it is the only one that keeps us there and makes us live in hope.

March 1977

235

JUSTIFICATION BY FAITH

ANGLICAN Evangelicals have expressed their hope that the classic Reformation theme of Justification should come up for study by the Anglican/Roman Catholic International Commission. The Eucharist, Ministry, Authority: satisfactory progress has been made towards a common understanding, and, indeed, agreement on these themes, but what about personal religion? What about the heart of the matter: the individual's relationship with God? *Sola Scriptura:* here, Catholic and Protestant do seem to be getting beyond the long-lasting oppositions and partial views to a joint recognition of the one source of authority for us all: the living Word, Christ himself, and his relationship with his Church. But what of *Sola Fide, Sola Gratia?* Are we not still as divided as ever when it comes to understanding our way to salvation?

Many theologians working in the ecumenical field will have breathed a somewhat despairing sigh when they heard of the Evangelical demand for yet more weary investigation of what they thought were such well-trodden paths. The joint Anglican Evangelical/Roman Catholic study group which met regularly for years in this country, from well before ARCIC and ARC came into being, seemed to have done all it possibly could to establish understanding. If the Evangelicals are still not satisfied after all that talk and study, how can agreement ever be reached?

The impression has been given that the debate between Hans Küng and Karl Barth settled it all, and that after that the way was wide open for the complete settlement of the Catholic/Protestant quarrel. Unfortunately, the work was not in fact completed; they showed that Catholics and Protestants share the conviction that justification comes from God alone, by his grace, but they did not reach a common mind over the effect of justification: over the holiness which we receive. The effect of grace in raising up and restoring us in our very selves, so that we do not simply enjoy a new relationship, but become new creatures: this was not agreed.

On this point, of course, hang not only the nature of the Church and of the sacraments, but the entire spiritual life of every Christian. It seems to Catholics that Protestants do not really believe in the triumph of God's grace, in his power to remake us in his image. They would therefore lack the essential basis for confidence, for hope, for growth in Christ. At any rate, this appears to be the consequence of Protestant theory: Protestant experience and testimony tell us otherwise.

And it seems to Protestants that Catholics rely too much on human effort, on physical demonstrations of devotion, on grace as a state rather than grace as a life and a power.

So perhaps we do need a Joint Statement on this theme after all. But not 'Justification by Faith': that sounds too much like morbid brooding over the past unhappiness of battles long ago. 'The Remaking of Man' would bring us more surely to the heart of the matter. What do we believe God to be doing in history? Is the Kingdom of Heaven effectively among us? Not conditionally, or hypothetically, but in a reality that anticipates and pledges our future?

Puritanism has often seemed to be more of a return to the Old Testament than a joyous acceptance of the new Dispensation. Within our English history, we now need to grasp more intelligently the full extent of the radical change in the human situation brought about by the birth of Christ for our salvation. The New Reformation of the late twentieth century will be the achievement of those Christians who are prepared to accept in themselves and for others the transforming power of their faith in the victory of the Cross.

December 1977

COMMUNION

THE social cohesion of the Catholic Church stems from a single, very simple, principle: our relationship with Christ is public as well as private. The Christian is not an isolated individual; he is part of a people.

This principle is vividly expressed in the 'body-language' used by the Church. The Body of Christ is both food and ourselves. To give or receive communion is to give or receive the community. Holy communion communicates everything. It must not be thought of as just one among God's many gifts; it contains everything else.

The Archbishop of Canterbury has asked us to give him and every Anglican holy communion. He has asked us for all we have. Those who receive communion at Catholic altars, those who concelebrate, or those who offer eucharistic hospitality in the community of which they have pastoral charge, must discern what it is they are doing. They are receiving, or they are giving, the whole Body of Christ; the Person, the food, the faith and the fellowship. Christ himself did not distinguish one from the other, and we are in no position to do anything different.

If this is indeed what Dr Coggan wants, then we must give it now. It is too easy just to say 'not yet' or to shelter behind church discipline. We must give the Catholic faith, whole and entire, to all who receive, or who ask to receive, holy communion; we must give them the grace of absolution in the sacrament of penance; and we must take them into the working family of the Church. Those who receive holy communion receive both its meaning and its practice.

Intercommunion could start tomorrow if the Anglicans or the Methodists or any other church made it clear that in coming to our altars they are ready to receive in faith all that we have to give. This is what every Catholic does; it is unthinkable that we should offer some partial gift. There is nothing one-sided about such a solution, for we ourselves are waiting to receive all they have to give. Not their denials, for no one can live on negation, but everything positive by which their Christian life is nourished and expressed.

Some Catholics talk of changing the regulations for holy communion as if what they really wanted were an easing of social relationships at their daughter's wedding. They regard hesitations as bigotry; they grow puzzled and indignant when their clerical friends accept the Church's discipline. But communion is no transitory relationship, and must not be reduced to the level of a one-night stand.

Communion means being one church. In the entire Christian scheme of things, we do not become what we are not; we become what we are. To become more united, we must start by being united. In true sacramental theology, 'sign' and 'means' are never separated. And the eucharistic sign includes the constitutional bonds that express our fellowship. Those who distinguish and oppose 'law' and 'love', 'canons' and 'communion', forget that the Eucharist was given to us in legal terms; expressing Christ's final and perfect will, it is his new and eternal testament. A loving father draws up his will in the strict legal forms that are needed to preserve order and charity in his family.

The discipline of Rome, we are told, both attracts and repels. When it attracts, it is because it is the yoke of Christ. When it repels, it may be because of human inadequacy. Christ asks us to recognise and live with such inadequacy, so as to overcome it, as he did. When it repels, it may also be because our own sin refuses the weight of the Cross. There is no easy way to the restoration of unity in England. People dislike talk of 'submission'. But submission is what holy communion means. It meant that for Christ himself; it means that for every Catholic, who sees obedience to the bishops of the Church as a necessary part of his obedience to Christ. Without them, he would have no access to Christ, who chose to communicate only through his witnesses. We cannot give more than everything that makes us what we are; and just as certainly we cannot give less.

April 1978

THE FIRST DISCIPLE

ARCHDEACON BERNARD PAWLEY has perhaps by now repented the extraordinarily unperceptive and ungracious words which he used in the General Synod of the Church of England on Thursday 22 February. The record of the Catholic Church in this country as elsewhere does not justify the remark that it is essential 'for the people of the great Roman Catholic communion to wake from their slumbers', or the suggestion that the small (*sic*) RC communities in England and Wales are 'untypical of their communion'. This is no way to talk at any time, least of all in a debate on the three joint statements of the Anglican/Roman Catholic International Commission. All those who have given their friendship over the years since the Council to Archdeacon Pawley must have been disappointed and grieved that after all this time he could dismiss them so sweepingly; and when they hear public statements of this kind, those who still doubt the value of spending time working for unity between Canterbury and Westminster must naturally and inevitably feel that their hesitations are well founded.

Straightforwardness, not size, is the key to truth; progress towards unity demands the total abandonment of the sectarian and condescending style of talk about one another of which this is so unfortunate an example. Of whom are the Catholics of England and Wales supposed to be 'typical', except themselves? It is with us, in the first place, since we are their closest neighbours, that Anglicans must be united. Catholics in different countries all have their own distinctive local personality, appropriate to their circumstances and derived from their history; and we are the ones who are most familiar with the particular problems facing us before unity can be restored. Difficult or not, the dialogue with the Catholics of England and Wales is the one that most needs developing.

One of the places where that dialogue is going ahead most fruitfully is the Ecumenical Society of the Blessed Virgin Mary. But even there, it must be plainly said, in the interests of frank recognition of the barriers set up by entrenched attitudes, there is still room for improvement. A group photograph printed in the papers after a recent conference gave us a line-up of the distinguished speakers and leading supporters, coming from a variety of churches. The problem in assembling the group had obviously been: whom shall we put in the middle? But instead of the natural choice, the one layman present, Martin Gillett, moving spirit of the Society, there appeared, as if he were chairman, the clerical representative of the Archbishop of Canterbury. Martin Gillett's modesty no doubt contributed to keeping him from his due place; but at the same time, a certain ecumenical tact should restrain the Church of England on this and similar occasions from putting itself into the centre of the stage. Any observer could be pardoned for thinking that Anglican ecumenism is nothing other than British diplomacy carried on by other means, especially if he knew that correspondence between Lambeth and Ambrosden Avenue is carried on through Dr Coggan's Foreign Relations department.

The Anglican/Roman Catholic International Commission is now addressing itself to the doctrine of the Church. This was in fact originally suggested at the very first meeting (Gazzada, 1967) as the point at which conversations should begin, but a long run-up appears to have been found necessary. Whatever people think about that, one thing is clear: the Commission, like Vatican II, should include Our Lady in whatever it decides to say. Any statement about the Church which did not include some reflection on the place of Mary in the scheme of salvation would be regarded by Catholics as so seriously defective as to be unacceptable as a basis for establishing unity.

'May it be done unto me according to your word'. Our Lady was the first disciple of the New Testament; and discipleship is the fundamental category of ecclesiology. It is by obedience to the Word of God that we are knitted into the fabric of the Church; all relationships in Christ stem from that central decision. Mary's assent of faith made her the Mother of Our Lord; and since then, all others who do the will of the Father also become 'mother, sister and brother' to him.

The Church lives by the pattern of Mary's life, receiving God's blessing as a consequence of hearing the Word of God and keeping it. That is the central happening of every Mass; the Church is called together to hear God's Word and to be united with the obedience that the Son of God, the Word himself, once offered and offers now to the Heavenly Father. Without Mary's obedience, freely given by Mary herself and by ourselves in imitation of her, there would be no Church and there can be no Christian unity.

The Church is a family; those who wish to be called by the Christian name will only be brought into that one family if they are able to recognise in Mary's life the pattern of their own. Devotion to Our Lady must pass from the domain of a private society, however august and well-supported, to that of public declarations of faith. When the Archbishops of Canterbury and York go on pilgrimage to Walsingham (for example), intercommunion may begin to appear possible.[1] But until we know to what kind of faith the Church of England is committed (and devotion to Mary has always been a sovereign test), we cannot know what meaning they attach to communion.

Meaning is all-important. Faith is the recognition of the source of truth and the acceptance of what it says, to the limits of our understanding. That was how Mary believed; all who see their own faith in hers and act upon it will certainly be

[1] See p. 322, entry for 26 May 1980.

made one. In this there is no doubt of the thoroughly typical character of the Catholics of England and Wales throughout their unbroken local history. The work of the International Commission must help the Church of England to see in our faith the continuation of the simple discipleship, in loving assent to the Word of God and to his Spirit, of the woman who in accepting him became our Mother.

May 1979

THE RULE OF FAITH AND THE RECOVERY OF UNITY

WHEN I arrived at St Edmund's College, Ware, in 1962 as a fledgling member of the seminary staff, I received a somewhat chilly welcome from one of my new colleagues, who informed me that amongst other disadvantages I suffered from the fact of having moved from Anglican to Catholic communion and was on that account rendered useless for ecumenical work. I forbore from saying that I had been involved in ecumenical work for at least twelve years already and had been writing on ways of promoting unity between Canterbury and Rome when he was still sitting on a school bench.

There is nothing I hope for more than the restoration of full unity among English Christians. In the remarks that follow, there is only the desire to further, not to hinder, the purpose of the Anglican/Roman Catholic International Commission.

The Commission has published three Agreed Statements, on the Eucharist, on Ministry and on Authority, and it has now published its replies to comments on the first two statements (*Elucidations*, CTS/SPCK, 1979).

Do these *Elucidations* satisfactorily solve the problems that many of us, in both churches, have posed about the statements? The members of the Commission are unanimous in considering that they do; respect for their authority and experience certainly incline one towards wanting to share their conviction that if the authorities of the two communions were to make their assent, unity and concord would follow.

The statement on eucharistic doctrine, together with the answers to comments and criticisms now given, can if taken as a whole certainly be interpreted as an adequate affirmation of

Catholic faith on the particular points with which it deals. If it has really removed the traditional Evangelical objections, which presented the main problem for the Commission, then it is a remarkable achievement.

A doubt, however, remains. It arises because of the admission in the section on Reservation that 'In spite of this clarification, others still find any kind of adoration of Christ in the reserved sacrament unacceptable' (*Elucidations*, n. 9). It has been suggested both in the document and in published commentary on it, that this is a divergence of devotional practice that does not affect substantial agreement in eucharistic faith. Within the Catholic Church itself one finds, of course, divergent devotional practice; while very many express their devotion to the Blessed Sacrament reserved, very many others do not.

But where among Catholics there is no divergence at all is in the adoration of Christ's real presence in the Mass. Adoration is indeed offered to the Father through Christ, as the *Elucidations* correctly say. But we cannot truly worship 'through with and in' Christ, unless we acknowledge him as God: unless we are prepared to offer our worship to him as we make the acclamations, or as the celebrant lifts the Host before communion with the words 'This is the Lamb of God'. That Presence and our response to it is the heart of every other mode of presence in the Mass; it is the supreme sign of our reception in faith of the Word of God.

Once doubt has crept in over this point, it grows over the affirmation that

> even though the Church is active in this celebration, this adds nothing to the efficacy of Christ's sacrifice upon the cross, because the action is itself the fruit of this sacrifice (n. 5).

This is confusing. By becoming efficacious in this Mass, in this celebration, Christ's sacrifice is producing more fruit and is therefore most certainly adding something, which St Paul described as ours, because of Christ's work in us.

It looks as if sacrament as well as sacrifice demands more investigation before we can be sure that agreement has been reached. This conviction is strengthened by the fact that Holy Order is never described either in the second Agreed Statement or in these *Elucidations* as 'a sacrament'. The adjective 'sacramental' is used, but not the noun; an ambiguity remains. If there really is agreement over the nature of a sacrament, then ordination would clearly be seen to be one, along with the eucharist and baptism. All that we are given here by way of a definition is the statement that

> Both traditions agree that a sacramental rite is a visible sign through which the grace of God is given by the Holy Spirit to the Church (*Elucidations*, n. 13).

As a definition of a sacrament this is clearly inadequate. Let us hope that by 1980 yet more progress can be made.

Since the Malta Report of 1968, which spoke of growing towards unity by stages, there seems to have been a certain shift of emphasis on the work of the Commission. The Report did not speak, for instance, of 'communion by stages', though that idea has since come to the fore, and it has even been suggested, by the Church of England General Synod earlier this year, that we could think of entering into such 'communion by stages' while study of the Agreed Statements is still going on and before an official verdict has been reached. Is the one thing necessary being forgotten: the priority of faith?

The union that is sought between the Anglican Communion and the Catholic Church is a union of faith, hope and charity. The doctrinal discussions and the Agreed Statements that come from them can clear away obstacles, but if the work is to come to a successful conclusion, they will have to be completed by a joint confession expressing that living faith, the ground of our hope and the source of our charity.

For that reason, the discussions must aim not at resolving conflicts by a compromise, not at any face-saving formulae that leave our private thoughts exactly where they were before, but at a genuine solution. Minds must be clarified through the discovery of a new and richer expression of the faith, resulting from a full appreciation of all the elements of our present problem.

The Agreed Statements on the Eucharist and on Ministry can be regarded as warming-up exercises enabling the two groups taking part in the discussions to become accustomed to one another's methods and dominant concerns before tackling the more central question of Authority, where the reasons for faith and the rule of faith itself are directly under scrutiny. The selection of these themes arose, no doubt, out of the fact that our division at the level of worship is the most obvious to the ordinary church-goer and the papal judgement on Anglican Orders the most touchy matter in the mind of the ordinary clergyman. But even if perfect agreement had been reached on these issues — and it has not — it would not have sufficed to bring about lasting union and the further growth of the Church. Union at the level of worship and at the level of ministry would be a union of externals, a ceremonial, cosmetic union, if the principles of faith itself are not fully engaged. We have seen enough of this kind of fancy-dress approach to the problem of Catholic unity, with the holiday tourist element now increasingly being added, for us to realise how frivolous it is, how ridiculously unreal in the eyes of those who expect the Church to produce a serious answer to the problems of human conflict.

The Anglican/Roman Catholic International Commission must try to ensure that whatever it says on the further subjects of Authority and of the Church leads us towards a joint definition and affirmation of faith. It may well turn out that it does not directly bear on any of the more obvious issues on which we have come to disagree. My expectation is that it will be on the Church as bearer and teacher of the faith: the living expression of the living Word.

I say a joint statement of *faith* because by making such a statement both sides would acknowledge themselves to have been led to accept and exercise the power given by God to his Church of declaring our faith without misleading those who are called to share it. A profession of faith commits and binds the Church: for the union of the New Covenant, anything less is not enough.

It would also be a statement of *hope* because it would lead us all to find in the one Church of God the way to live our lives with confidence in the present and with no fear of the future: it would give us the fundamental reason for persevering in expectation of all the benefits unity would bring.

And it would be a statement of *charity* because it would be a single expression of minds, wills and hearts: communion in God, not a conference-table handshake.

Past Councils have produced their formulae, usually simple and brief ones, which, once accepted in faith, have given us unity and growth. These formulae have arisen out of conflict, out of the confrontation of views, within and without the Church, and out of the intense labour and suffering of those whose intellects and entire lives were given to finding them, in loyalty to the faith they had received and in answer to problems that their predecessors had not had to face.

I do not think that ARCIC can stop short now of looking for such a formula of union. If they find one, then four hundred and fifty years of church history will have ended by teaching us something fresh. It took as long to reach Chalcedon, and a great deal longer to arrive at other judgements which are now permanent acquisitions in the life of faith.

The alternative to such a clearing of minds would be shared ceremonies but an obscured Christ: devotion without doctrine, Scripture without a Saviour, the lessons of archaeology without teachers for today. Such solutions are already familiar; some people have fallen for them. They do not take the sixteenth-century conflicts or our past history since then, let alone the demands of Christ himself, with sufficient seriousness.

When Word and Church have come into focus as one reality, not two, the rest will follow. Until we come to share that clear vision, our paths may continue to converge, but they will not be one.

October and November 1979

THE MINISTRY AND SERVICE OF THE WORD

IT is unfortunate that many of those who have worked long and patiently to restore the unity of the Christian Church in this country should have concentrated their thoughts (and their votes) around the single question of the validity of ministerial orders. Solve that problem, it has been said, and all others will be solved. The Second Vatican Council had only to reverse *Apostolicae Curae*, and it would have taken its place for ever in the annals of English history. John Paul II has only to do what the Council failed to do, and his coming visit will be even more momentous than the sending of St Augustine by St Gregory the Great. Dr Runcie has only to stand by his side and say the same words of eucharistic consecration in Canterbury Cathedral, and the *Ecclesia Anglicana* will once again be *Romana* as well.

Such a solution is at once too simple and not simple enough. It is too simple in that it sees the Church as dependent entirely on the possession by individuals of special sacramental powers, so that wherever these powers are being correctly used, the Church is being built up, and wherever these powers are not possessed and in action, the Church is not being built up. An Anglican clergyman, for instance, can be convinced that he has these powers, and that he is doing for his church exactly what a Greek Orthodox or a Roman Catholic clergyman is doing in Athens or Rome. He may not be satisfied that a Methodist, for example, has them, and therefore does not want to envisage union with the Methodists without requiring some form of re-ordination. Another Anglican clergyman can be equally convinced that such powers as he has are already shared by the Methodist clergy; he therefore may not favour a scheme of union requiring any kind of re-ordination, lest his own present status be interpreted in an exclusive sense that he repudiates. And schemes can founder because rejected at the same time from these two contrary points of view.

But suppose the Church is not really centred upon clergymen requiring (or not requiring) these sacramental powers at all: what then? Is not this approach far too mechanical, fostering clericalism and irresponsible eccentricity, and reducing the sacraments to a kind of white magic?

It must be abundantly clear to any reader of the Acts of the Apostles that the means by which the Apostles gathered the Church together was their service of the Word of God. That was the priority required of them: only by communicating the message could the Church come into existence. They were creating a new human society by preaching the message committed to them. That society retained the pattern that originates in the Gospels: crowds gathering round Our Lord and his apostles. After the Ascension and Pentecost, that pattern remained. It was still Our Lord himself, the Word of God, who was at the centre, present now in a different way; and the communities built up by the apostles, as well as the community formed by the apostles themselves, reproduced the gospel pattern, grouping themselves round the pastors whom he chose and sent out.

247

Apostolic succession since that time is not a succession of a hereditary kind. The continuation of the New Testament pattern is typological, not genealogical: the preservation of the same type, the same recognisable set of relationships. The Word himself is received in that context: he is seen to be Lord because he is acknowledged and effectively obeyed by people who express his way of life in families he brings into being.

Ministry is nothing if it is not the service of the Word. Ministers of whatever church are in the first place commissioned to pass on the Word as understood by that church. It is not mutual recognition of orders that is required, so much as mutual recognition of the faith and teaching of other churches, on which orders depend. Every minister is a valid minister of his own church, since he has, by due authority, to speak in its name.

Unity must therefore come not by a recognition of one church's authority by another, not by borrowing systems of government, not by acquiring or sharing a validity of a restrictedly sacramental kind, but by a joint act of obedience to the same Word who is sovereign over all churches. Such an act of obedience would not be a repudiation of those who went before us: they had their decisions to make in their time, and their loyalty to the light that they saw was what was required of them in their own generation. In our own time, other decisions have to be made.

Each church must decide whether the living Word of God is not now asking it to receive in faith from a church now separate from it everything that church has to give, everything that it already gives, out of its hearing of the Word, to its own members. Churches do not live by negations; we can forget the denials we have made and which have led us apart. These denials have never provided the life-giving truths by which we have developed as Christians; it is only the positive, the affirmative, that we can give or receive.

Full theological agreement is not possible; it does not exist anywhere, in any church, and it is not even desirable. The simple question is not 'do we recognise one another's orders?' but 'do we recognise one another's faith?' If we do, then the further step of faith, of obedience to the Word as we hear him today, can confidently be taken.

The Times, 14 February 1981

VIII

THE POPE: ROMAN SYNODS

THE MESSAGE OF JOHN PAUL I

THE late Pope indicated in several ways and on several occasions his desire to be a pastor among pastors, a bishop among bishops. He would not govern alone. In his first message to the Catholic world, he spoke of his reliance on

> all the Bishops of the Church of God 'who represent their own particular Church and who together with the Pope represent the whole Church which is bound together in chains of peace, love and unity' (LG, n. 23). Their collegiality we wish strongly to emphasise and we want to make use of their efforts in the government of the Universal Church, whether through the Synod or through the structures of the Curia in which they take part by right according to the norms already laid down.

For the future development of the Church, no theme is more important. The Catholic Church does not 'descend' from Rome like some ever-broadening family tree, any more than it 'ascends' from Rome as if it were a cone balanced on its point. The Church, spread throughout the world, holds together because of its extremely simple and yet immensely strong cellular structure. As a living organism, it is at any one time and in any one place made present by each one of its local churches, with the bishop as nucleus. To see one part is to see and comprehend the whole, equally present in other parts of the world, with its centre (not its 'summit') in the Bishopric of Rome. It is Christ, in the midst of the Church, who gives it this pattern and this consistency; the rock-like certainty of each individual's faith in him is the characteristic also of the entire community into which he calls them.

Every enhancement of respect for the office of Supreme Pastor which each successive Pope is able to win from the world by his gifts and his labours enhances at the same time the standing everywhere of the office of bishop. Every strengthening of the Church of Rome means a corresponding strengthening of each local church. It is the task of each Pope not to make one man omnipresent and omnicompetent in the Church, but to make one charism truly effective in each place to which it has been given: to confirm his brethren, the successors of the Apostles, in the work they have to do together in the service of the Word of God.

This means that to look to Rome for everything weakens Rome itself and the whole Church of God. The health of the body is the health of every one of its parts. A strong Church in England and Wales means a correspondingly strong Church in Rome; an actively united Church in England, Ireland, Scotland and Wales would reinforce the unity of the Church everywhere else. Rome expects everyone to make their own distinctive contribution, and must not be looked to for everything that happens in the Church. John XXIII said that he was, after all, 'only the Pope'; Paul VI indicated that he did not intend to implement Vatican II with Vatican I methods; John Paul I remarked on the incongruity he saw in calling his blessing 'apostolic' when he gave it to his fellow-apostles, the bishops.

For the ecumenical effort, which the Pope considered 'the ultimate task of our immediate predecessors', and wished to continue, this means in the first place a fresh appreciation of the Catholic presence in this country. We must ask our fellow Christians to look once again at what we are trying to do by way of building a local Church in total obedience to the Gospel. Unity does not depend on whether or not we have a good Pope, a Pope with a sense of humour, an affable Pope or a liberal one. English people have welcomed and appreciated all these qualities of mind and heart in Popes from Pius VII to John Paul I without coming a whit nearer restoring communion with them. It is no use anyone imagining that if one day an ideal Pope came along, a Gregory the Great as opposed to a Leo the Great, a Pope of love as opposed to a Pope of law, a Pope of exhortation, not a Pope of jurisdiction, a Pope content with honour and unconcerned about obedience, then all at once the obstacles to unity would be removed. Pope-fancying will get us nowhere. Unity results from discovering the pastoral office of the universal

Church in one's own street, not from admiring its benevolent attributes on a package tour stop-over in Rome.

The unity of the Church does not depend on the human qualities of the Pope, or on any sort of new theory or practice of collegiality. Important as these things are, they are bound to fluctuate: to know periods of decline and eclipse as well as times of brilliance and achievement. The unity of the Church depends on man's acceptance of the ties of communion that God has given in order to remedy human sin. This is the essential part, so often forgotten: the need to discover and to obey the will of God, to take part in his plan, if we are to escape from the consequences of our own sins, to be restored and ultimately to be saved.

The unity of the Church is not an end in itself. It exists in order that the message of salvation may effectively be given to the world. The arguments that go on about the proper blend of spiritual inspiration and juridical organisation, of the precise interplay of the *potestas ordinis* and the *potestas jurisdictionis,* of centralisation and of delegation, often miss the main purpose of the authority given by the sacrament of Order throughout the Church (spreading *outwards,* let it be said, again, not 'up' or 'down', from pope, bishops, presbyters, deacons . . .), which is the communication of truth, of doctrine, of the Word.

When it drew up its agreed statement on Authority in the Church (Venice 1976), the Anglican/Roman Catholic International Commission did not pay sufficient attention to this perpetual dependence of the Church on the living Word of God. The dominant theme of this document was communion, and the way in which the governing authority of the Church maintains communion, including its activity in expounding and preserving true teaching. This made it seem as if teaching were a function of government. In fact, the New Testament order of priorities reverses these roles. The Word has the initiative; service of the Word comes first. Obedience to the Word creates community. The people of God only obey their recognised and appointed authorities because they accept the overall authority of the Word.

The authority of the bishops of the Catholic Church is given them in the first place for proclamation and teaching, for kerygma and catechesis. The Joint Statement on Authority made

252

it sound, on the other hand, as if they were primarily concerned with internal government; this imbalance will need correcting if their present investigation of the doctrine of the Church is to help us further forward towards unity.

In the short time he was with us, John Paul I set an example as preacher and catechist to all other bishops, both in his prepared statements and in his informal, impromptu, conversational remarks to those whom he has received in audience, from Cardinals to choirboys, journalists and married couples. The welcome he was given sprang most certainly from the affection inspired by his own cheerful and engaging personality; but it arose above all from the context of faith within which his office is accepted and understood. The currents of history will affect the manner in which that office comes to be exercised, and those whose preparedness to recognise and accept the God-given function of the Bishop of Rome depends upon niceties of theological perfectionism are bound to go on being disappointed, as they always have been in the past. Where unity is concerned, it is unlikely that John Paul I would have succeeded where John XXIII and Paul VI did not succeed before him, nor Pius XII before them, because so many people let unity wait upon human qualities and the fruitless search for an ideally-run Church.

What is certain is that he wanted us all to look away from him to the Christ who founded the Church, and to recognise in the Pope and in all other bishops with him the successors of those whom he first called to be Servants of the Word. By that focusing of our faith, and by that alone, the unity of the Church is still continually being created.

November 1978

MANKIND REDEEMED

THE first encyclical of Pope John Paul II has now given us a clear indication of the strong outlines of his understanding of the Christian mystery and of his approach to the work that lies ahead. He speaks in his own person, directly, without any of the blurring and softening produced by the papal and episcopal plural of former times. He calls Christ unambiguously 'a man', putting aside the theology that used to tell us that while he had a human nature, he cannot strictly speaking be called a man, since the subject of his being is the Second Person of the Blessed Trinity. Nestorius, as scholarly re-appraisal of the Council of Ephesus now tells us, had a point. The lurking monophysitism that has persisted so damagingly in Catholic theology clearly has no place in the thinking of the present Pope. One would not expect the author of *The Acting Person* to want to go on giving houseroom to those spiritualities that saw in the 'absence of human person' in Christ the supreme sign of his sacrificing self-denial and demanded as much from those called to follow him in the clergy of the second order.

The Pope sees man as *the primary and fundamental way for the Church* (his italics; n. 14). Clearly he is unperturbed by any possible accusations of being too 'horizontal' in his thinking. He expressly follows the way of Christ himself, 'the way that leads invariably through the mystery of the Incarnation and the Redemption', in search of man 'in all the truth of his life'. Some people have cavilled at the translation of *pro multis* in the Eucharistic Prayer as 'for all men'. They will find no support in this encyclical, for we are clearly told that 'every man without exception whatever' has been redeemed, and that Christ is united 'with each man without any exception whatever . . . even when he is unaware of it'.

It cannot be said that by this emphasis on man the Pope has fallen into the trap of trying to get the Church accepted by addressing himself only to themes made fashionable by contemporary humanistic demands. The divine dimension is paramount; Christ is the revelation of the Father's love, and it is to the Father that he has reconciled us in the new and definitive Covenant (n. 9). This is the origin and permanent purpose of the Church's mission; the love of God for man drives and directs everything we do in obedience to his will.

He thus provides a new inspiration and foundation for the movement towards the full communion in faith of all Christians: unity in mission. This, he says, already unites us. We are already bound together in the search for 'the magnificent heritage of the human spirit that has been manifested in all religions' (n. 12). The missionary attitude, exemplified by St Paul in his Areopagus address, 'begins with a feeling of deep esteem for what is in man' (John 2:26). The missionary must demand

and defend human freedom, the freedom that is needed to embrace the Gospel, and the freedom that is given by acquiring a knowledge of the truth.

My response to the Holy Father's first encyclical would however be less than honest, and therefore less than what he so clearly expects, if I did not voice my disquiet about one aspect of its expression that is of deep importance for the present mission of the Church. Although throughout the hundred pages the principal concern is for man, 'man in all his truth, in his full magnitude', 'the real, "concrete", "historical" man' (n. 13), no indication is given that this 'man' to whom Christ was sent is of more than one kind:

God created man in the image of himself,
in the image of God he created him,
male and female he created them (Gen 2:27).

The whole encyclical can be read as if it applied only to one half of the human race; and in these times, that is not enough. The permanent significance of the fact that man has been created male and female must be made abundantly clear. Distinctions and differences are not suppressed in Christ; they are enhanced, and they are transcended. They cease to divide, but they do not cease to exist. There will be no marriage in Heaven, but men will still be men, and women will still be women. Creation and Redemption mean infinitely rich diversity in perfect harmony, not a return to the chaos and the anonymity from which we came.

Unless the Pope can help the Church to interpret and to situate in Christ the present demand for a proper understanding of the share of women in our common humanity and above all for an effective realisation of the teaching that the Gospel contains on this theme, then we shall once again miss the tide, as we missed it over other issues: over slavery, for instance, over freedom of conscience and over humanity itself.

The balance of the Gospel on these themes has at long last been restored: where fundamental humanity is concerned, for example, in this very encyclical. But for many generations, in these matters as in others, the Church reinforced, or was used to reinforce, the limited views and the prejudices of human selfishness and human systems. Only slowly were the full implications of the Gospel realised. We must now all ask ourselves whether we are not, where men and women are concerned, simply accepting and making more rigid the false relationships set up in the culture of the Mediterranean or in that of Northern Europe, which have been given credence and respectability over the centuries by our foot-dragging reading of the Old Testament, by our refusal to move forward into the epoch of the New.

Pope John Paul II needs to beware lest by his policies he should do no more than bring an attitude to women inherent in Polish culture to the support and confirmation of the machismo of the Latin races. The fear that this may be the case is given strength by the manner of his references to Our Lady at the end of his encyclical. Mary is indeed Mother of the Church; but to honour her truly, we must take Our Lord's words to heart; she is blessed not so much because of her physical motherhood as because she heard the Word of God and kept it (Lk 11:27-8). If that is the ground on which she is given honour by God, it must be the ground on which we too give her honour. Before the Apostles, she was an Apostle; she accepted her vocation to be a Servant of the Word (Lk 1:38; Acts 6:2, 7; 11:20; 12:24).

The attitude to the mother — a certain fixation and dependence — adopted in certain cultures and by many individuals in all societies must not be mistaken for true devotion to Mary, the Mother of Our Lord. She was chosen to set us free from the chains of physiology and psychology. Just as there is a strong and fundamental sense in which we must 'call no man father' (Mt 23:9), so too we must call no woman mother. Instead we must learn to live our own lives in freedom through the knowledge of the One who is Father and Mother to us all, for he made us male and female 'in his own image'. In that we shall imitate Mary in what made her truly Mother: her faith, lived in the obedient acceptance she gave at the Annunciation, in the Temple, at Cana, before the Cross, and at Pentecost. Only that faith can enable us to escape from those limited views of life on this earth that we owe not to our Creator but to the inherited cultural patterns that we have made and must one by one discard, as we grow, slowly but surely, into his image and resemblance.

One final niggle. The title 'Supreme Pastor', expressly chosen by John Paul I in preference to 'Pontiff', and taken explicitly at his inaugural Mass by John Paul II, no doubt for the same reasons, has disappeared from the introduction and conclusion of this encyclical: 'Pontiff' is back. But the Imperial theme must never again be allowed to overlay the Christian one: John 21 and 1 Peter 5 are decisive.

June 1979

PETER AND THE PRESBYTERS

IF this *Review* is to make its proper contribution to the work of the Church, it must persistently be concerned with one particular mystery of faith: Holy Order in the service of the Word and of the People of God. The crisis among those who have received this sacrament, the intense search in recent years for a clearer understanding of its nature and its relationship to the other sacraments and to those who are united by them, the need to find and to train many more in order that they may be given ordination and sent to build up the Church, all of this has long been familiar — only too familiar — to everyone holding responsibility for our life and growth.

The all-round talents and pastoral appeal of the present Pope cannot by themselves restore the situation. The double-edged appreciations of his ministry that are published in the press would, if taken seriously, leave Catholics as uncertain as ever about the way forward either for the Church in general or for its ministry. We must all think for ourselves, going far more deeply than either journalists or ecclesiastical bureaucrats are able to do, if we are to arrive at a shared understanding of ministerial identity and a common policy for the service of the People of God.

The need for using (and keeping) our heads is always with us, but it is particularly pressing just now because the sound from Rome is still so uncertain. There is plenty of it, of course: the slam of the door on laicisation, the reiterated insistence on the law of celibacy, the rejection of the ordination of women, the exhortations, messages and synodal decisions. Firmness, a clear policy line, an appeal to loyalty; these things are needed, as prerequisites for advance. But they do not show the way forward, and that way will not be seen until we have in the Church a more detailed and more generally agreed understanding of the precise role of those whom St Peter called his fellow presbyters.

Roman uncertainty can be seen in the way in which the title chosen by both John Paul I and John Paul II as the best expression of their function — Supreme Pastor — has so rapidly been displaced in official documents by the old title of Supreme Pontiff, non-Christian in origin and misleading in meaning. It can be seen in the way in which the term 'presbyter', deliberately chosen in preference to 'cleric' or 'priest' (*sacerdos*) in the conciliar document *Presbyterorum Ordinis,* and correctly employed in the renewed rite of ordination, is still too often neglected in favour of 'priest'. And it can be seen in the feeble vagueness on this particular subject of the document promulgated by the Special Synod of Dutch Bishops in January this year.

In his homily at the closing Mass of this Synod, the Holy Father singled out for special emphasis 'one particular point which emerged at the centre of all the other questions raised and which will have a profound impact on the future of the Church' and this particular point was 'the authentic ministry of priests, both in itself and as it is related to the bishops and the commitment of lay people in all the dioceses of the Netherlands.' So there is no doubt of the hopes placed by the Pope in what the Synod has done for the ordained ministry, seen as standing at the heart of renewal; and there can equally be no doubt that in his emphasis he is right.

This *Review* must therefore point out the failure of the Synod in this respect to match up to its responsibilities. The section on the bishops is thorough and positive: a balanced statement of essentials. But the next section has been skimped; it falls far short of what is so urgently needed at the present time.

It begins (n. 17) by declaring 'the unanimity of the Synod in professing the distinction between the ministerial or sacramental priesthood and the priesthood common to all the baptised'; one would hope so, since it was the teaching of the Vatican Council in 1965 (LG, n. 10). But it has been pointed out over and over again since then that the identity-crisis for thousands who have abandoned this ministry and, no doubt, for thousands more who hesitate to enter it, has arisen because the nature of this distinction is not clearly seen. Cardinal Kim of Korea said as much at the Third Synod of Bishops, held in Rome in 1972:

> We humbly ask that the meaning of this essential difference should be made clear.

But the Synod did not produce the clarification needed; and eight years later, in spite of an immense campaign of research into the question, which has established some very clear, constructive, deeply traditional answers, providing us with the exact guidelines and profound inspiration we need for the future, this document contents itself with a bare recall of the statement that, sixteen years ago, raised so many problems, and then goes on to what amounts to no more than a plaintive hope that things will be better in the future, proposing some practical measures, which, lacking as they do the essential understanding of this Gospel ministry, amount to no more than whistling in the dark.

The Synod should have developed a theology of the presbyterate which showed the way in which presbyters share in the service of the Word of God and the pastoral functions which give to those who receive the sacrament of Holy Order their specifically priestly role. That 'essential difference' must be spelt out; and it should be abundantly clear by now that it is not by reflecting simply on priesthood in general that it will be seen, but by reflecting on that which, within the shared priesthood that Christ confers on the whole Church, is the special consecration of this group of his disciples: the role of shepherds and fishermen. The ordained bishop's or presbyter's sacrifice is a sacrifice offered by a shepherd of the flock; it is as pastor that he is marked out within the New Testament priesthood, not as priest, and to search for a 'distinctly priestly' kind of priesthood is to introduce inextricable confusion into the whole issue.

The way in which documents from Rome are still insufficiently imbued with this thoroughly pastoral understanding of the presbyteral ministry and cling instead to a narrower sacerdotal theory is shown by the lack of clarity over the corporate nature of the eucharistic sacrifice to be found in the Pope's letter to bishops for Maundy Thursday 1980. It appears there (n. 9) that a distinction is to be made between the sacrificial act performed by the celebrant and the separate spiritual sacrifices which all others offer with him. It would have been much better to say clearly that all together offer one sacrifice — the Body and Blood of Christ — and that this one sacrifice is made present as God's gift only through the action of the bishop or presbyter acting in virtue of his apostolic and pastoral character. Once again, as soon as you try to work out the unique role of the principal celebrant of the Eucharist and other sacraments in sacerdotal terms, you are back in the state of confusion from which Vatican II began to rescue the Church, providing the basis for the renewal of ministry that we all desire.

John Paul II hit the nail on the head when he told the seminary rectors of England, Scotland and Wales that:

The first priority for seminaries today is the teaching of God's word in all its purity and integrity, with all its exigencies and all its power.
The Word of God — and the word of God alone — is the basis for all ministry, for all pastoral activity, for all priestly action.

It is therefore disappointing to find that in the letter for Maundy Thursday this line of thought was not followed up; instead, we have a return to the theme of the 'Two Tables' in the presentation of the Eucharist: the Table of the Word of God and the Table of the Bread of the Lord. One is aware that this theme can claim patristic and counter-reformation precedent. But it would have been far more telling to draw on the authentic biblical theme of the One Table to which Wisdom invites us, a theme to which scholars have been drawing attention for years now, notably in their exposition of St John's Gospel, where Word and Body are shown to be a single mystery, in the Person of Christ.

The renewal of the liturgy since the Council depends absolutely on the putting into practice of this central intuition, that the Mass, from beginning to end, is one action, originating in and shot through by the presence of the Word of God. And the renewal of the Church in the 1980s depends with equal urgency on the conviction that the People of God is a single priestly people, in which those who have received the sacrament of Holy Order are still priests, but in a new and distinct way: they are not bigger and better priests (there is no difference of degree), but are now, as Peter said, 'shepherds of the flock of God' that is entrusted to them (1 Pet 5:2). A theology of ministry that is totally pastoral is the only one that can renew the ordained ministry, in numbers and in quality. Those who give their lives for the flock are rightly called good shepherds.

June 1980

WHAT THE WEST HAS WON

NO one possessing the slightest acquaintance with human behaviour other than his own, whether white, black, brown, red or yellow, can be under any illusion about the universal spread of original sin. The disease from which he suffers is no isolated or private affair. Putting self first is not restricted to any one person, tribe, race or people. The television documentary that can show us even half-an-hour of unflawed human behaviour has yet to be made.

In responding to the breadth and depth of human need, the Church of Christ cannot make selective or preferential judgements. No nation can be singled out for special blame or special favour. Salvation is offered to all; the love of God is given to all.

For all its self-seeking, the West holds no monopoly in materialism. And even in the West, materialism is constantly being overcome. The Third World is not the only place that knows self-sacrifice. Those who romanticise over rustic Catholicism follow Rousseau, not Christ.

At the present juncture in human affairs, churchmen who fail to appreciate what has been achieved, in spite of everything, in the West, and the essential, irreplaceable part that the Church has played in that achievement, are betraying their own cause. They sin against the light.

In the last forty years of European history, organised barbarity has been overthrown and in its place there has come into existence a society equipped as never before to make possible for its members a free, happy and genuinely human way of life. In the struggle that has brought that about, keeping totalitarian dictatorship, whether of the right or of the left, at bay, and resisting all temptations to return to the crude nationalisms and limited party loyalties of the past, the Church has been the principal inspiration and guide.

The Church of twentieth-century Europe has refused to claim for herself the place of privilege that was given her or that she sought to secure in the past, to the persistent damage and disruption of human affairs. The Church has realised how many of her opponents were born out of her own family and were recalling her to elementary duties she had forgotten. Europe's Communists and Socialists themselves now recognise from what stock they have come. The Church has set about reintegrating into her understanding, preaching and practice of the Gospel those many elements that should never have been forgotten or suppressed. And at the same time the Church has seen more clearly her own distinctive place in human history as the pilgrim People of God, never to be captured and used in the service of any one nation's cause.

The Church has fought many intellectual battles as well. Atheist humanism has been out-thought in the West. Our scholars and thinkers are the ones who have led the way in the investigation of Christian origins, confirming and enlarging our biblical faith. They have worked over the new problems posed by the human and physical sciences, showing the reliability of Christ and the way in which his teaching, like that of no one else, meets human needs and makes possible the attainment of human aims.

The Christianity of Europe, Eastern and Western, Catholic and Protestant, has in the twentieth century won at least as many victories as at any other time for God and for the human spirit. It has vigorously set about restoring its own unity. It has renewed its life in the light of its original inspiration. It must not now lose its nerve and sink back into a mood of denunciation and fear, of distaste for the world to which it has been sent, or preoccupation with its own failings and weaknesses, of mistrust of itself and suspicion of everyone else.

So many voices are at present to be heard — from behind — crying 'Back' that well-informed observers begin to fear the onset of a real crisis in Church affairs. The Holy Father, who in Paris had some wise things to say about progressives and integrists, should be wary of being used by those whose personal insecurities and shallow faith would, if they took control, severely damage the life of the Church.

When he was sent to the West from Poland to study theology — one of a privileged three whom one Polish bishop at least, Cardinal Sapieha, did not want to keep insulated at home — he went to Rome; but he went, as he said the other day in front of the Hôtel de Ville, by way of Paris.

Those who, in the 1980s, follow his example may well still be the ones who have most to contribute to the work of the Church, leaven of the world. The Pope does not give to opulent prelates or to career ecclesiocrats the warmth of encouragement that he has given to worker-priests. If in continuing to travel by way of local churches he can fulfil his intention of listening to what those local churches have to say, and does not take repetitive flattery for the mind of the Church, then we may hope that the victories won in the last forty years, and still being won, will not be thrown away. He will only succeed in doing that if he seeks out those who, in the West, are prepared to do as he did as a young priest; to think, to look beyond national frontiers, and to make detours, seeing for themselves.

It is always sad when a curate of promise settles for less than the original goal of his pilgrimage. It would be a great mistake if the Pope or any of our leaders made us slacken our march. Some of the wanderers in front may need recalling before they get too far out of sight; but those who want us all to mark time or even retreat, present, now as always, the real threat to the Church, to the West and to the world.

August 1980

JESUS AND THE CROWDS

ONE outstandingly significant feature of Our Lord's life that many commentators hardly seem to notice, but which came across with great force in Alec McCowen's delivery of St Mark's Gospel, is the fact that crowds followed him everywhere. He attracts not just a chosen few, listening quietly and attentively to his words, but a jostling throng, with many motives but one common aim: to see and hear him.

His Church is still a mass phenomenon. Some of his disciples disdain the crowd. But they are wrong. Christianity is a popular religion through and through. The intellectuals, the aristocrats, the highly gifted, cannot, in the Church, set themselves apart. They must identify with the rest of us. The Church offers to all a common faith.

The millions that want to see the Pope reveal the continuity between twentieth-century Catholicism and the first-century Gospel; then they wanted to be close to Christ, now they want to be close to Peter, whom Christ has chosen and sent. John Paul II attracts by the person that he is; but he attracts still more because of the Person whom he represents. If Jesus had no place in men's hearts, how many would make room there for Karol Wojtyla? The encouragement derived from the visits made by the Pope comes in large part from the reminder they give us that we are not isolated in our faith. The crowd of Christ's followers is not a lonely crowd.

The sheer numbers brought together by the presence of the Pope should make his critics hesitate before making their selective judgements on what he has to say. Unwelcome and puzzling as it may be, it is at least possible that his words about marriage, for instance, are as welcome to those who go to hear him as are his words about social justice. He may have a better sense of what the public wants — or what, in its heart of hearts, it knows it needs — than some of those who are all for accommodation.

Some people try to explain away bits of papal teaching by suggesting that John Paul II is being hoodwinked by his entourage: 'It is commonly accepted, and probably true, that most of the Pope's relationship with the world is in the hands of a small group of predominantly conservative curial officials in the Vatican, who tell him what they think he ought to know'. 'It is commonly accepted, and probably true': the phrase has a delightfully Gilbertian ring; it could become a sort of chanted anti-motto for aspiring reporters.

A much sounder basis for interpreting the mind of John Paul II is to be found in his own statement that he makes his visits abroad in order to reach out beyond the information offered by the curia: to see and hear the local churches for himself.

Certainly curial officials are made uncomfortable by his travels, feel themselves overlooked, and have grown uncertain of their role; they stick more closely than ever to the old, safe lines, simply because they are not too sure which way the Pope will jump next.

If the bishops of a particular country give the Pope guidance on the way he may best fulfil his pastoral role when he visits their country, he is ready to take it. The success of his visit to England, Scotland and Wales next year depends at least as much upon us as upon him. But he will certainly be himself, and he will certainly say what he wants us to hear and not what we or the publicists would like to hear. If he speaks about marriage, then positive teaching about the normal, healthy conduct of a normal, healthy marriage, from which any Catholic with faith and a properly functioning conscience will draw the appropriate conclusions, will get his message across better than negative rulings and condemnations. But this is in fact the way he is accustomed to teach; it is those who write about him who are concerned to tell us, with approval or disapproval, what he is against rather than what he is for.

We shall have had more time to prepare the Pope's visit than any other country so far. We need to help him to know what our needs are and then listen hard to the remedies he himself proposes. We want his own words, whatever they are; there have been times when he could have spoken more out of his personal experience than he has in fact done. But if he is to know what to say, and how to say it, then we must make known to him our hopes and our problems.

Above all, the divided Christians in this island need his help towards becoming one Church, capable of uniting and giving hope and purpose to our disordered and demoralised national life. His visit can drive the last lingering traces of that bogeyman Giant Pope from the national imagination.

There will be crowds. They will not all be converted. But they will be signs, as always, of the living presence of the Lord.

May 1981

THE TRUTH THAT SAVES

PAPAL infallibility is still widely regarded as a major obstacle to the reunion of all Christians. The topic recurs with monotonous regularity in practically every conversation that takes place about turning the divided state of English Christendom into something a bit more presentable. Catholics are asked to explain themselves, and manifestly fail to do so, since they are asked yet again the next time round. Whether the final ARCIC document will button the whole thing up for us remains to be seen. Even if it does, there will remain plenty of people, both inside the Anglican Communion and outside, for whom papal claims of any kind will take a lot of swallowing.

There is a danger that in trying to untie every ecumenical knot and resolve every ecclesiastical tension we may forget that faith itself will always be a stumbling block for any human mind that wants to remain totally in command of its own reflections and opinions. In the life of anyone finding his or her way to God there are many crises, many barriers to be negotiated, before ease, maturity and comparative peace are attained. Confrontation with infallibility and living with infallibility make up a considerable part of that painful readjustment of the mind, soul and heart that cannot be by-passed if we are ever to arrive at our destination.

Before accepting and understanding papal infallibility, there is the infallibility of the Word and the Church of God to be accepted and understood. That is the theme that needs to be discussed in the first place. Papal infallibility, as should be well known, is itself defined in terms of that general infallibility of the Church. It cannot ever appear to be even remotely acceptable unless it is first of all granted that the Church as a whole is to be believed with absolute certainty in its proclamation of the faith: that the Church cannot let us down as it communicates to us the saving message that Christ came to teach and to express in his own Person.

This is where the real divide comes in Christendom: believing the Church or not believing the Church. The reliability of the Church as teacher and as visible sign of the presence of Christ is not something added to the authority and reliability of Christ himself. It is not an optional extra. It is much more than a

266

consequence, even a necessary consequence, of the coming of Christ. The extraordinary truth that we must learn to grasp and to live with is this: God has so committed himself to mankind that he has associated us irrevocably with our own salvation. Christ gave himself no other means of communicating with us in our twentieth-century generation, and in every other generation past and future, than men and women like ourselves. 'He who hears you, hears me, and he who hears me, hears him who sent me.' Those words must be taken seriously. We cannot find Christ unless we are prepared to believe the witness of those who speak for him to us. And this is not because of some accident, some loss of manuscripts and files, some chance forgetfulness on the part of Christ, omitting to make sure that what he had said was properly preserved from the damage and decay that afflicts all human history. It was part of Christ's own deliberate plan, that we should live together in his Church in the light of a message within which we are ourselves incorporated. If the Gospels are properly read, the fact is quite inescapable: to believe the Gospel, to believe Christ and to believe the Church are all one.

It is because the Gospel is for our salvation that it does not fail us. Human salvation cannot be made to depend on faulty instructions or flawed instruments. And it cannot come from a message that is beyond the reach of the human mind: if it has been given to human beings, it must be expressed in human language.

Those whose minds draw back from the idea that Christian faith has been and can still be stated in sentences that, if they do not exhaust the truth, at any rate do not mislead us by conveying falsehood, have failed to see that truth cannot be stated in any other way, and that the Bible itself reveals God to us in propositional terms. 'You are the Christ, the Son of the Living God': Peter's confession of faith, the archetypal utterance of every Christian disciple, is a proposition just as much as it is an invocation. Faith combines the two movements of the mind in a single action. It is a prayer, and it is at the same time a statement of fact: it is addressed to Christ and it is said about Christ. To attach oneself to God is at one and the same time an act of public witness to God, by which we say to the world who he is.

As a disciple of Christ, among Christ's disciples, the successor of Peter still makes the same confession. It is fundamental to the Christian faith that those who serve with Christ share in his authority. Only when we have discovered those whom he has chosen to be with him as his disciples do we really discover the unfailing depth and truth of his saving love.

June 1981

THE RULE OF THE SHEPHERD

WHEN John Paul II comes to this country next year, he will be present among us as the bishop who, according to the express will of Christ, is directly concerned not just for his own diocese of Rome, but for the whole Church of God. That is what it means to say that his visit has a pastoral character and purpose. We will receive him not because he is the ruler of the Vatican State, or because he is a bishop of the Church in another country with whom we wish to maintain amicable relations, or because of his personal gifts and achievements, but as the Supreme Pastor of the Church of Christ. The six days will be quite different in their significance from the State visit of a foreign king or president, or from the welcome given to some conquering hero in whatever field. The Pope will be here because he is the chief shepherd of the Catholic Church in England, Scotland and Wales: because he has received from Christ responsibility for the care of the Church in this island and is coming to see us for himself, to strengthen and encourage us, and to do all he can to help forward the mission we have received.

The primacy of the Pope means that Christ has provided for the pastoral supervision not just of each separate local community, but of all of them together as one communion, single yet diverse. The bishops themselves have a bishop to look after them. Each local church has a head, its bishop; the universal church also has its head, the Pope. As a bishop rules his local church, so the Pope rules in the whole Church. And rule is exercised through laws, as it is guided by them.

The hesitations over papal primacy being voiced in this country by Anglicans and others derive for the most part from an unfamiliarity with the idea the Christian faith and communion can and must be expressed in legal terms. People shy away from the word 'juridical' and want everything to be run by simple mutual esteem and affection. But it must be said with the utmost clarity and persistence that while it is true that laws, including ecclesiastical ones, if administered without regard to their full human context of reason, understanding and free acceptance, can never create a proper society, it is also above all true that laws are the highest, utterly essential, expression of real relationships between God and man, and that to forget or minimise their importance is to impoverish, to diminish and ultimately to destroy any kind of civilisation.

The very sacrament by which we are held together in the Church was delivered to us in legal terms and as a legal bond: 'the New Testament in my Blood'. A last will and testament protects the love in a family, whose relationships, without such a document, are inevitably put under strain.

The Law of Christ is still a law. And as long as we are imperfect, it will remain, to a greater or lesser extent, external to us. We are trying to practise it so that it becomes second nature, to interiorise it so that we can obey it without thinking. But whether it has become habitual or whether it remains to be incorporated in our being, it is still a law.

The rule of the shepherd is part of that Law. The primacy of Peter, the primacy of John Paul II, must be exercised through law if it is to be real and if it is to be just. Every Catholic recognises in the Pope the one who is there to defend individual rights when other Catholics, bishops or others, abuse them. The world-wide jurisdiction of the Pope is no arbitrary dictatorship or unwarranted intrusion, but an expression of the universal character of the pastoral care made available for genuine human living by the intention and the will of Christ. The servant of the servants of God is pastor of the pastors of God. There is no contradiction in the fact that individuals are called to be both bishop and deacon, overseer and under orders.

The rights and laws of Catholic communion, the *venerandae communionis iura* that, as St Ambrose pointed out, stem from the Roman See and the faith of the apostles, should not be suspect, but understood and accepted, in a country that prides itself on its defence of the rule of law. A Christianity without law may flatter whatever religious aspirations we may have, but will soon leave us floundering in our own feebleness. The Christianity that still uses law to discipline our wayward-ness and accordingly has pastors who make laws by which to govern, will ultimately prove itself to be the real source, guaran-tee and living strength of the constitution and laws of this country.

Papal monarchy and British monarchy, Catholic collegiality and British parliamentary government, must now learn to live and work together. When this country rediscovers the place of law in Christian faith and practice and thereby relates Church and State for their distinct but mutual benefit, we may even be able to help in ridding the world of the hatred and violence bred by nationalism, that pagan survival, that corruption of Christianity, that major pestilence of the modern world.

July 1981

IX

RENEWAL AND DEVELOPMENT

TOWARDS A THEOLOGY OF DEVELOPMENT

IF action in favour of development is to find its true orientation and impulse, it must be the expression of a doctrine not simply of man, not simply of created reality, of the world, but of God. We need a morality, we need a philosophy of history, we need theories of different aspects of the social order, we need techniques; and from beginning to end of all this we need a spirituality. If we appeal only to the love of our neighbour as our motive for contributing to aid programmes in undeveloped countries, without acquiring a conviction about the relationship of that love to the love of God, then we shall be unintegrated, schizophrenic. We shall, literally, be half-hearted; the love which is our gravity, our dynamic, our energy, our polarising force, will not be properly harnessed and directed.

In our thinking and action in favour of development, we are not trying to prove that the Church can be some use to the world after all; we are not trying to use Catholicism as an ideology which can trigger off the kind of social change we particularly want; we are not trying to devise a new humanism superior to that of political rivals. In all that the Church is attempting to do in this field, there is, however obscure and fumbling it may be, a new effort to grasp the reality of God and to understand the world as the place where he is active.

Our action will have one character and quality if we see this world as no more than a vale of tears, if we see people as no more than souls to be snatched as brands from the burning, if we think of heaven as the blissful reward for an austere and unhappy struggle. It will have another character if we think as cheerfully as possible about our surroundings and our neighbours and try to do the best we can in this world without attempting to strain our minds after the incomprehensible reality of God, whom we can safely leave until the hereafter, when we shall have plenty of time to get acquainted. And if these two lines of approach leave us unsatisfied, as being pragmatically ineffective or intellectually restricted, then we need to look once again at the content of our faith in search of a better one.

Christ our Beginning

Christian thinking about the development of the world starts from the fact that Christ is not simply an example to men, a manifestation within history of the nature of God, but the principle of creation itself. In him, creation finds more than its meaning; it discovers its existence. The hymn in honour of the primacy of Christ in St Paul's Epistle to the Colossians (1:15-20) speaks of him as 'the image of the invisible God' and 'first-born of all creation'. As image, Christ is the perfect revelation of God; he does not simply speak about him, but is, in his entire being, the expression of God. Through Christ and in him, says St Paul, all things were created (v. 16). The background of his thought here is the understanding of the creative work of the Wisdom of God contained in Proverbs 8. God's Wisdom, independent of the cosmos and of man, originating from God and acting as the associate of God in a way that man does not, co-operates with God in making the world. As God's Wisdom, Christ expresses God himself and is active with God in creation; all things, including man, were made, not for man, but for Christ as image of the invisible God.

At the same time, Christ is 'the first-born of all creation'. In a context which sets Christ firmly outside the created universe ('He is before all things and in him all things hold together', v. 17), this title attributes to Christ another aspect of the divine Wisdom: as well as being transcendent, he is the principle of all created things (Prov 8:22). In making the universe, God saw in Christ his own self-expression and his own Wisdom, the pattern of his work, and the manifestation of his glory. Creation depends upon Christ and refers constantly to him as its means of coming into being and of completion.

The establishment of the Kingship of Christ will be the ultimate manifestation of the imprinted pattern of the Christ-life which the whole universe has received by its creation in him. It will be the complete working-out of a creative process the fundamental lines of which were established at the beginning. In Christ we see God as distinct from the world and as pre-existent; and in him also we see the start and the completion of creation. Because of Christ, the love of God and the love of the world cannot be separated. Our way to the invisible God, the homing point of our love for him, is given to us by Christ himself, who makes him visible; and the same Christ is the first principle of creation in its origin, consistency and aim. God sees the world in Christ; if we love God, we look at the world in the same way. Christ is the image of God, not of the world; he is separate from the world, transcendent. At the same time, the world exists in him, and we cannot approach him without at the same time approaching the world.

The next part of the hymn develops the theme of Christ's second title to the primacy of all things. As well as being the first-born of all creation, he is the first-born from among the dead, and, as first-born, head of the Church. The Church is the product of a second course of action, distinct from the act of creation, undertaken by God in Christ to reconcile those who had become strangers and enemies (v. 21), through the blood of the cross (vv. 19, 20). Salvation through the Cross drives out the discord which had entered the created order and puts peace in its place. Redemption in Christ is added to creation in Christ as the basis of a correct understanding of the world.

Action in the world will therefore be inseparable from attachment to God. And it is more than a duty laid upon us, a condition of salvation, a means of fulfilling our destiny. Action in the world is christocentric. It is not aimed at the promotion of man or at the development of man as such; nor is it just an act of obedience to a God who is 'outside' the world. It is part of creation by, in and for Christ, and part of redemption, reconciliation, through his work on the Cross. It flows from and expresses the love of God as life-giving and death-destroying. Mortification, in Christian spirituality, is the slaying of death, that life may be liberated, and never the slaying of anything created. We cannot give glory to God in Christ, image of God,

274

first-born of all creatures, and first born from the dead, unless we are affirming and promoting created life.[1]

Christ our End

It has often been held that Christian eschatology deflects man's attention from this world, rendering his belief in the goodness of the created order notional rather than real by focusing his attention on a transcendent source and a heavenly goal. Does it, then, contradict what we have just seen of the relationship of Christ to the world? Does Christ set us within the world, only to take us out of it again in order to save us? Is the Christian attitude to the world fully represented by the prayer that

> among the changes of this world, our hearts may be set on the one true home of joy (Collect, Easter 4)?

In both *Lumen Gentium* and *Gaudium et Spes*, the Council showed its desire to bring out the significance of belief in heaven and heavenly fulfilment for our present concern with the temporal order. Chapter VII of *Lumen Gentium*, on the pilgrim church, speaks of the ultimate completion and perfection of the created order, the whole universe as well as the human race, as something only to be reached 'in the glory of heaven when the time comes "for establishing all" (Acts 3:21)'. But this ultimate completion is not to be seen as an opening of prison-house doors or as a longed-for demobilisation, with 'Roll on, Blighty' setting the tone for Christian prayer. 'The promised restoration to which we look forward has already had its beginning in Christ. It receives impetus on the sending of the Holy Spirit and is continued by his efforts in the Church . . . We, meanwhile, in expectation of a good future, are bringing

[1] This examination of Col 1:15-20 is very much indebted to A. Feuillet's *Le Christ Sagesse de Dieu dans les Epîtres Pauliniennes* (Paris, Gabalda, 1966). As Fr Congar points out in his preface, this highly technical work of exegesis establishes some of the fundamental principles of a theology of the temporal order, setting our understanding of man and the world clearly in the framework of Christology.

to completion the work in the world entrusted to us' (LG n. 48).

The future restoration has already begun, and, far from distracting our attention from work in this world, is a most powerful stimulus to our involvement in the development of this world. 'The end of the ages has already reached us (cf. 1 Cor 10:11) and the world is already irrevocably set on the renewal which is anticipated in a real way in this life' (LG n. 48). The end of the ages is both completion and judgement, as ch. VII reminds us at some length; if this end 'has already reached us', then there is a process of renewal going on in the world, with its source in the creative and redemptive action of God, a process to which we can commit ourselves or to which we can refuse our co-operation; and by our present attitude and action we are already judged, we are already moving towards our own perfection or away from it. The fact of creation, re-creation and fulfilment in Christ has set the true pattern and provided the energy, motive and stimulus for human activity in the world. The correct expression of Christian hope is our firm grasp of present time and our extroverted involvement in our present situation.

Gaudium et Spes rejected any idea that the Christian life is a matter of saving one's soul by walking unscathed through the gin-traps of this world:

> They are wide of the mark who think that because here we have no lasting city but we seek the city that is to come, they can neglect their duty here on earth; they forget that the faith increases their obligation to fulfil those duties in accordance with their vocation (GS n. 43).

> The Christian message does not distract men from building up the world nor induce them to neglect the welfare of their fellows, but rather obliges them more strictly to these tasks (GS n. 34).

> Faithful Christians making their way to heaven should look for and set their minds on the things that are above. But this increases rather than diminishes the importance of their task of co-operating with all men in building a more human world (GS n. 57; cf. n. 39).

Those who speak of the Church as 'bowing down before the world' since the Council have quite misunderstood the bearing of these texts. There is no question of putting the world in the place of God or of regarding the exploration and use of the world's resources as a sufficient religion for modern man. The Council is asking us to act on the fundamental Christian belief that we cannot love God without loving what he has made. Far from being an attempt to find the world sufficiently meaningful without God, *Gaudium et Spes* sees that the world can only take on its full significance in the light of Christian faith. And in saying this, it makes clear the fact that Christian faith itself is empty unless the world is taken seriously as the field of God's activity, of which we are part and in which we are consciously, rationally and freely involved.

What is 'The World'?

'The World of Today' which the Council had in mind is the world of men, the entire human family, its whole environment; the world which is the theatre of human history, marked with man's industry, his triumphs and disasters (GS n. 2).

This is the world as made by God through Christ (Jn 1:10), the world into which Christ was sent and into which he sent the Apostles (Jn 17). It includes 'all things', not simply the human race (Col 1:15-20; Rom 8:19-22). Now this world can certainly be seen as hostile to God; it is deeply scarred by sin and is under the influence of enemy powers. 'World' is used by both St John and St Paul in this sense; there can be no naïve acceptance of it on the part of the Christian, who must in fact, on account of the corruption running through the world, distrust it and turn aside from it. The Council did not forget this; the world 'was enslaved indeed to sin' (GS n. 2). But the dominant thought of the Christian, which guides his discernment in the midst of the alternatives offered him by the world, is his conviction that the world has been freed from this slavery by Christ crucified and risen from the dead 'so that according to God's design it may be transformed and achieve its fulfilment' (GS n. 2).

Now this liberation was prepared for and brought out, and is at present being carried to completion, within the world, within the created temporal order. This is one of the great contemporary mutations in Christian thinking, clearly visible in the Council documents: the Church and the world, the spiritual and the temporal, are not separate juxtaposed powers or organisms which must necessarily be rivals. *Lumen Gentium* quotes the well-known affirmation of the *Epistle to Diognetus*: 'Christians must be in the world what the soul is in the body' (LG n. 38). This can all too easily be understood in a Platonist or Cartesian sense: the soul is 'superior' to the body, the spiritual must 'rule' the temporal. But the power which rules in the world is not a jurisdiction, a 'sword', whether temporal or spiritual: it is the power of the Risen Christ. Christ is both temporal, or material, and spiritual; his power is that of an order of existence, a total life, which is working in the world to transform it as a whole.

> The Church, at once 'a visible assembly and a spiritual community' marches with the whole of humanity, shares the fortunes of the world here below, exists as the leaven, we might say the soul, of human society, to renew it in Christ and transform it into God's family (GS n. 40).

There is no service of the Risen Christ which is not service of the world which he has raised up. The power of the Spirit is a power effective in the penetration and transformation of the world, not set beside the world, but its living principle.

The unity of world and Church is not brought about by the control of one sphere by another, by the clericalisation of the world or the secularisation of the Church. The unity of the world and the Church already exists in Christ, in whom it is constantly growing in depth and extent.

It is important to remember that the Church's attempt to understand and guide its activity in the world in the light of the fundamental principles of its belief does not simply produce a new theory, a new ideology, a speculative basis for correct behaviour. A theology without faith and devotion can be a dangerous cutting intrument. Theology is only the Church's means of getting a clearer vision of the Lord of the Church, of Jesus of Nazareth. Our Christology can easily be no more than a transliteration of our own private theories about the cosmos; our doctrine of man a repetition of well-meaning commonplaces. We have to return constantly to the fact that the Christ for whom the world was made is the Jesus of the Gospels, and that the man in whom all men should see themselves is the Son of Man who came to serve and to save mankind. In such a perspective, development will be seen to be not any and every sort of 'promotion of the human', control over natural resources, or enrichment in knowledge, property and experience, but only those human actions which fit in with the mission and programme of Christ.

> The Spirit of the Lord is upon me,
> because he has anointed me to preach good news to the poor.
> He has sent me to proclaim release to the captives
> and recovering of sight to the blind,
> to set at liberty those who are oppressed,
> to proclaim the acceptable year of the Lord.
>
> (Isa 61: 1-2; Lk 4: 18-19)

These are the categories of human being in whose favour the fundamental principle of the universe is at work. The Sermon on the Mount is a statement of the law which rules creation and which says that the fruits of development are reserved for certain categories of men and women and for those who identify themselves with these categories in the search for an order in harmony with the love of God. In his description of the Last Judgement (Mt 25:31-46), Our Lord showed that precisely the same cosmic law will be at work in the final winding-up of all things. All will work out in favour of those whose relationship with the world has been expressed through feeding the hungry, welcoming strangers, clothing the naked, and visiting those in prison; they are the ones who, even though they did not know it, were serving Christ, were obedient to the first principle of life and were contributing towards the attainment of its final end. The kingdom which they will enter is the one which has been prepared for them from the foundation of the world (Mt 25:34), the kingdom of the Christ who is 'before all things' (Col 1:17); and this kingdom was proclaimed by the same Christ from the beginning of his ministry in Palestine (Mt 4:17).

Development is based on far more than a vague moralism, a desire to share with others the goods of this world, or even the hope for the establishment of world-wide peace. Its dynamic is the energy of God himself and its growing point is human poverty. There can be no true prayer which does not focus on this source, which does not turn our attention to God-with-us in human destitution and promote his saving purpose in his world. Christian humanism involves the poverty of ourselves for the enrichment of others. It involves the reversal of our present instincts, which develop the world by gathering it in towards ourselves, because it knows that the world only develops if our energies are released into it, if we fall into the ground and die.

If violent revolution means that we use force to ensure that someone else gives up riches for the sake of others, then we should beware of it, for it could be a return to that exterior domination, to the theory of the two swords, which we are trying to reject. We cannot harness the energy of God and direct it against others. The judgement of God is not ours to control. The violence must be done to ourselves, if the world is to be changed.

And if development were taken to mean that superior should help inferior, but not change places with him, then we should have missed the point again; we should be attempting to annex and make private use of the goodness of God.

Revolution and development are neither of these things. They are conformity with the law that rules creation, from beginning to end: the law of Christ, that in this world we should die with him, so that others, with him and with us, should rise again.

July 1969

SOCIOLOGY AND THEOLOGY

THE frustrations of sociologists who try to work in the service of the Church in this country are by now well known; for years their constant difficulties have provided something of a counter-witness in the eyes of the world. This is very far from being the case elsewhere; there are few countries where Catholics are not making good use of sociological techniques in sizing up their problems and where scholars trained in sociological method are not deepening our understanding of the Church both as it has lived in its history and as it exists at the present day. Boulard, Le Bras, Comblin, Carrier, Pin, Houtart, Greeley, are among those who have established themselves as scientific commentators and prophets in the modern Church.

If we think exclusively in theological terms, we elaborate from Scripture and the relevant documents of the Church an ideal theory of the Church which we treat as an absolute and even normalise as law, trying to fit human reality into our pattern as into a Procrustean bed. If we think simply in sociological terms, we take observed patterns as our norms and, seeing only man's limited achievements, lose sight of his orientation and the goals he is trying to achieve. In both cases we are involved in the old and elementary mistake of extrapolating beyond the bounds of our scientific discipline, trying to make its findings apply in areas outside its specific angle of vision.

It is also possible to make the mistake of being empirical in one area and idealist in another. Sometimes statistics about education, marriage or the priesthood, for example, are contrasted with an ideal, theoretical situation and we feel disquieted or shocked by the size of the lapsing rate, particularly if we have the notion that this ideal situation existed at some time in the past. But sociology only upsets us if we have false ideas of what we are and always have been. Ten per cent of fervent practice, forty per cent regular, forty irregular, ten completely lapsed: a Catholic parish today? In fact these statistics come from Flanders in the fifteenth century. Fr Lavery's remarks this month about greater attendance in church on Good Friday than on Easter Sunday reflect a modern parish priest's experience; a fifteenth-century parish priest would have said the same.

Sociological enquiry can be, after all, a useful reminder and confirmation of the parable of the Sower. One has to be ignorant, as well as absurdly short-sighted, to take misuse of it for the real thing. It is an essential aid to the understanding and renewal of the Church. Sociologists can most forcefully correct some of the more uncontrolled statements of our modern prophets.

'Let them grow together till the harvest'; the Church was founded as the most open and permissive of all societies. Heresy means a restriction somewhere; the Church can only be intolerant of that which narrows her horizons and her concern. Sociology helps to tell us how people can grow together. It makes possible that confrontation between theological theory and real-life experience which this *Review* seeks to promote and which is the way of growth both for science and for society.

Sociology has nothing to do with apologetics or propaganda; some of those who distrust it still think in ecclesiastical 'public image' terms. They should be more concerned about what lies behind the image, or, more simply and straightforwardly, with reality. Sociology, with the other human sciences, must be taken seriously by those who believe in God made Man, in the real humanity of Christ, and in men and women renewed and reconciled with the Father by the power and gift of the Spirit. In this country, it stands in long need of the respect, the study and the use which it deserves.

March 1970

CHRIST IS OUR CONTEMPORARY

THERE is a great deal of 'waiting for something to turn up' among Christians. They look at modern society and talk of a moral breakdown or, not wishing to appear censorious, of a mutation. They look at the Church, find a great deal they dislike, and express the hope that things will settle down and that the graph will reverse its trend.

However, cultural swing should not be taken for Providence, and no one should place their Christian hope in the reaction that follows revolution. The flow of influence is hard to discern; so much depends on one's point of view, so that apparent success for the Church may represent victory for the world at least as much as for the Gospel. If people take a Christian option today because they think the historian will show that they have backed the winning side in social change, we can fully expect that secular disappointment will make them abandon their position or find other reasons for it.

Hope in revolution or in evolution, whether social or, on a longer term, biological, is about as satisfying as the old pie-in-the-sky doctrine. The only reality we can know and enjoy is the reality of our present life, and the test of Christian faith is its ability to give us happiness here and now. If heaven is to be desirable, we must have access to at least a foretaste of it, and preferably rather more. No sensible man works for an entirely problematic reward.

Attraction to the person of Christ must be the sufficient motive for Christian faith, which has nothing to do with theories about religion and culture or religion and morals, or with ideas about what is desirable for psychological health. It is a matter of attachment to Christ simply because, in the search for happiness, we cannot conceive of finding fulfilment in any other way. Christianity is credible not because it is good for others, not because it promises future benefits, but because it gives me what I want today.

Truth does not mean crawling along a dangerous knife-edge between precipices of error. The balance of a believing mind is not the idleness of sitting still at a dead centre. The narrow gate is a way into the city, not a place of permanent confinement — a barrier we must pass in order to move more freely, not a place where we stay fixed for ever. Orthodoxy means grasping the whole meaning of life; orthopraxy means living life to the full.

Theologians so often write for or against other theologians. One trend sets another in motion; a Harvey Cox can confine himself to political and social action for a while but the need to cultivate leisure, feast and festival catches up with him in the end. In striving after original insights, the would-be prophet loses the vision of the whole. We do not need fresh emphases from our theological writers so much as an understanding of Christ and his teaching which situates us accurately in the real world and gives us proper access to the breadth of all that there is.

Normality is not mediocrity; equilibrium is not inactivity. There is a classic quality about human greatness which makes us see the hero as the true man, not as an eccentric. When we say that Christ was both God and man, we recognise him as summit and standard of all achievement. If theologians will simply say who Christ is, drive home his teaching and illuminate our problems by it, they will fulfil their vocation; they will help us to make our way in the world. Too many Christian teachers fit Christ into their systems, instead of making themselves his pupils; and the temptation of those who read theology is to be more interested in what men have made of Christ than in Christ himself. But Christ himself puts human teachers in their place.

The authentic believer subordinates himself to Christ and does not use his faith in the service of personal theories; he does not turn the Church into his own private world; he does not alienate himself from human affairs. He directs his activities within this world, fully aware of its death-traps, in terms of the practical wisdom made accessible to man in Christ's teaching. If belief depends upon a new theology or denominational unanimity or tomorrow's Church, then we shall never believe.

In prison or in prosperity, men need the same Gospel. It is no good waiting for the Church or the world to change; if Christianity is true, then Christ is our contemporary, as available now as much as he ever has been, and as credible now as much as he ever will be. His time, not ours, decides who is out of date.

The Times, 5 September 1970

THE CHURCH IS CIVILISATION

MANY of the difficulties, both intellectual and practical, which arise in the course of our efforts to understand and practise Christianity arise out of mistakes over the relationship between the Church and the various cultures and societies which have flourished in the past and continue to exist at the present day.

Historians, anthropologists and observers of human affairs are all inclined to identify the Church with the manifestation of it they happen to be investigating. This has occurred particularly in the case of students of the Western Middle Ages and of Byzantium; while this situation is now changing, we are still left, in the scholarly as well as in the popular mind, with the idea that society and the Church were at one time co-terminous and that the time when this happened is either an ideal epoch which we should for ever imitate or else a phase in human affairs which is best forgotten about and left behind. More than we realise, our attitudes are still moulded by the idea that there was a real Christian society at some time in the past and that the modern world is in various ways the result of the break-up of that society, or worse still, of a revolt against it. The Protestant Reformation, the French Revolution, the rise of modern science, the spread of Communism, or the development of technology are all seen as stages in that break-up or revolt, to be resisted in the name of an alternative form of society which we call Christian civilisation.

When made by historians or anthropologists who have no belief in Christianity or are opposed to it, this incorrect assumption about the place of the Church in society has led them to reject it, along with their rejection of a particular social pattern now held to have outlived its usefulness. And even when they have been favourable to the influence of religion, and especially to the influence of Christianity, as is the case, for instance, with Professor Arnold Toynbee, they have often maintained that along with the decline and disappearance of one civilisation there must also come the end of the particular religion which was its support and inspiration. A new civilisation can only come about through the rise of a new religion. Professor Toynbee has had highly appreciative things to say about Christianity as a religion and as a civilising force, but he thinks, all the same, that it will be replaced by something else, by a new, higher, synthesis to which Christianity will contribute but which it is not capable of creating by the application of its own interior strength, power of discernment and methodological resources.

When Christian thinkers, preachers or publicists make the same mistake, the result is, in the long run, equally unfavourable to Christianity. They identify Christian civilisation with one particular example of it; any departure from this ideal is then bound to be a decline, any novelty dangerous, any change in social habits an attack on accepted morality. Over and over again, Christian apologists have defended not the real Church but an order of society which they regarded as God-given and which the Church was expected to promote and protect. They have thereby involved the Church in the defence of party interests or of social attitudes which were either neutral options for a Christian or else indefensible.

It has, of course, been pointed out often enough that we must not in fact identify the Church with the patterns of civilisation which it brings into existence. With the break-up of these forms, or their falling into disuse, the Church itself continues to exist and lives on to see the day when new patterns can be created. But I am not sure that theologians have made clear how it is that the Church as an institution and as a social organism persists through the various ups and downs of civilisation and can also be found existing as an identical and identifiable society in the midst of human groups contemporary with each other, but living according to different patterns of civilisation. They have written of the way in which Christianity as a set of doctrines or ideas exists coherently and separately in its own right, but they have not shown how the Church itself possesses an independent existence of the same kind, to be distinguished from particular forms, liturgical or otherwise. The mental and spiritual distress caused by the massive cultural shifts which are going on at present show how difficult it is for people to change these forms, once their Catholic faith has come to be identified with a particular way of ordering their public life and personal devotion.

But the Church will not be correctly understood until it is seen as a society independent of all others, with its own means of cohesion and its own aims, to be distinguished from 'the medieval world', or 'Byzantium' or 'the Baroque' or from 'patriarchal tribalism', for instance, and as a society which is civilisation itself, which has carried the meaning of the term to a new level, giving it an expression in the light of which, in fact, truly human behaviour can best be discerned and estimated.

Civilisation, Society and the Individual

By 'civilisation', I mean a form of individual and organised social life which brings out and expresses man's nature, enabling him to live in such a way as to produce the fruits of his diverse abilities. A particular civilisation gives him both the means of discovery and creation and those of communication with his fellow men.

History can be said to have thrown up a number of such civilisations, living next to one another or succeeding one another with more or less progress, according to one's point of view. Historians write about their rise, their achievements and their decline and fall: more about their decline and fall than about their achievements, with the result that for a long time now we have been obsessed with the idea of decline within our own society.

But in spite of all this study of the civilisations of the past, it often seems to be very difficult to see whether the time in which one is living is a period of civilisation or not. Talk of civilisation leaves one with a feeling of nostalgia; it all belongs to days long ago, and is absent, perhaps not even possible, in our own day. Even when one's own period is not actually one of decline, it is seen as one of transition. Civilisation has existed in the past and may exist again in the future; jam yesterday and possibly tomorrow, but never jam today.

This suggests that historians have in fact not given us much of a definition of civilisation. They have not got much beyond the position of those who 'know what they like'. The Church itself can provide a definition: one which is not purely verbal and fixed, but which can be pointed to in history and which is available for further study, for the continual revision and enrichment of our understanding what we mean by civilisation and are ourselves trying to achieve.

The essential life of the Church, which, I am suggesting, is to be regarded as the key to the definition of civilisation, is best discerned not through an examination of the organisation of the clergy (so often this is what historians mean by 'the Church'), nor through a study of its liturgy (though here we are closer to the heart of the matter), nor yet through an examination of the cultural forms through which it communicated its teachings. In his television lecture series on civilisation, Sir Kenneth Clark rightly drew attention to the way in which the Counter-Reformation threw up new architectural styles, new visual symbols and a wealth of fresh spiritual writing which enabled ordinary people to find themselves within the household of faith, giving them ready access to the truths and moral principles of the Gospels. Achievements of this kind in the history of the Church are certainly worthy of our appreciation and study, but we need to push our researches further and to try to understand what the Church is, that it should be capable of expressing itself in this way.

Christ and Civilisation

If we start from the notion that the Church itself is civilisation, we may get nearer the mark. The essential achievement of the Church is not the building up of an efficient organisation, nor even administering the sacraments to large numbers of people, nor the monuments of intellectual and artistic endeavour: it is the lives which people have been enabled to live under the influence of the Christian Gospel. To study the Church as civilisation we need therefore to look above all at the teaching of the New Testament and see how far this has been understood and practised by those people who have accepted in one way or another the message of Christ. The Sermon on the Mount is the key document of civilisation and of the Church. A man may be accounted civilised to the degree in which he has shown himself to be, in practice, a disciple of Christ.

This means that our criterion for deciding what constitutes civilisation will be an overall human one. We shall not look to see how efficiently a given society was organised, how far it was ruled by law, how coherent were its ideas, how splendid its artistic achievement, though answers to these questions will lead us to the ultimate answer. In order to evaluate the place of the Church within society, we shall not be looking at its official standing in the eyes of the state or of public opinion, nor at the degree of power of one kind or another which its officials may have exercised. We shall see the Church rather in the quality of personal life which it was able to foster.

Intellectuals judge the state of health of the Church by the level of its theological writing, and specialists of other kinds will always have their particular standard by which to judge the achievement of the Church. But the presence or absence of the Church, its effectiveness or ineffectiveness, must be judged rather by its own standards, by the way in which individuals and corporate groups show themselves to be penetrated by the life-pattern of Christ.

To study the Church in this way does not mean simply looking to see whether this or that Christian virtue was practised or not at a particular time and place. Such an investigation might well be rather difficult. It is a matter, rather, of examining the way in which individuals manage to find themselves and grow as human beings in the light of Christian teaching. It is fully formed human persons, not organisations or intellectual structures, who will provide the object of study

This evaluation of civilised behaviour through reference to the New Testament does not mean that our estimate of human development will be individualistic and will simply be an expression of moral judgement. It is a matter of examining the way in which new sets of human relationships come into being and transform those involved through the establishment of links with Christ; it is this pattern of human relationships and achievement which constitutes the Church as civilisation. Because, from the time of Christ, there have always been people who assimilated his life-pattern, releasing their personal energies and abilities through accepting the principle of death to self, so that life may take over, civilisation in the true human sense has always existed, persisting through the upheavals and collapses which historians have often regarded as signs of the break-up or decline of civilisation, but which were often in fact crises which brought the individuals who coped satisfactorily with them to the height of civilised behaviour. True civilisation can exist in a recognisable way within a variety of cultural patterns and even, perhaps especially, in circumstances in which normal cultural manifestations and potentialities are absent: in war-time, concentration camps, prisons, hospitals, or among those who are in need of every kind.

Breaking and Making Relationships

Patterns of civilisation can be seen in kinship patterns, in family and social relationships, and in the attitudes or groups and generations to one another to which anthropologists, psychologists and sociologists devote their attention. Now it is particularly striking that the example of Christ and the demands which he makes involve entering into a particular range of kinship patterns which have adopted sonship, in union with him, as their basis and centre, and obedience to the word of God as their condition and principle of exercise. 'My mother and my brothers are those who hear the word of God and put it into practice' (Lk 8:21). This new set of relationships may involve the breaking of the various kinds of relationship studied by the social scientists and anthropologists: 'Anyone who prefers father or mother to me is not worthy of me. Anyone who prefers son or daughter to me is not worthy of me' (Mt 10:37). The one episode recorded of the time of Christ's growth to maturity shows that he himself broke the family pattern in order to live out the one relationship which was essential to his own life and to our own: 'Did you not know that I must be busy with my Father's affairs?' (Lk 2:49).

It is precisely this fundamental pattern of relationships, made possible through Christ and through the gift of the Holy Spirit, which makes possible personal fulfilment in freedom and which constitutes the new society and civilisation of the Church, open, like other societies, to the investigation of the social scientist and student of human culture, but so far hardly understood or investigated from this point of view.

Even the all-important chapter two of *Lumen Gentium*, on 'The People of God', does not bring out the novelty, where the style of personal living and where true civilisation are concerned, of Christ's call to follow him and to imitate him in his relationship with his Father in heaven, a heaven which is now present on earth as an active, transmuting force in human relationships. It tells us that the Church is grounded in the human reality which makes up its essential membership, but it does not bring out the way in which this new human reality comes into being and continues its existence: the establishment, through personal response, of a relationship with God on which all links with other people then depend. Following the example of Christ, the individual has to find himself or herself through the love of God without deferring to parental or any other human ties. This principle was emphasised by Christ in his reply to Peter, who, with the other apostles, had left everything to follow him. 'I tell you solemnly, there is no one who has left house, brothers, sisters, father, children or land for my sake and for the sake of the gospel who will not be repaid a hundred times over — now in this present time and, in the world to come, eternal life' (Mk 10:29-30). This suggests the breaking of existing given relationships which are then replaced by new ones, all based on the fundamental new relationship which is described as life 'for the sake of the Gospel' or 'for the sake of Christ'.

The Church therefore consists of a number of individuals who are trying to live out the demand of Christ and are doing this in a corporate and conscious way in terms of relationships with one another, and also in terms of relationships with all other human beings in whom, in one way or another, they expect to find Christ.

When we study the Church as civilisation, this is the kind of human reality which we shall be examining, and not the organisation centred on the pastoral activity of the clergy and involving the practice of a number of rites and duties, of which even *Lumen Gentium* speaks when giving a picture of the people of God. Unless we are aware of the type of continually renewed free decision which brings individuals into the Church and which keeps them there we shall always tend to assimilate the Church to other types of human society.

We shall on that account be failing to apply the essential category which enables us to distinguish the Church from its subsidiary cultural manifestations and to discern its true originality. This is important where history and apologetics are concerned; but what is of far greater importance is the fact that we shall fail to see how Church life itself should work, how individuals are related to the Church and how they fulfil themselves within it.

The relationships brought into existence by the Church are not relationships of a purely natural kind. The Church does not exist to reinforce those ties in which we find ourselves involved in spite of ourselves: it is a principle of disorder at least as much as a principle of order. By enabling people to establish the fundamental relationship correctly, it makes it possible for them to bring all other relationships into harmony, to reconcile the claims of individual and society, to use their freedom in a creative and constructive way.

Attempts to identify Church and state, Church and social order, Church and family and so on, must necessarily break down, through a failure to understand the independence and distinctively transforming role of the Church. The authority of the Church must not be called upon to reinforce the authority of governments or of parents, and it is not primarily the task of the Church to build up a particular pattern of human society — except, of course, its own constantly growing and changing pattern.

Even those who have remembered to stress the independence of the Church in relationship to the diverse human cultures have not always avoided making this mistake. They have continued in spite of themselves to regard the Church as the most important element in an over-all system of social order, and they have not given sufficient thought to the fact that an essential preliminary condition for belonging to the Church is, in the mind of Christ, the breaking of every personal link.

Practical Consequences

The consequences of this where our thought about education, for example, is concerned are far-reaching. Young people need to be shown that the Church is just not one more stifling aspect of parental or scholastic environment which can appear to them to be hindering their true development. They need to be shown that a proper relationship with God through Christ is the real way of finding themselves, instead of allowing themselves to be moulded into the sort of image which their parents or teachers may have devised for them. There is an entirely legitimate personal break which has to be achieved and this can be carried out in a constructive and healing way if Christianity is properly taught, instead of in the destructive and dissolving way which so many people follow, to the great hurt and damage of all concerned. To understand the Church as a civilisation is to understand the way in which individuals become civilised.

The acceptance of celibacy for the sake of the Kingdom of God must be also understood against this background, and not simply in the narrower perspective of giving up the support and comfort of marriage and the family. Celibacy is a means of putting oneself outside the ordinary structures of society, which involve professional ties, links of inheritance, the stamp of social class, the building up of a career, the acquisition of real estate and all the other necessary ways of constructing a regular and fruitful way of life, in order that one may establish one's roots in the teaching and practice of the Gospel, the supreme means by which all of these other things are kept healthy and flourishing and can continually be renewed. When the clergy become a set and accepted order within society, as with the *Ordo clericorum* of the Middle Ages or with the moral gendarmes of Joseph II or the Napoleonic régime, then celibacy has lost its point, which is that of freeing men and women to act as a ferment of inspiration and criticism in society.

If we adopt this point of view of looking at the Church as civilisation, we shall be preserved both from identifying the Church with a particular historical age and from the anxiety which arises when one imagines that contemporary civilisation is in a state of decline. Instead of shaking his head over the wretched state of the time in which he lives and hankering over some past age, held to be truly civilised, the correct attitude for any Christian is the conviction that civilisation is available to him at any time and in any place. Christian civilisation does not belong to the thirteenth or the seventeenth centuries, but can be found at all times in Church history.

Christ was the completely civilised man, and those who have imitated him closely have achieved civilisation in their lives, whatever their social status or degree of education. One aspect of civilisation, for example, is being able to get on with other human beings of any kind: to put them at their ease and to make them feel able to expand and develop with the aid of your acquaintance and association. This can be seen happening very clearly in the life of Christ. At the same time, the civilised man can cope with every situation in which he may find himself, rising above hostility and persecution. This again can be seen in the life of Christ.

Civilisation is more clearly seen in individuals than in societies. An individual is capable of rounded and complete achievement, the pattern of which is visible in the whole of his life. This is not true of societies, which may help individuals to develop by means of their organisation, language, cultural achievements and so on, but which cannot be said to constitute complete achievements in the same way. An indication of this is the difficulty historians have in establishing chronological divisions in the sections of human life that they are studying. Birth and death are quite definite for individuals; they are not for societies. Historians preoccupied with the rise and fall of civilisations, especially those who turn prophet about the age in which they are living, may be doing no more than project their own political and cultural preferences, their own optimism or pessimism, or the infinitely varied stream of human existence. If the essentials of civilisation are to be found in the life of the Church, properly so called, then they are available everywhere and at all times. Most ages have seemed to those who lived through them to be ages of precipitate change and of disaster; but some men in every age, despite their circumstances, achieved civilisation.

Nineteenth-century Catholicism was dominated by the idea of rebuilding Christian society, of the formation of the entire life of a country by Catholic principles. Churchmen may have put the kingdom of God first, but they spoke and worked as if their effective patriotism was focussed on an earthly city.

Sauvez Rome et la France
Au nom du Sacré-Coeur:

the words of the pilgrimage hymn had their echo in other countries besides France.

Cardinal Newman was by no means convinced that we should seek to build a Christian civilisation, as something expressed in the whole ordering of society, so that the State comes to be regulated as though it had been swallowed up by the Church. When T. W. Allies declared that 'Catholic civilisation . . . was the ideal which the Church aimed at in the middle ages, and which she worked into the laws, manners, institutions, public policy, and public opinion of Europe', Newman expressed his scepticism about the value of such an aim.

I do not see my way then to hold that 'Catholic civilisation' as you describe it, is in fact (I do not say in the abstract but in a world like this), is, or has been, or shall or can be, a good or *per se* desirable . . . Now, that it is the tendency of Christianity to impress itself on the face of society, I grant; but so in like manner it is the tendency of devotion to increase Church lands and property, and to multiply religious houses; but as the state of the recipient (i.e., a given people, *hic et nunc*) may hinder the latter tendency from working well, e.g., may lead to secularity and corruption in the clergy, so may certain peculiarities in this or that age or place, interfere with the beneficial effects of the former; that is, it is not necessarily good.[1]

It may well be said that this is too easy a solution to the problem of what constitutes authentic Christian living. If the only way of keeping one's equilibrium is the way of not expecting too much, of retreating into Church life, of looking at the world with a pessimistic and even rather jaundiced eye, this seems too great a price to pay. Newman once wrote on these lines to a friend disturbed by the state of the Church:

As to your question, the Church has ever seemed dying, and has been especially bad (to appearance) every 300 years. Think of it when the whole force of the Roman Empire was against it. Well, they triumphed, against all human calculations. Hardly had things got into shape, when down came the barbarians and all was undone and then they had to begin again. Would not the prospect of the future look as terrible to St Augustine or St Leo (humanly) as it does to our generation? It is impossible to forecast the future, when you have no precedents, and the history of Christianity is a succession of fresh trials, never the same twice.[2]

He does not accept a façile theory of man's evolutionary progress: nor does he go over into the group of those who always see the world as going from bad to worse. But he only avoids these extremes by appearing to be uncommitted, by never expecting too much.

[1] Newman to Allies, 22 November 1860, Orat. P. C.; quoted in MacDougall, H. A., *The Acton-Newman Relations*, Fordham U. P., 1962, p. 173.
[2] Newman to Monsell, 30 April 1877, Orat. P. C.; ibid., p. 172.

We can be more confident than Newman was about the extent to which the life of the Church can be given social and cultural expression in this world. But that expression will come about as a by-product of seeking the Kingdom of God, of living the essential life of the Church. Those who seek first a Christian civilisation will find it eludes them just as surely as civilisation itself eludes those who leave the Church out of their calculations.

June 1971

ENVOI

RESTAURANTS AND REDEMPTION:
THE THEOLOGY OF CUISINE

I suppose everyone should be grateful to *The Good Food Guide* for bringing *ratatouille niçoise* to the English countryside. It would be absurdly snobbish to despise the fact that one can now enjoy Provençal cooking at the restaurant tucked away behind the cut-price petrol station. But the cosmopolitan invasion is getting out of hand. It is possible that one day, like every good conquered people, we shall end by mastering our conquerors, but at present we are going through a phase of indigestion.

If we heard that the Italians were combing the Umbrian hills for Yorkshire pudding or savouring kippers and bloaters in Amalfi, we would consider them to be suffering from some bizarre gastronomic madness. But spaghetti bolognese in a West Country farmhouse is really just as odd. Devon is no doubt full of people who want to spend their evenings reminiscing about package holidays in nostalgic surroundings, so it may well be profitable to lay on the saltimbocca and the cannellone and hang up a few straw-covered bottles. The thing is bogus just the same.

Even when our eating out is not given a foreign flavour, and an attempt is made at a local English style, the effect is spoilt by a lack of straightforwardness; everything has to be done in fancy dress in a folksy or medievalising way, with comely wenches offering love apples instead of tomatoes, or coneys in tansy sauce. Wheeling out the roast beef of Old England in a flurry of white napery, silver dish covers and ample waistcoats may seem a trifle better, as a more established way of doing things, but, as décor, it can still be overdone.

If there is to be a renaissance of civilised eating and drinking in England, this sort of thing is not what we want. It is just as outlandish to recreate a Victorian dining room or a Chaucerian hostelry for browsing in as it is to set up a Marseilles bistro in Friern Barnet. The fun is that of a fancy dress ball; all right for an occasional change, but it has no more to do with cooking or hospitality than disguise has to do with dancing. Let the French give us French restaurants and the Italians *trattorie*, along with the Chinese, Indians, Vietnamese, Japanese, Germans, Spaniards and all the rest. But Englishmen who hand out menus in which Crete, Vienna, Lancashire, Polynesia and Maryland jostle for attention, all in the context of ribbon curtains, oilcloth, chopsticks, toothpicks and other picturesque impedimenta associated with warmer places, are furnishing evidence of the triumph of tourism, but are doing nothing at all for the enhancement of the English way of life.

The one country restaurant I know which does attempt to stay native, with a deployment of seafood, steaks and Stilton, falls into vulgarity through the sheer quantity it provides. The butcher who runs it staffs the place with cousins, aunts and daughters, all buxom evidence of the value of his fare, but eating there is rather like taking part in a holiday-camp eating race. At a similar place I know in Normandy, working men take hours over their lunch, vigorously debating the menu with Madame and forcefully discussing the food when it arrives; they are uninhibited all right, but the whole performance is thoroughly civilised, since taste and variety, not mere size and weight, have governed the selection.

The new wave of English restaurants — places like Crispins and Bumbles — have brought in a readiness to mix foods and flavours and a style of cultivated casualness, youthful ease and politeness, which is refreshing when people know what they are doing, but which is disastrous in the wrong hands. If you are going to have 'Trinity College Cream' on the menu, your waitresses in their long dresses must at least know that there is more than one Trinity College. It will take more than a few charming undergraduates to give our eating an identity of its own.

The good foreign restaurants in England are, like the ones abroad, family affairs. However grand they may be, there is always an old lady in a knitted jumper hovering somewhere in the background. Only when restaurant cooking becomes an extension of home cooking, and when home cooking and eating become a family custom, will we have any real progress. When sixth-formers learn how to assess materials instead of spending hours arranging prawn cocktails, and when Sunday lunch gives time for conversation — including talk about food — then perhaps public eating will acquire a sense of style.

As things are at present, in spite of *The Good Food Guide*, eating in England remains awkward and unnatural, an exotic pleasure, even a guilty one, untouched by grace. When a puritan tries to break out, he often falls into barbarity. And there is more than a touch of barbarism around at present. Clothes as well as food reveal it, in the King's Road or Kensington High Street.

Good food in France is still the expression of a robust, highly moral, classless common sense. When we can eat out well in England without being insulted by formica, package foods, artificial flavouring or the bill, then we shall be able to stand on our own feet in Europe, and shall enter a better world in which dining will be part of our redemption. Everyone will at last know how to use this essential way of restoring our good nature.

Catholic Herald, 10 August 1973

CHRONOLOGY

A PERSONAL SELECTION OF SIGNIFICANT DATES IN THE
HISTORY OF THE CATHOLIC CHURCH FROM 1958 TO 1982
WITH PARTICULAR REFERENCE TO ENGLAND AND WALES.

PETER JENNINGS

Keep Thou my feet; I do not ask to see
The distant scene — one step enough for me.

John Henry Newman

16 June 1833

1958

9 October: Death of Pope Pius XII at Castel Gandolfo, aged eighty-two. Elected Pope 2 March 1939.

28 October: Cardinal Angelo Roncalli, Patriarch of Venice, is elected Pope by a Conclave of fifty-five Cardinals at the eleventh ballot, and takes the name John XXIII.

15 December: Archbishop Giovanni Montini of Milan created Cardinal.

1959

25 January: After Mass for Christian Unity at the Benedictine monastery adjoining the Basilica of St Paul's Outside the Walls, Pope John first announces (to a private gathering of eighteen Cardinals) his intention to summon a Council of the Church.

29 June: Publication of Pope John's first Encyclical Letter *Ad Petri Cathedram* (on truth, unity, peace).

1960

5 June: Pope John establishes the Vatican Secretariat for Promoting Christian Unity under Cardinal Augustine Bea.

2 December: Meeting between Pope John and the Archbishop of Canterbury, Dr Geoffrey Fisher at the Vatican: the first between the Pope and an Archbishop of Canterbury since the Reformation.

1961

5 May:	Meeting between Pope John and Her Majesty Queen Elizabeth II at the Vatican.
15 May:	Publication of Pope John's Encyclical Letter *Mater et Magistra* (on Social Justice).
27 June:	Dr Michael Ramsey enthroned as the 100th Archbishop of Canterbury.
26 August:	Bishop John Murphy appointed Archbishop of Cardiff.
25 December:	Pope John, in the apostolic constitution *Humanae Salutis*, convokes the Vatican Council.

1962

20 July:	Invitations are sent to separated Christian Churches and Communities to send delegate-observers to the Council.
11 October:	The Second Vatican Council solemnly opened in St Peter's Basilica by Pope John. The Church's Twenty-First Ecumenical Council and the first since Vatican I of 1869-70.
20 October:	The Council issues a *Message to Humanity*.
8 December:	The first session of the Council is concluded without any completed results.

1963

22 January:	Death of Cardinal William Godfrey, Archbishop of Westminster, aged seventy-three.
28 March:	Pope John establishes a commission for the revision of the Code of Canon Law.
11 April:	Publication of Pope John's Encyclical Letter *Pacem in Terris* (Peace on Earth). On 13 May, at the request of Pope John, Cardinal Suenens, Primate of Belgium, hands the encyclical to the U.N. Secretary General U Thant, and addresses the U.N. Assembly.

3 June:	Death of Pope John XXIII at the Vatican, aged eighty-one.
21 June:	Cardinal Giovanni Battista Montini, Archbishop of Milan, is elected Pope by a Conclave of eighty Cardinals and takes the name of Paul VI. He announces his intention to continue the Vatican Council.
30 June:	Pope Paul VI solemnly crowned in St Peter's Square.
2 September:	Archbishop John Heenan of Liverpool succeeds Cardinal Godfrey as eighth Archbishop of Westminster.
29 September:	The Second Session of the Council opens.
5 October:	Archbishop Cardinale takes up appointment as Apostolic Delegate to Great Britain.
11 November:	Cardinal Suenens proposes that an age-limit of seventy-five be set for the retirement of bishops.
4 December:	The Second Session of the Council closes with the promulgation of the *Constitution on the Sacred Liturgy* and the *Decree on the Instruments of Social Communication.*

1964

4 to 6 January:	Visit of Pope Paul to Jordan and Israel.
5 January:	Historic meeting between Pope Paul and Ecumenical Patriarch Athenagoras of Constantinople on the Mount of Olives in Jerusalem.
13 January:	Bishop Karol Wojtyla, auxiliary of Cracow, Poland, since 1958, is appointed Archbishop of Cracow.
29 January:	Bishop George Beck of Salford is appointed Archbishop of Liverpool.
2 April:	Pope Paul establishes a Pontifical Commission for means of Social Communication.

19 May:	Pope Paul establishes a Vatican Secretariat for Non-Christians.
14 September:	Pope Paul opens the Third Session of the Council.
21 November:	The Third Session of the Council closes with the promulgation of the *Dogmatic Constitution on the Church (Lumen Gentium)*, the *Decree on Ecumenism* and the *Decree on the Eastern Catholic Churches*.
2 to 5 December:	Visit of Pope Paul to India, where he attends the thirty-eighth International Eucharistic Congress in Bombay.

1965

22 February:	Archbishop Heenan created Cardinal by Pope Paul and appointed Vice-President of the Secretariat for the Promotion of Christian Unity. (Twenty-seven new Cardinals increase the number in the Sacred College to 103, representing forty-three countries).
28 May:	The diocese of Southwark is raised to Metropolitan rank, and Bishop Cyril Cowderoy is named first Archbishop.
14 September:	The Fourth and final session of the Council opens.
15 September:	Pope Paul in the Apostolic Letter *Apostolica Sollicitudo* sets forth the norms governing the new Episcopal Synod established to assist the government of the Church.
4 October:	Pope Paul addresses the United Nations General Assembly in New York at the invitation of U Thant, the Secretary General.
7 October:	Bishop George Patrick Dwyer of Leeds is appointed Archbishop of Birmingham.
28 October:	The following documents are promulgated by the Council: *Decree on the Pastoral Office of Bishops in the Church (Christus Dominus), Decree on the Renewal and Adaptation to*

Modern Times of the Religious Life, Decree on the Training of Priests, Declaration on Christian Education, Declaration on the Relation of the Church to non-Christian Religions.

18 November: Promulgation of the *Dogmatic Constitution on Divine Revelation* and the *Decree on the Apostolate of the Laity*.

Pope Paul announces the beginning of a reform of the Roman Curia.

4 December: A Service of Prayer for Christian Unity at St Paul's Outside the Walls is attended by the Pope, Council Fathers, observers and guests at the Council.

7 December: Promulgation of the *Declaration on Religious Liberty, Decree on the Priestly Ministry and Life, Decree on the Missionary Activity of the Church,* and the *Pastoral Constitution on the Church in the Modern World* (*Gaudium et Spes*).

7 December: Pope Paul begins the reorganisation of the Roman Curia — The Holy Office is given the new title of the Sacred Congregation for the Doctrine of the Faith.

7 December: Common Declaration of Pope Paul and Patriarch Athenagoras of Constantinople lifts the mutual excommunication imposed in 1054 by the Papal Legate Cardinal Humbert and Patriarch Michael Cerularius.

8 December: The Second Vatican Council solemnly closed by Pope Paul.

28 December: The Queen attends a special service at Westminster Abbey to celebrate the 900th anniversary of its consecration.

1966

22 to 24 March: Meeting between Pope Paul and the Archbishop of Canterbury, Dr Michael Ramsey at the Vatican.

24 March:	Common Declaration between Pope Paul and the Archbishop of Canterbury at St Paul's Outside the Walls.
6 August:	Pope Paul in the Apostolic Letter *Ecclesiae Sanctae* makes it obligatory that all Bishops should offer their resignation on reaching the age of seventy-five.
21 October:	Publication of *The Jerusalem Bible*.
20 December:	Father Charles Davis resigns as Editor of *The Clergy Review* and announces his intention to leave the priesthood.
21 December:	Abbot Basil Christopher Butler, OSB, of Downside is consecrated Bishop by Cardinal Heenan and becomes an auxiliary bishop in the Diocese of Westminster.
23 December:	Cardinal Heenan invites Father Michael Richards of St Edmund's College, Ware, to take over the Editorship of *The Clergy Review*.

1967

9 to 13 January:	First meeting of the Anglican-Roman Catholic Joint Preparatory Commission (established by Pope Paul and the Archbishop of Canterbury, Dr Ramsey) at Gazzada, Italy.
30 January:	President Podgorny of the Soviet Union becomes the first communist head of state to have an audience with the Pope.
26 March:	Publication of Pope Paul's Encyclical Letter *Populorum Progressio* (on the Development of Peoples).
13 May:	Visit of Pope Paul to Fatima, Portugal, for the fiftieth anniversary of the apparitions of 1917.
14 May:	Publication of Directory Concerning Ecumenical Matters by the Secretariat for Promoting Christian Unity.

14 May:	Consecration of the new Metropolitan Cathedral of Christ the King, Liverpool, by Cardinal Heenan.
26 June:	Archbishop Wojtyla of Cracow created Cardinal.
25 to 26 July:	Visit of Pope Paul to Patriarch Athenagoras in Constantinople.
15 August:	Pope Paul sets out details of the reform of the Roman Curia which comes into force on 1 January 1968. (Constitution *Regimini Ecclesiae Universae*).
31 August to 4 September:	Second meeting of the Anglican-Roman Catholic Joint Preparatory Commission held at Huntercombe Manor.
29 September to 29 October:	First General Assembly of the International Synod of Bishops held in Rome, with 197 participants, on the Revision of the Code of Canon Law, Seminaries, Mixed Marriages and Renewal of the Liturgy.
30 December to 3 January 1968:	Third meeting of the Anglican-Roman Catholic Joint Preparatory Commission held in Malta.

1968

16 to 18 April:	First meeting of the Roman Catholic-Anglican Commission on the Theology of Marriage at Windsor Castle. The Commission was established in 1967 by the Secretariat for Promoting Christian Unity and the Archbishop of Canterbury with particular reference to the problems in 'mixed marriages' between Catholics and Anglicans.
2 June:	Whit Sunday — Cardinal Heenan preaches in Westminster Abbey, the first Cardinal to do so since the Reformation.
30 June:	Pope Paul issues his *Credo of the People of God*.
29 July:	Publication of Pope Paul's Encyclical Letter *Humanae Vitae* (on the Regulation of Births)

which condemns all forms of artificial birth control.

22 to 24 August:	Pope Paul visits the Eucharistic Congress at Bogota, capital of Colombia.
22 to 24 November:	Association of Interchurch Families — First conference held at Spode House.
29 November:	Publication of The Malta Report in *The Tablet*.

1969

4 March:	Foundation of the Ecumenical Society of the Blessed Virgin Mary. Mr Martin Gillett Secretary until his death on 23 April 1980.
28 April:	Archbishop Gordon Gray of St Andrews and Edinburgh created Cardinal.
10 June:	Visit of Pope Paul to the World Council of Churches and the International Labour Office in Geneva.
29 June:	Archbishop Enrici takes up appointment as Apostolic Delegate to Great Britain.
7 to 10 July:	Symposium of European Bishops in Chur, Switzerland.
8 July:	The General Synod of the Church of England votes to reject the Anglican-Methodist Unity Scheme.
31 July to 2 August:	Visit of Pope Paul to Uganda; the first by a Pope to Africa.
10 October:	The Anglican-Roman Catholic International Commission (ARCIC) is appointed by the Archbishop of Canterbury and the Vatican Secretariat for Christian Unity.
11 to 28 October:	Extraordinary General Synod of Bishops in Rome, with 146 participants, to study the improvement of collegial understanding between the Holy See and National Bishops' Conferences. A Synod Council is established.
29 November:	Opening of the Catholic Radio and Television Centre at Hatch End.

30 November:	The New Order of Mass (a revision of the Roman Missal promulgated by St Pius V in 1570), approved by Pope Paul, comes into effect. (Apostolic Constitution *Missale Romanum*, of 3 April 1969).

1970

1 January:	Reorganisation of the liturgical year and calendar for the Roman Rite comes into effect. (Approved by Pope Paul in *Paschali Mysteri*, of 9 May 1969).
9 to 15 January:	First meeting of the Anglican-Roman Catholic International Commission held at Windsor Castle. The Commission, following the Malta Report, examined eucharist, ministry and authority in relation to the overall concept of *Koinonia*.
31 March:	Publication of Motu Proprio *Matrimonia Mixta* (on mixed marriages).
1 to 5 June:	First National Conference of Priests (convened by the Hierarchy of England and Wales) held at Wood Hall. Father Sean Kearney elected chairman.
21 to 28 September:	Second meeting of the Anglican-Roman Catholic International Commission held in Venice.
27 September:	Pope Paul proclaims St Teresa of Avila as the first woman Doctor of the Church.
25 October:	Canonisation of the Forty Martyrs of England and Wales in St Peter's Basilica by Pope Paul: 'May the blood of these martyrs be able to heal the great wound inflicted upon God's Church by the separation of the Anglican from the Catholic Church'.
21 November:	Pope Paul announces that, after 1 January 1971, Cardinals over the age of eighty will be excluded from future Conclaves. Apostolic Letter *Ingravescentem Aetatem* (*The Growing Weight of Age*).

26 November to 5 December:	Visit of Pope Paul to Samoa, Sri Lanka, Indonesia, Philippines, and Hong Kong from where he broadcast to the people of China.
27 November:	An attack is made on the life of Pope Paul as he arrives at Manila Airport in the Philippines.
4 December:	Visit of Pope Paul to Australia.

1971

11 April:	Publication of General Catechetical Directory by the Sacred Congregation for the Clergy.
14 May:	Heythrop College granted a Royal Charter and becomes part of London University. (The College moved from Oxfordshire to London during 1970).
1 to 8 September:	Third meeting of the Anglican-Roman Catholic International Commission held at Windsor Castle.
6 to 10 September:	Second National Conference of Priests held in Liverpool. Constitution accepted by the priests and by the Bishops' Conference at their November meeting.
30 September to 6 November:	The Second General Assembly of the International Synod of Bishops in Rome, with 210 participants, on the Ministerial Priesthood, and International Justice.
31 December:	The Anglican-Roman Catholic International Commission publishes its First *Agreed Statement on Eucharistic Doctrine.*

1972

14 March:	A Service of Intercession for Peace in Northern Ireland held in Westminster Cathedral attended by Cardinal Heenan, the Archbishop of Canterbury, and the Prime Minister, Mr Edward Heath.
7 July:	Death of Patriarch Athenagoras of Constantinople aged eighty-six.

30 August to 7 September:	Fourth meeting of the Anglican-Catholic International Commission held in Gazzada, Italy.
11 to 15 September:	Third National Conference of Priests held at Newman College, Birmingham.
14 September:	Cardinal Heenan addresses the First National Church Leaders' Conference, held in Birmingham.
4 October:	Cardinal Jan Willebrands, President of the Secretariat for Promoting Christian Unity, gives a lecture in the Great Hall of Lambeth Palace.
5 October:	The Congregational Church and the Presbyterian Church in England and Wales unite as the United Reformed Church.

1973

5 March:	Patriarch Albino Luciani of Venice created Cardinal.
25 April:	Mother Teresa of Calcutta presented with the Templeton Foundation Prize for Progress in Religion by Prince Philip at the Guildhall, London.
21 June:	Publication of *The Church 2000*, an Interim Report on pastoral strategy offered by the joint working party set up by the Bishops' Conference and the National Conference of Priests.
14 July:	Cardinal Mindszenty, Primate of Hungary, visits England.
28 August to 6 September:	Fifth meeting of the Anglican-Roman Catholic International Commission held at St Augustine's College in Canterbury.
3 to 7 September:	Fourth meeting of the National Conference of Priests held in Birmingham on the theme of Co-responsibility. Chairman: Mgr Philip Cronin.

| 16 October: | Archbishop Bruno Heim takes up appointment as Apostolic Delegate to Great Britain. |
| 13 December: | The Anglican-Roman Catholic International Commission publishes its Second *Agreed Statement on Ministry and Ordination.* |

1974

4 July:	Publication of *Ground Plan*, a suggested reorganisation of the diocesan structure of the Catholic Church in England and Wales.
27 August to 5 September:	Sixth meeting of the Anglican-Roman Catholic International Commission held at Grottaferrata, Italy.
2 to 6 September:	Fifth meeting of the National Conference of Priests, held in Birmingham.
27 September to 26 October:	The Third General Assembly of the International Synod of Bishops in Rome, with 209 participants, on Evangelisation of Today's World.
7 November:	Bishop Alan Clark, Co-Chairman of the International Commission, addresses the General Synod of the Church of England in London.

1975

24 January:	Enthronement of Dr Donald Coggan as the 101st Archbishop of Canterbury.
16 June:	Publication of *A New Pentecost?* by Cardinal Suenens.
18 to 20 July:	Meeting of the fifteen National Commissions of the Bishops' Conference of England and Wales at Newman College, Birmingham.
29 August to 5 September:	Seventh meeting of the Anglican-Roman Catholic International Commission, held at St Stephen's House, Oxford.
1 to 5 September:	Sixth meeting of the National Conference of Priests, held in Birmingham on the theme of Education.

23 September:	Due to ill-health, Cardinal John Heenan writes to Pope Paul to offer his resignation as Archbishop of Westminster.
1 October:	Pope Paul issues Apostolic Constitution *Romano Pontifici Eligendo* (on the election of the Roman Pontiff). The maximum number of Cardinal electors at a Conclave must not exceed 120.
7 November:	Death of Cardinal John Heenan aged seventy. Solemn Requiem held in Westminster Cathedral on 14 November.
8 December:	Publication of Pope Paul's Apostolic Exhortation *Evangelii Nuntiandi* (on Evangelisation in the Modern World).

1976

7 February:	Bishop Derek Worlock of Portsmouth appointed Archbishop of Liverpool. Installed on 19 March.
17 February:	Abbot Basil Hume, OSB, of Ampleforth, appointed Archbishop of Westminster.
25 March:	Episcopal Ordination and Installation of George Basil Hume, OSB, (53) as the Ninth Archbishop of Westminster in Westminster Cathedral.
	Benedictine monks sing latin plainsong vespers for the Feast of the Annunciation in Westminster Abbey.
29 April:	Bishop Langton Fox of Menevia appointed Ecclesiastical Assistant to the Catholic Charismatic Renewal in England and Wales by the Bishops' Conference.
24 May:	Archbishop Hume, OSB, created Cardinal.
31 May:	Death of Father Charles Stephen Dessain of The Oratory, Birmingham, aged sixty-eight. A distinguished Newman scholar, he edited twenty-one volumes of *The Letters and Diaries of John Henry Newman*.

29 June:	Dissident Archbishop Marcel Lefebvre ordains thirteen men to the priesthood at his seminary in Econe, Switzerland and is suspended from the licit exercise of holy orders by the Vatican.
24 August to 2 September:	Eighth meeting of the Anglican-Roman Catholic International Commission held in Venice.
6 to 10 September:	Seventh meeting of the National Conference of Priests held in Birmingham on the theme of Justice and Peace.
16 October:	Publication of the *Good News Bible*.
16 November:	Publication of *A Time For Building*, the Final Report of the joint working party set up by the Bishops' Conference and the National Conference of Priests in 1971.

1977

20 January:	The Anglican-Roman Catholic International Commission publishes its Third *Agreed Statement on Authority in the Church*.
23 April:	Bishop Michael Bowen of Arundel and Brighton is appointed Archbishop of Southwark. Installed on 23 April.
28 April:	Meeting between Pope Paul and the Archbishop of Canterbury, Dr Donald Coggan, at the Vatican.
29 April:	Common Declaration signed by the Pope and Archbishop of Canterbury after a service in the Sistine Chapel.
1 to 5 August:	International Conference on Charismatic Renewal, *Growing In The Church*, held in London, sponsored jointly by the Catholic Committee for Charismatic Renewal and the Fountain Trust.
30 August to 8 September:	Ninth meeting of the Anglican-Roman Catholic International Commission held at Chichester Theological College.

5 to 9 September:	Eighth meeting of the National Conference of Priests held in Birmingham on the theme *A Time For Building*. Chairman: Father Tom Shepherd. Mgr Joseph C. Buckley expresses his hope for a National Congress to be held in 1980.
19 September:	Publication of *Searching For God* by Cardinal Basil Hume, OSB.
30 September to 29 October:	Fourth General Assembly of the International Synod of Bishops in Rome, with 204 participants, on Catechetics.
13 October:	Ecumenical Service in Westminster Abbey to dedicate a memorial to all martyrs of the Reformation, Catholic and Protestant.
21 November:	Mgr Cormac Murphy-O'Connor, Rector of the Venerable English College in Rome, appointed Bishop of Arundel and Brighton. Installed on 21 December.
November:	The Revised (1977) Directory on Mixed Marriages issued by the Episcopal Conference of England and Wales.

1978

25 January:	The Archbishop of Canterbury, Dr Donald Coggan, preaching at an ecumenical service for Christian Unity in Westminster Cathedral makes a plea for intercommunion.
1 February:	Cardinal Basil Hume, OSB, addresses the General Synod of the Church of England.
9 March:	Death of Mr Douglas Woodruff, Editor of *The Tablet* from 1936 to 1967, aged eighty.
17 March:	Start of a thirty-day vigil of prayer for Northern Ireland, inaugurated by Cardinal Hume in Westminster Cathedral.
10 to 13 April:	The first all-European ecumenical meeting of the Conference of European Churches (CEC), and Council of Bishops' Conferences in Europe (CCEE) held at Chantilly near Paris.

28 May:	Vespers sung in Latin in Canterbury Cathedral for the first time since 1540, by Benedictine monks and nuns recalling the Benedictine contribution in England.
6 July:	Cardinal Hume, OSB, celebrates Mass and preaches in honour of St Thomas More in the crypt chapel of the Houses of Parliament.
23 July:	The eleventh Lambeth Conference of the Anglican Communion opens with a service in Canterbury Cathedral.
6 August:	Death of Pope Paul VI at his summer residence of Castel Gandolfo at the age of eighty.
12 August:	Funeral of Pope Paul VI in St Peter's Square.
26 August:	Cardinal Albino Luciani, Patriarch of Venice, is elected Pope by a Conclave of 111 Cardinals at the fourth ballot, and takes the name John Paul I.
27 August to 8 October:	The Turin Shroud on public display in Turin Cathedral to mark the 400th anniversary of its arrival in Turin during 1578.
3 September:	Inaugural Mass of Pope John Paul I in St Peter's Square: the first Pope since Nicholas II in 1059 not to be crowned.
4 to 8 September:	Ninth meeting of the National Conference of Priests, held in Birmingham. Chairman: Father Gerard Burke.
28 September:	Death of Pope John Paul I at the Vatican aged sixty-six.
4 October:	Funeral of Pope John Paul I in St Peter's Square.
7 to 8 October:	Second International Scientific Congress on the Shroud in Turin followed by five days of scientific tests. A Carbon 14 date test is not allowed.
16 October:	Cardinal Karol Wojtyla, Archbishop of Cracow in Poland, is elected Pope by a Conclave of 111 Cardinals at the eighth ballot,

and takes the name John Paul II. He is the first non-Italian Pope since Adrian VI (1522-23) and, at the age of fifty-eight, the youngest Pope to be elected since 1846.

22 October: Inaugural Mass of Pope John Paul II in St Peter's Square.

1979

12 to 20 January: Tenth meeting of the Anglican-Roman Catholic International Commission held at Salisbury and Wells Theological College, Salisbury.

25 to 26 January: Visit of Pope John Paul to the Dominican Republic. His first overseas visit as Pope.

27 January to 2 February: Visit of Pope John Paul to Mexico.

28 January: Pope John Paul addresses the General Assembly of the Latin American Bishops meeting at Puebla (27 January to 12 February).

26 February: Publication of the *New International Version* of the Bible.

15 March: Publication of Pope John Paul's first Encyclical Letter *Redemptor Hominis* (on the Redemption of Man).

30 April: Archbishop Agostino Casaroli is appointed Secretary of State by Pope John Paul following the death of Cardinal Jean Villot on 9 March. Created Cardinal on 30 June. Cardinal Paolo Bertoli named Cardinal Camerlengo.

15 May: Letter from Pope John Paul to Archbishop George Patrick Dwyer of Birmingham, President of the Bishops' Conference of England and Wales, to mark the Centenary of the Elevation to the Cardinalate of John Henry Newman by Pope Leo XIII on 12 May 1879.

2 to 10 June: Visit of Pope John Paul to Poland. He celebrates Mass in Victory Square, Warsaw at the start of the visit.

21 June:	Cardinal Hume, OSB, elected President of the Council of European Bishops' Conferences at the end of the fourth Symposium of European Bishops in Rome.
30 June:	Archbishop Tomás Ó Fiaich of Armagh and Primate of All Ireland is among fourteen new Cardinals created by Pope John Paul in his first Consistory, raising the membership of the Sacred College to 135.
13 July:	The Queen visits the Flower Festival in Westminster Cathedral.
30 July to 3 August:	International Conference on Charismatic Renewal, *Joy In The City*, held in London, sponsored by the Catholic Committee for Charismatic Renewal and the Fountain Trust.
28 August to 6 September:	Eleventh meeting of the Anglican-Roman Catholic International Commission held in Venice.
3 to 7 September:	Tenth meeting of the National Conference of Priests, held in Birmingham on the theme of Priesthood and Spiritual Renewal. Chairman: Father Gerard Burke.
29 September to 1 October:	Visit of Pope John Paul to Ireland: Phoenix Park, Drogheda, Clonmacnois, Galway, Knock, Maynooth and Limerick.
1 to 8 October:	Visit of Pope John Paul to the United States of America.
2 October:	Pope John Paul addresses the United Nations General Assembly in New York.
16 October:	Publication of Pope John Paul's Apostolic Exhortation *Catechesi Tradendae* (on Catechesis in our time).
17 October:	Mother Teresa of Calcutta is awarded the 1979 Nobel Peace Prize.
1 November:	The Cause for the Beatification and Canonisation of John Henry Cardinal Newman is resumed, with Mgr Anthony Stark as Vice-Postulator.

5 to 9 November:	First Plenary assembly of the College of Cardinals convened by Pope John Paul to review the financial and other problems of the Vatican.
28 to 30 November:	Ecumenical pilgrimage of Pope John Paul to Turkey.
29 November:	Meeting between Pope John Paul and Ecumenical Patriarch Dimitrios I in Istanbul. Establishment of a Catholic-Orthodox theological commission for the beginning of official dialogue in quest for unity of the two Churches.
6 December:	Visit of Pope John Paul to the Venerable English College, Rome, on the occasion of the fourth centenary of its foundation.
13 to 14 December:	Dutch theologian Father Edward Schillebeeckx, OP, questioned by members of the Congregation for the Doctrine of the Faith concerning the contents of his book, *Jesus: An Experiment in Christology.* English language publication on 12 February 1979.
18 December:	The Sacred Congregation for the Doctrine of the Faith declares that Father Hans Küng 'can no longer be considered a Catholic theologian nor function as such in a teaching role'.

1980

14 to 31 January:	Extraordinary Synod of Dutch Bishops convoked by Pope John Paul in Rome on the problems of the Church in Holland.
15 February:	Father Agnellus Andrew, OFM, President of the International Catholic Association for Radio and Television since 1968 named Vice-President of the Pontifical Commission for Social Communications. Consecrated Bishop in Westminster Cathedral on 26 March and took up appointment in the Vatican.
16 March:	Cardinal Tomás Ó Fiaich, Archbishop of Armagh and Primate of All Ireland preaches at

a special ecumenical service of prayer for peace in Northern Ireland held in Westminster Cathedral.

24 to 27 March:
Extraordinary Synod of Bishops of the Ukrainian Rite in Rome to elect eventual successor to Cardinal Josyf Slipyi.

24 March:
Murder of Archbishop Oscar Romero of San Salvador while preaching at a Mass he was celebrating in the chapel of Divine Providence Hospital in San Salvador.

25 March:
Enthronement of Dr Robert Runcie as the 102nd Archbishop of Canterbury.

3 April:
Letter from Pope John Paul to all Bishops of the Church on the Mystery and Worship of the Holy Eucharist.

2 to 6 May:
The National Pastoral Congress of the Catholic Church in England and Wales held in Liverpool, with 2100 delegates representing every level of Church life.

2 to 12 May:
Visit of Pope John Paul to the African countries of Zaire, the People's Republic of the Congo, Kenya, Ghana, Upper Volta and Ivory Coast.

9 May:
First meeting between Pope John Paul and the Archbishop of Canterbury, Dr Robert Runcie, in Accra, Ghana, while on separate tours of Africa.

26 May:
The Archbishop of Canterbury, Dr Robert Runcie leads an Anglican national pilgrimage to the shrine of Our Lady of Walsingham.

30 May to 2 June:
Visit of Pope John Paul to France.

30 June to 12 July:
Visit of Pope John Paul to Brazil.

11 July:
1500th anniversary of the birth of St Benedict in 480. Cardinal Basil Hume, OSB, preaches at a special Mass in Westminster Cathedral. Benedictine monks and nuns of

	the forty-four monastic communities in the United Kingdom, including some Anglicans, sing Vespers in Latin for the Feast of St Benedict in Westminster Abbey, attended by the Archbishop of Canterbury, Dr Robert Runcie.
14 to 16 July:	The Bishops' Conference of England and Wales meet in special session to prepare their message in the light of the National Pastoral Congress. All forty-three bishops take part.
1 August:	Fortieth anniversary of the founding of the Catholic Institute for International Relations (CIIR). Inaugural meeting of 'The Sword of the Spirit' took place in Archbishop's House, Westminster on 1 August 1940.
19 August:	Publication of *The Easter People*, a message from the Roman Catholic Bishops of England and Wales in Light of the National Pastoral Congress.
23 August:	Cardinal Hume, OSB, and Archbishop Worlock of Liverpool, present a copy of *The Easter People* to Pope John Paul during a private audience at Castel Gandolfo. They give the Pope a full report of the Congress and invite him to visit England and Wales.
26 August to 4 September:	Twelfth meeting of the Anglican-Roman Catholic International Commission held in Venice.
31 August:	Announcement that Pope John Paul had agreed to make a Pastoral Visit to the Catholic Church in Great Britain.
1 to 5 September:	Eleventh meeting of the National Conference of Priests, held in Birmingham on the theme of One People One Mission. Chairman: Father Robert Spence.
26 September to 25 October:	Fifth General Assembly of the International Synod of Bishops in Rome, with 216 participants, on the Role of the Christian Family in the Modern World.
28 September:	Pope John Paul joins the European Bishops in a pilgrimage to Subiaco to mark the fif-

teenth centenary of the birth of St Benedict, patron saint of Europe. Declaration of the European Bishops' Conference on *The Responsibility of Christians in the Europe of Today and Tomorrow.*

17 October: The first State Visit by the Queen to the Vatican.

25 October: The Synod issues *Message to the Christian Family in the Modern World.* Cardinal Hume, OSB, is elected to the Council of the Secretariat-General of the Synod.

15 to 19 November: Visit of Pope John Paul to West Germany.

21 November: Publication of an *Instruction On Infant Baptism* by the Sacred Congregation for the Doctrine of the Faith.

27 November: The Bishops' Conference of England and Wales issue statements on unemployment, moral issues surrounding the possession of a nuclear deterrent and the racial situation in South Africa.

3 December: Publication of Pope John Paul's second Encyclical Letter *Dives in Misericordia* (on the Mercy of God).

1981

12 January: Bicentenary of the death of Bishop Richard Challoner on 12 January 1781.

17 February: The Church's teaching forbidding Catholics to enrol in masonic or other similar associations reaffirmed by the Sacred Congregation for the Doctrine of the Faith.

16 to 27 February: Visit of Pope John Paul to the Philippines, the island of Guam and Japan.

25 February: The Church of England General Synod votes to give provisional approval to the Proposals entitled *Towards Visible Unity: Proposals for a Covenant.*

15 March:	Archbishop Godfried Daneels of Malines-Brussels becomes the first Catholic Archbishop to preach at an Anglican Eucharist in Canterbury Cathedral.
30 April:	Bishop Victor Guazzelli, Bishop in East London, appointed Ecclesiastical Assistant to the Catholic Charismatic Renewal.
7 May:	Pope John Paul meets with some 600 participants at the fourth International Leaders' Conference of the Charismatic Renewal held in Rome 4 to 9 May.
13 May:	Assassination attempt on the life of Pope John Paul while he was being driven through the crowds in St Peter's Square at the start of a General Audience. The Pope is rushed to the Gemelli hospital in Rome where he undergoes an emergency operation.
28 May:	Death of Cardinal Stefan Wyszynski, Primate of Poland, aged seventy-nine.
3 June:	Pope John Paul leaves the Gemelli hospital and returns to the Vatican.
20 June:	Pope John Paul is readmitted to the Gemelli hospital.
1 July:	Tercentenary celebrations of the martyrdom of St Oliver Plunkett at Tyburn on 1 July 1681. Cardinal Tomás Ó Fiaich, Archbishop of Armagh and Primate of All Ireland preaches at a special Mass in London.
3 July:	Publication of *Signposts and Homecomings*, the report of a study group on Catholic Education set up by the Bishops' Conference of England and Wales.
3 July:	Publication of *Living Liturgy*, a report prepared by Father Anthony Boylan, National Adviser for Liturgical Formation.
7 July:	Bishop Józef Glemp of Warmia in Poland is appointed Archbishop of Warsaw.

11 July:	First-ever ecumenical pilgrimage to Walsingham, led by Bishop Cormac Murphy-O'Connor of Arundel and Brighton and Bishop Eric Kemp of Chichester.
13 to 14 July:	Special council of Cardinals appointed by Pope John Paul to study the financial and organisational problems facing the Holy See announce that the Vatican expects a deficit of more than £12 million for the year 1981.
16 to 23 July:	Forty-second International Eucharistic Congress held in Lourdes. (First Congress held at Lille in 1881).
29 July:	Wedding of His Royal Highness, the Prince of Wales to The Lady Diana Spencer in St Paul's Cathedral. Cardinal Hume, OSB, says one of the prayers during the service.
14 August:	Pope John Paul leaves the Gemelli hospital and goes to Castel Gandolfo to convalesce.
25 August to 3 September:	The final meeting of the Anglican-Roman Catholic International Commission held at Windsor Castle. Final report completed and submitted to Pope John Paul and the Archbishop of Canterbury, Dr Robert Runcie.
1 September:	Pope John Paul accepts the resignation of Archbishop George Patrick Dwyer of Birmingham who had asked to be allowed to retire for reasons of ill-health.
7 to 11 September:	Twelfth meeting of the National Conference of Priests, held in Birmingham; the Conference prepared material to be included in the general brief to be given to Pope John Paul before his Pastoral Visit to Great Britain.
15 September:	Publication of Pope John Paul's third Encyclical *Laborem Exercens* (on human work) to mark the ninetieth anniversary of the Encyclical *Rerum Novarum* of Pope Leo XIII, 15 May 1891.

3 October:	Letter from Pope John Paul notified the convalescent Fr Pedro Arrupe, superior general of the Society of Jesus, that he had appointed Fr Paolo Dezza, SJ, as his personal delegate to the Society.
4 October:	Celebrations to mark the opening of the eighth centenary of the birth of St Francis of Assisi. Pope John Paul celebrates Mass in St Peter's Square.
7 October:	Pope John Paul holds his first General Audience in St Peter's Square since 13 May.
21 October:	Statement from Cardinal Hume, OSB, and Cardinal Gordon Gray, Archbishop of St Andrews and Edinburgh, to confirm that Pope John Paul would visit Great Britain in 1982.
29 October:	The work of the revision of the Code of Canon Law comes to an end and the commission's president, Cardinal Pericle Felici, presents the draft document to Pope John Paul for Promulgation. The Code now in force was promulgated by Pope Benedict XV in 1917.
16 to 20 November:	The second all-European ecumenical meeting of the Council of Bishops' Conferences in Europe (CCEE) and Conference of European Churches (CEC) held at Løgumkloster, Denmark.
15 December:	Publication of Pope John Paul's Apostolic Exhortation *Familiaris Consortio* (on the Role of the Christian Family in the Modern World).
24 December:	Pope John Paul lights a candle in his study window for Poland which came under martial law on 13 December.

1982

16 January: Pope John Paul announces that he has up-
graded the status of diplomatic relations between the Holy See and the United Kingdom
to ambassadorial level. In London the Apostolic
Delegation has become a Nunciature, and the
British Legation to the Holy See is now an
Embassy.

Publication of the Final Report of the Anglican-Roman Catholic International Commission.

28 May to 2 June:	**PASTORAL VISIT OF POPE JOHN PAUL II TO GREAT BRITAIN**
28 May:	Pope John Paul arrives at Gatwick Airport. Mass at Westminster Cathedral, with all the Bishops of England and Wales. Service for the sick, handicapped and disabled at St George's Cathedral, Southwark.
29 May:	Pope John Paul takes part in a service at Canterbury Cathedral at the invitation of the Archbishop of Canterbury, Dr Robert Runcie. Private meeting at Canterbury with leaders of other Christian Churches. Mass at Wembley Stadium.
30 May:	Whit Sunday — Mass at Coventry Airport. Visit to Liverpool.
31 May:	Mass at Heaton Park, Manchester. Visit to York.
	SCOTLAND Addresses young people at Murrayfield. Addresses Religious Brothers and Sisters at St Mary's Cathedral, Edinburgh.
1 June:	Meeting with leaders of Scottish Churches. Meeting with severely handicapped at St John's Hospital, Rosswell. Visit to St Andrew's College of Education, Glasgow. Mass at Bellahouston Park, Glasgow.
	WALES
2 June:	Mass at Pontcanna Fields, Cardiff. Youth Event at Ninian Park Stadium, Cardiff, for young people from the whole of England and Wales. Pope John Paul returns to Rome from Cardiff.

329